"According to the Psalter, 'th[...] this book, Dr. Benjamin Saunde[...] and just. Saunders provides an [...] [...]ces it in relation to both natural and civil law. He covers topics from the Decalogue to civil disobedience from Theonomy to Two-Kingdoms views of church-state relationships. A superb primer on biblical law and its meaning in a world desperately hungry for the justice of God."

—MICHAEL F. BIRD, deputy principal, Ridley College,
Melbourne, Australia

"In light of the Covid pandemic and intrusive new laws regarding gender and sexuality, Christians have many questions regarding the role of civil government and rule by law. In *The Crisis of Civil Law*, Benjamin Saunders combines robust theological analysis and keen academic knowledge of the Western legal tradition to provide Christians with a very helpful and accessible resource. This timely work provokes Christians to think more critically regarding the intersection of Christian ethics and civil law."

—ALAN BRANCH, professor of Christian ethics,
Midwestern Baptist Theological Seminary

"In an age when Christians are confronted by a chaotic mix of mutually exclusive claims about the role of God's law in their own lives and in wider society, Benjamin Saunders's book offers clarity in the midst of that confusion. In place of the simplistic caricatures which too often appear when engaging such complicated subjects, Saunders draws on a wide variety of legal and theological themes to provide his individual readers and the wider Church with a constructive tool for both understanding the discussion of law and moving forward from that understanding to a healthy application in their own contexts. Perhaps the best way to describe his approach is that it is nimble, carefully balancing an awareness of the distinctive natures of specific situations while appealing to the common source of God's law. I highly recommend this work to laity and specialists alike."

—TIMOTHY PADGETT, resident theologian,
The Colson Center for Christian Worldview

"At a time of considerable controversy over Christians' relationship to civil law, Ben Saunders's new contribution is very welcome. He encourages Christians to avoid simplistic answers and charts a levelheaded course that's both theoretically informed and practically insightful. Even when readers disagree with his conclusions, they will find him a thoughtful, charitable, and edifying guide."

—DAVID VANDRUNEN, Robert B. Strimple Professor of Systematic Theology
and Christian Ethics, Westminster Seminary California

"*The Crisis of Civil Law* is a commendable volume detailing the many questions—theological, moral, and political—pertaining to Christianity's reflection upon the substance of the moral law and its application to legal statute. I am happy to recommend this volume, not because I agree with every last sentence, but because Saunders has provided an excellent resource that covers all the areas worthy of our consideration. The reader walks away doubtlessly better informed as to the historic importance and dire relevance of Christian thought to civil order."

—ANDREW T. WALKER, associate professor of Christian ethics
and public theology, The Southern Baptist Theological Seminary

"An accessible and authoritative guide to the enduring wisdom of Scripture and tradition on the 'weightier matters of the law' and on many legal aspects of public and private life. Law professor Ben Saunders combines real-world legal expertise with refined theological wisdom in delivering this refreshing and rewarding title. This book can be read in an evening but pondered for a long time."

—JOHN WITTE JR., Robert W. Woodruff Professor of Law,
McDonald Distinguished Professor of Religion,
and faculty director, Center for the Study of Law and Religion,
Emory University

The Crisis
of Civil Law

What the Bible

Teaches about Law

and What It Means Today

The Crisis of Civil Law

What the Bible
Teaches about Law
and What It Means Today

Benjamin B. Saunders

LEXHAM PRESS

The Crisis of Civil Law: What the Bible Teaches about Law and What It Means Today

Copyright 2024 Benjamin B. Saunders

Lexham Press, 1313 Commercial St., Bellingham, WA 98225
LexhamPress.com

Print ISBN 9781683597568
Digital ISBN 9781683597575
Library of Congress Control Number 2023943165

Lexham Editorial: Elliot Ritzema, Elizabeth Vince, Stephanie Juliot
Cover Design: Sarah Brossow
Typesetting: Mandi Newell

23 24 25 26 27 28 29 / US / 12 11 10 9 8 7 6 5 4 3 2 1

"Hear, O Israel: The Lord our God, the Lord is one.
You shall love the Lord your God with all your heart and with all
your soul and with all your might. And these words that I command
you today shall be on your heart. You shall teach them diligently to
your children, and shall talk of them when you sit in your house,
and when you walk by the way, and when you lie down, and when
you rise. You shall bind them as a sign on your hand, and they
shall be as frontlets between your eyes. You shall write them
on the doorposts of your house and on your gates."

—Deuteronomy 6:4–9

"Take away from the magistrate, who is above the fear of man,
the fear of God, and you make him a tyrant. Infuse into the tyrant
the fear of God, and of his own accord he will do more freely and
faithfully what the law orders than any terror could have caused
him to; and out of a tyrant you will make a father on the
pattern of Him whom as a result of faith he begins to fear
and to serve, namely, God."

—Ulrich Zwingli

CONTENTS

Introduction - 1

   I. Foundational Principles of the Christian View of Law - - - - 9

   II. Law and the Bible - 37

   III. The Ten Commandments and Civil Law - - - - - - - - - - - - - 73

   IV. Moral Law and Civil Law - 109

   V. Obedience and Disobedience - 145

   VI. Errors to Be Avoided - 175

Conclusion - 187

Acknowledgments - 195

Further Study - 197

Subject and Author Index - 201

Scripture Index - 209

INTRODUCTION

I t is not difficult to see that law is in crisis in the West. In 2019, an English judge said that the belief that sex is unchangeable is a belief that is "not worthy of respect in a democratic society" and is "incompatible with the human rights of others."[1] In the same year, a Canadian court held that referring to a child by the child's birth name and sex and attempting to persuade the child to abandon treatment for gender dysphoria would be considered family violence.[2] The child's father was jailed for speaking publicly about the case.

During the Covid-19 pandemic, a woman from northern New South Wales, Australia, who was pregnant with twins needed urgent medical attention. She was told by government officials that if she entered the neighboring state of Queensland for medical treatment, she would have to be quarantined for fourteen days under border rules. She decided to fly to a hospital in Sydney to avoid crossing the border, resulting in a delay of sixteen hours. Tragically, one of the babies died—while she was obeying a law that was intended to protect life and health.[3]

---

1. M Forstater v. CGD Europe, United Kingdom Employment Tribunal (18 December 2019). This was overturned on appeal: M Forstater v. CGD Europe, ICR 1 (2022).

2. AB v. CD, BCSC 604, 10 [46] (2019).

3. Australian Associated Press, "Queensland minister says NSW woman whose unborn twin baby died was not denied healthcare," *The Guardian*, August 29, 2020, https://

Those hoping for greater clarity within the church would be disappointed. The global Covid-19 pandemic exposed fault lines among Christians about how to think about civil law. In response to the pandemic, governments across the world locked down entire communities for months on end, closing churches, schools, and businesses, with harsh penalties for noncompliance.

Christians responded to these laws in radically different ways. In Canada, church leaders vocally opposed government restrictions on gathering for worship, citing Christ's lordship over his church, and some were jailed for their stance.[4] In Australia, many churches enthusiastically implemented government restrictions by (among many other things) requiring those who wished to serve in any capacity to get vaccinated and dividing their congregations according to vaccination status, citing the mandate to obey government in Romans 13.

There is a crisis within Western legal systems and little unity within the church. Underlying the crisis in the Western view of law is a rejection of any sense of higher law or moral order to which lawmakers are subject. Law is simply whatever the lawmaker declares to be law. More than this, it is widely held that God's moral order is actually harmful and needs to be suppressed. What are Christians to make of this? How can we respond to the crisis in law and confusion among Christians about what law is?

Prior to the twentieth century, there was much more agreement among Christians about questions of law. While of course there were differences, writers within the Roman Catholic, Lutheran, and

---

www.theguardian.com/australia-news/2020/aug/29/queensland-minister-says-nsw-woman-whose-unborn-twin-baby-died-was-not-denied-healthcare; "Queensland Chief Health Officer says NSW woman whose baby died could have crossed border, did not require exemption," *ABC News*, August 28, 2020, https://www.abc.net.au/news/2020-08-28/queensland-coronavirus-nsw-baby-dies-border-exemption/12605554.

4. See, e.g., Wyatt Graham, "What You Should Know about the Release of Pastor James Coates," *TGC Canadian Edition*, March 23, 2021, https://ca.thegospelcoalition.org/columns/detrinitate/what-you-should-know-about-the-release-of-pastor-james-coates.

Reformed traditions all held similar principles about law.[5] I suggest that there is a need to recover the historic understanding of the Christian tradition regarding law, and those principles can provide valuable guidance in helping us to think well about law today.

This book aims to help Christians to think about civil law. It sets out key principles to guide Christians in their thinking, drawing on the catholic teaching of the Christian tradition regarding law. It aims to answer the following questions: What does the Bible have to say about law? What is the relationship between Scripture and civil law? How should lawmakers go about making law? Should Christians obey all laws, even unjust ones?

CHALLENGES IN THINKING ABOUT LAW

Law is a difficult subject to think well about. The first reason for this is that law often conflicts with Christian values. Law tends to follow societal trends, although at a fairly leisurely distance, and a change of law can be the outcome of a process of societal change in attitudes toward things like sexuality, human rights, or the sanctity of life. Law functions as a kind of barometer of community views and can be the focal point for Christian concerns with the direction of society.

More than this, law is increasingly being used as an instrument to suppress Christianity and Christian views. Western society has been deeply influenced by Christianity, reflected in such principles as the idea of a higher law and the presumption of innocence. But now the sword of the state is increasingly being turned against Christianity, especially for what are now considered to be intolerant and bigoted attitudes in matters of sexuality and gender. In many

---

5. See J. Daryl Charles, *Retrieving the Natural Law: A Return to Moral First Things* (Grand Rapids: Eerdmans, 2008), 114; Stephen J. Grabill, *Rediscovering the Natural Law in Reformed Theological Ethics* (Grand Rapids: Eerdmans, 2006), 2; John T. McNeill, "Natural Law in the Teaching of the Reformers," *Journal of Religion* 26, no. 3 (July 1946): 168; Richard A. Muller, *Post-Reformation Reformed Dogmatics: The Rise and Development of Reformed Orthodoxy, ca. 1520 to ca. 1725*, 2nd ed. (Grand Rapids: Baker Academic, 2003), 1:97.

ways, law is no friend to the church today. Given this, it is perhaps unsurprising that Christians often have a suspicious attitude toward governments and law.

A common strategy adopted in response to feeling threatened by law is to seek to influence the political process to enshrine Christian values in law, whether this be through lobbying politicians or getting the right candidates elected. Now, of course, a Christian voice in the public square can be extremely valuable. The difficulty with this approach, however, is that it does not challenge the dominant narrative about law but simply subsumes Christians within it. While Christians may be successful from time to time in enshrining "Christian values" in various pieces of legislation, this approach does not challenge the fact that law is often seen as little more than the product of the political process, and "Christian values" are simply one of many potential sources of influence on the law. The long-term fruit of such an approach is an increasingly bitter polarization of warring political camps who do battle to have their values recognized in law.

Second, Christians rightly have a high view of the Bible and are accustomed to resolving disputes by appealing to Scripture. Some Christians argue that there is a distinctive Christian viewpoint on issues of law and that Christians should be having a transformative effect on the culture. Christians often look to Scripture for an authoritative, objective standard against which to measure human laws, and, as a result, Scripture is called upon to resolve everything from gun rights to refugee laws to how to respond to a pandemic.

While seeking to be faithful to Scripture is of course a good thing, there are clear limitations to such an approach to law. While the Bible contains many laws, it is not intended to be an exhaustive legal code and does not contain all the answers to the questions we might have about law. It would be silly, for instance, to suggest there is a distinctly Christian perspective regarding which side of the road we should drive on. And we hardly need the Bible to tell us that there should be a law requiring all road users to drive on the same side of the road.

Thus, while there is clearly a distinctly Christian viewpoint on many issues, especially questions of life and sexuality, on many other questions it is much harder to discern a distinctly Christian viewpoint. It is not clear, for example, that there is only one scriptural answer to the question of whether company directors should owe fiduciary duties to their shareholders, or only to the company. Or what non-statutory powers the executive ought to possess. Or whether non-parties to a contract ought to be able to enforce that contract. Or what disclosure obligations should apply when companies make a public offer of securities.

In this way, the notion that we can look to Scripture's commands to resolve our legal crisis eventually comes up short in the face of reality. And yet Christians have not been provided with any other tools for thinking about law. In practice, transformational approaches tend to lead to a deflated withdrawal in the face of most questions of law because we lack the categories to think about law in terms other than scriptural faithfulness.

A third challenge to thinking about law well is the complexity of biblical law and its remoteness from our own context. Some parts of scriptural law can make us decidedly uncomfortable, being far removed from our modern-day values. Exodus 21:7 appears to condone—or at least it does not clearly prohibit—the practice of fathers treating their daughters as disposable property, to be bought and sold for profit. Deuteronomy 25 states that "when men fight with one another and the wife of the one draws near to rescue her husband from the hand of him who is beating him and puts out her hand and seizes him by the private parts, then you shall cut off her hand. Your eye shall have no pity" (Deut 25:11–12). To say the least, it is difficult to know what to make of laws such as these.

A fourth challenge is the tribalism of Christians themselves, given that many Christians today identify strongly with one or the other side of the right-left divide in politics. Ideally, Christians ought to be disposed to accept truth wherever it may be found, but in practice that is often not the case. Some perspectives on law are associated with a particular side of politics, so even though they may be true, that association can hinder their acceptance, especially if we see those on the other side of the divide as our enemies.

However, the Bible does not neatly fall into either the left or right wing of politics. Scripture shows great concern for the weak and underprivileged (a typical preoccupation of the left) and is also the source of many "traditional values" (a typical preoccupation of the right). While it is true that both left and right express something of the truth, neither side is a full statement of the truth, and both need correcting at points. Reading Scripture through ideological blinkers can blind us to the full force and import of the scriptural teaching about law.

A fifth challenge is that of context: we are deeply shaped by the historical and geographical context we live in, and it is difficult to escape that context. Many American Christians strongly object to gun regulation as a violation of their constitutional rights. Most Australian Christians cheerfully submit to a system of extensive gun regulation in the interest of a safe society (which, by and large, it is). Many things that we are inclined to consider necessary, universal, even obvious, are in fact much more subjective and context-bound than we like to admit.

A final challenge is that of over-regulation. There is an increasingly prescriptive regulation of every aspect of society in the West, and the church is not exempt from this. Because of the loss of a shared morality, governments respond by imposing prescriptive and detailed rules directing people how to behave.[6] Church life is

---

6. Ross Grantham, *The Law and Practice of Corporate Governance* (London: LexisNexis Butterworths, 2020), 469.

now shrouded in a thick fog of government regulation. This presents the church with an unenviable choice: Should we resist or even disobey these regulations? This carries risks, and it is not always clear at what point disobedience is warranted.

On the other hand, complying with every directive means that the church responds to the issues it faces (whether the Covid-19 pandemic or abuse within the church) by adopting a baptized secularism: simply follow the government's direction, on the basis that we should "be subject to the governing authorities" (Rom 13:1). The result is that in practice government regulations dictate much of church life, and the institutional church is run by bureaucrats who advise on compliance with those regulations.

These are some of the challenges that Christians face when thinking about law. Can we think positively about something that is increasingly used as a weapon against the church? Can we maintain the radical distinctness of the Christian message and avoid simplistic triumphalism? Can we navigate between the unchanging truthfulness of the Bible and the application of those truths in the context of our own age?

THE AIM OF THIS BOOK

In this book, I will lay out a series of foundational principles, drawing from the wealth of the historic Christian teaching regarding law, to provide a coherent framework by which Christians can think about law. As a lawyer and legal academic, my primary interest is civil law—that is, the law enacted by civil governments. However, it is not possible to think about civil law from a Christian perspective without first considering the biblical material about law. The Bible contains a lot of material about law, and Christianity has deeply shaped the Western legal tradition. Therefore, I will first examine how to understand biblical law and the biblical teaching about law. Chapter 1 sets out foundational principles which, I argue, ought to guide how Christians think about law. Chapters 2 and 3 discuss biblical law; chapter 2 shows how to understand and interpret biblical law and its place in the Christian life, and chapter 3 is an exposition of the Decalogue.

With that foundation in place, I then consider how to think about civil law from a Christian perspective. Chapter 4 discusses the making of civil law, including two case studies that show how my argument could be applied in the areas of gun control and abortion. Chapter 5 discusses obedience and disobedience to civil law, and particularly the question of when it might be appropriate for a Christian to disobey an unjust law. Chapter 6 discusses errors to be avoided when thinking about law.

This book is not an exhaustive treatise of jurisprudence, nor is it a blueprint for what civil law ought to look like. It sets out foundational principles for how to go about the task of thinking about law from a Christian perspective rather than attempting to give the answers to every question. I hope that this book will give you greater clarity in your thinking about law and will contribute to unity among Christians as we navigate this complex topic.

I

FOUNDATIONAL PRINCIPLES
of THE CHRISTIAN VIEW *of* LAW

The Bible contains a great deal of teaching relevant to law. Christians recognize the lordship of Christ over everything and that civil lawmakers are accountable to God for the laws they make. Christians will therefore think about law in very different ways to non-Christians. And yet there seem to be many things that the Bible does not specifically address. How do we maintain a distinctively Christian view of law while recognizing the intentionally limited scope of scriptural teaching? This chapter sets out foundational principles which I argue should guide Christian thinking about law.

FOUR KEY PRINCIPLES

THE MORAL LAW

Perhaps the most significant principle of the Christian view of law is that humans are subject to a moral law, given by God. The moral law consists of the unchanging and universally applicable obligations

9

owed by all people as a rule of conduct by virtue of their creation in God's image. The moral law is revealed by God, distinguishes right from wrong, and directs what must be done and what must be avoided. This moral law is written on the heart and in principle is knowable by all people (Rom 2:14–15), and it provides (or should provide) the foundation for all human civil laws. Although it is knowable through reason and the conscience, that knowledge is corrupted by sin, and so the moral law is revealed more clearly in Scripture.

Not every law or command in Scripture is part of the moral law—only those things that are applicable to all people at all times. For example, in Deuteronomy 14:1 God commanded the Israelites, "You shall not cut yourselves or make any baldness on your foreheads for the dead." This was a specific command given to the people of Israel for a particular reason, and so it is not part of the moral law. By contrast, "You shall not murder" (Exod 20:13; Deut 5:17) is an unchanging and universal obligation applicable to all people, and so it is part of the moral law. The moral law, then, is a subset of the law revealed in Scripture. The Decalogue is considered to be a perfect summary of the content of the moral law.

Closely related to the moral law is the concept of natural law. Natural law is controversial in Protestant circles, as many people are cautious about the existence of moral truths outside the authoritative revelation in Scripture. Nevertheless, as I will discuss in chapter 2, Scripture clearly teaches that there is a universal moral standard, applicable to all people at all times. This law is written on the heart and is therefore knowable, at least in principle, outside the revelation of the moral law in Scripture, although the knowledge of that law has been obscured by sin. This is traditionally known as the natural law. Natural law and Scripture are both means of knowing the moral law, although Scripture is a much clearer and more authoritative statement of the moral law.

TRANSFORMATION

The second principle is that the Christian faith is radically transformative for a person's worldview and beliefs about reality, and specifically about law. Scripture commands Christians not to be "conformed to this world, but be transformed by the renewal of your mind, that by testing you may discern what is the will of God, what is good and acceptable and perfect" (Rom 12:2). The minds of Christians are to be transformed as they "take every thought captive to obey Christ" (2 Cor 10:5).

It is possible for unbelievers as well as believers to perceive truth and the principles of the moral law, even if distorted by sin. As such, there are areas of common ground between Christian and non-Christian views of law. As discussed later in this chapter, it is therefore better to think of the distinctiveness of Christianity for law as a spectrum—that is, the Bible will impact the way we think about some areas of law more than others. Christians disagree about the precise extent to which the Christian view of law is radically distinct. Nevertheless, it seems difficult to disagree with the proposition that the way a Christian thinks about law will be deeply impacted by the Christian faith.

FREEDOM

The third principle is that lawmakers have a large amount of freedom in constructing a system of government and law. This freedom is not total, because lawmakers are constrained by the moral law and by Scripture. Nevertheless, within the constraints of the moral law, there is considerable space for human creativity and wisdom in enacting civil laws. This freedom exists because of the intentionally limited scope of Scripture: by design, Scripture does not prescribe all the laws necessary for a modern nation state. This is of course not to say that the Bible is deficient or lacking in some way, or that it is irrelevant to modern law.

Christians are sometimes tempted to want to make the Bible a detailed blueprint for contemporary society, arguing that the Bible (and in particular the Mosaic laws) provides all the answers to every question of law. However, this is not how Christians have typically understood biblical law. The Christian tradition has overwhelmingly affirmed that the Bible is not, and is not intended to be, a comprehensive legal code for every human society throughout history.[1]

The moral law is relatively indeterminate. That is, it gives general principles rather than their precise application in every situation.[2] The moral law does not prescribe the details of the civil laws necessary to give effect to its principles. The Mosaic laws are often selective and illustrative rather than exhaustive, and there are many situations which are not specifically addressed. Many of the Mosaic laws assumed the applicability of various norms and obligations which existed among the people of Israel, and do not purport to regulate comprehensively the relationships of, for example, commercial dealings, property, or marriage.[3] That is, they are not a detailed blueprint of the laws governing these matters.

By contrast, human laws need to be detailed, prescribing what is to be done, by whom, and when, so that those subject to the laws know what they must do in order to comply with the law. To take an example, consider how people accused of murder should be treated

1. E.g., Martin Luther, "How Christians Should Regard Moses," trans. E. Theodore Bachmann, in *Luther's Works, Volume 35, Word and Sacrament I*, ed. Theodore Bachmann (Philadelphia: Fortress, 1960); Philip Melanchthon, *The Chief Theological Topics: Loci Praecipui Theologici 1559*, trans. J. A. O. Preus, 2nd ed. (St. Louis: Concordia Publishing House, 2011), 90–91; John Calvin, *Institutes of the Christian Religion*, ed. John T. McNeill, trans. Ford Lewis Battles (Louisville: Westminster John Knox, 1960), 4.20.15; Zacharias Ursinus, *The Commentary of Dr. Zacharias Ursinus on the Heidelberg Catechism*, trans. G. W. Willard (Eugene, OR: Wipf & Stock, 2020), 492–97; Jonathan Burnside, *God, Justice, and Society: Aspects of Law and Legality in the Bible* (Oxford: Oxford University Press, 2011), 5, 18–19; James B. Jordan, *The Law of the Covenant: An Exposition of Exodus 21–23* (Tyler, TX: Institute for Christian Economics, 1984), 72.

2. David VanDrunen, *Politics after Christendom: Political Theology in a Fractured World* (Grand Rapids: Zondervan, 2020), 135–36; Girolamo Zanchi, *On the Law in General*, trans. Jeffrey J. Veenstra (Grand Rapids: Christian's Library Press, 2013), 28.

3. Examples include Exod 21:7–11; Deut 21:10–14.

by the judicial process. It is not controversial that civil law should prohibit murder and that those accused of crimes should receive a fair trial. Scripture has many things to say that are relevant; it draws a clear distinction between intentional and accidental killing, and it provides other relevant principles, including stipulating that a charge shall only be established on the evidence of two or three witnesses (Deut 19:15). From this we can deduce the key principles that a person must be deemed innocent until proven guilty, and no person may be convicted without reliable evidence.

However, these principles do not tell us what the standard of proof is, how evidence is to be gathered, what evidence is admissible and what is not, what weight to give DNA evidence, whether a judge or jury should pass verdict, how a jury is to be instructed (if there is a jury), whether a decision must be unanimous, and what rights of appeal exist, among many other things. Matters such as these are within the realm of human decision—and so they are matters about which lawmakers have freedom.

A better way of thinking about biblical law is to see it as a foundation rather than a blueprint. In medieval times, Christian thinkers described the moral law as the foundation and human civil law as the building.[4] When constructing a building, there are certain principles that must be adhered to, but provided that these constraints are observed, there is considerable freedom.

A legal system can be viewed in a similar light. The Bible and natural law provide the foundational principles that must be realized in any just legal order but not the detail necessary for an adequate legal system. The moral law imposes constraints which must be adhered to, but lawmakers have freedom in building on this foundation to design a legal system and enact laws. There is not one way to construct a legal system or to enact the principles of the moral law into civil law. This means that many questions of law are questions of

---

4. See Brian M. McCall, *The Architecture of Law: Rebuilding Law in the Classical Tradition* (South Bend, IN: University of Notre Dame Press, 2018).

wisdom, and civil rulers have a level of freedom in determining how to enact civil law.

One implication of this is that in many situations a range of possible human laws will be legitimate. There will not be only one correct answer, and reasonable Christians might disagree. In America, people drive on the right-hand side of the road, while in Australia we drive on the left. It would be absurd to suggest that one of these is "right" and one "wrong." To take a more complex example, should a person be liable for damage she caused but that was not reasonably foreseeable?[5] Or should company directors owe fiduciary duties to shareholders, or only to the company?[6] These are difficult questions, and a range of different answers are possible. Many other examples could be given.

The principles of transformation and freedom must sit together. A Christian approach to law must affirm both radical distinctiveness on the one hand and non-distinctiveness on the other. To deny the distinctness of the Christian message would be wrong; yet, on the other hand, to say that there is a distinctive Christian view about every conceivable issue is equally unhelpful. How might we navigate between these apparently contradictory principles? I will discuss this later in this chapter.

CONTEXTUALIZATION

The fourth principle for thinking about law is contextualization. Christians have typically thought that human civil laws ought to be based on the eternal moral law—indeed, this is one of the distinctive contributions of Christian jurisprudence. Some Christians take this in a universalizing direction: because the *moral law* is universal and does not change, there must be something universal and unchanging about *civil law*. However, this is not the case.

---

5. Palsgraf v. Long Island Railroad Co., 248 NY 339, 162 NE 99 (1928).

6. See Benjamin B. Saunders, "Putting the Spoils of Litigation into the Shareholders' Pockets: When Can Shareholders Bring a Personal Action against the Directors of their Company?" *Company and Securities Law Journal* 22 (2004): 535.

Timothy Keller's concept of gospel contextualization provides a helpful analogy. Keller argues that while there is only one true gospel, "there is no culture-transcending way to express the truths of the gospel." The gospel must be freshly articulated in each cultural context. The precise practices adopted by any particular ministry depend not only on foundational doctrinal truths, but also a "theological vision" for bringing the gospel to bear within a particular cultural and historical setting.[7]

Something similar is true for law. The principles of the moral law do not change. However, human circumstances vary considerably. This means that there is not one single way to implement the moral law; the way the moral law is implemented within a particular legal system will depend on the circumstances and context. Therefore, law cannot be static, but must continually be adjusted to changing circumstances.[8] While the moral law is universal, there is not one way of implementing the principles of the moral law within a legal system.

In his treatise on law, Girolamo Zanchi provided the following example: "There is a law that in a besieged city no one is allowed to open the city gates."[9] In a time when people lived within walled cities and were subject to attack from enemy armies, the purpose of this law was to prevent enemies from gaining entry into the city and slaughtering the inhabitants. This law is an example of the wise application of the natural law in the context of that time. However, this law would be utterly pointless in many parts of the world today. Most people do not live in walled cities and are not subject to attack from enemy armies. Applying the underlying moral principle today would require rulers to respond to the very different threats to safety which now exist.

---

7. Timothy Keller, *Center Church: Doing Balanced, Gospel-Centered Ministry in Your City* (Grand Rapids: Zondervan, 2012), 17, 93.

8. See Johannes Althusius, *On Law and Power*, trans. Jeffrey J. Veenstra (Grand Rapids: CLP Academic, 2013), 21.

9. Zanchi, *On the Law*, 36.

The sixth commandment states, "You shall not kill." In ancient Israel, where people spent a lot of time entertaining on their roofs, this commandment required people who built a house to install a parapet (Deut 22:8). In other times, it would require people chopping wood to secure their axe heads and people living within a walled city not to open the gates during a siege. In still other times, it would require mining companies to support mine shafts to prevent collapse; it would require automobile drivers to be licensed, to adhere to road rules, to drive within the speed limit, and to refrain from driving while intoxicated; it would require airplane pilots to be properly trained, safety equipment to be fitted to dangerous machines, naked flames to be prohibited near explosive substances, safety switches to be fitted to electrical systems, poisonous substances to be stored safely—and the list could go on.

This illustrates that, while the moral law is unchanging, what it requires in specific contexts varies widely depending on the circumstances. What "you shall not kill" required of a woodchopper in ancient Israel is very different from what it requires of a worker on a modern gas rig. A law requiring people in ancient Israel not to drive while intoxicated would have made little sense, and a law requiring people in modern Australia to build parapets around their roofs would also make little sense. What laws ought to be implemented to give effect to this principle will vary significantly depending on the circumstances. The principles of morality do not change, but their application to specific situations does.

THE NEED FOR WISDOM

One important implication of these principles is that many, if not most, questions of law are questions of wisdom. Enacting laws, and thinking well about law, requires a great deal of wisdom. Wisdom is not reducible to a list of rules or a series of propositions that one can learn. It could be defined as understanding the nature of reality as God has created it and living well within that reality.[10] The creation has been ordered by God in a certain way, and that order can be perceived through Scripture and by reflection on its nature. Wisdom means being attuned to that order and navigating life in a complex world successfully.

Wisdom is sometimes defined as knowing what to do when there is no clear moral rule dictating what to do. While this is perhaps not wrong, a better view of wisdom is that it is an understanding of how the world works and of what conduct is fitting in a particular time or place. Wisdom does not merely fill the gaps, but grasps the gravity of certain courses of conduct and what will be beneficial or destructive.[11]

True wisdom is based on the fear of the Lord (Prov 1:7; 9:10). In Christ are the treasures of wisdom and knowledge (Col 2:3), and so wisdom is something that comes from God (Jas 1:5). A virtuous character is an essential part of wisdom. Foolishness and wickedness are connected in Scripture; as such, wisdom is not separable from character and virtue. Wisdom involves humility, recognizing the limitations of our knowledge and understanding (Prov 3:7; 11:2). A wise person is prepared to be instructed and corrected when needed (Prov 13:1; 15:31; 19:20).

There are different dimensions to wisdom. Wisdom comes from meditation on Scripture (Ps 19:7), which is sufficient to thoroughly equip the Christian for every good work (2 Tim 3:17). Given that there is a moral order in creation, the world has much to teach us, and wisdom may be gained from reflection on the created order (Prov 6:6–8). Wisdom is acquired through experience and learning from wise people (Job 12:12; Prov 13:20). Wisdom seeks the truth from a wide range of counsel and does not ignore contrary advice (1 Kgs 12:6–19; Prov 11:14; 15:22). Scripture also describes the skill of artists and craftsmen as a type of wisdom (Exod 35:10, 26, 35).

---

10. See chapter 3 in Simon P. Kennedy, *Reimagining Worldview: Wisdom and Formation in Christian Education* (Bellingham, WA: Lexham Press, 2024).

11. VanDrunen, *Politics after Christendom*, 140.

Thus, true wisdom does not come from one source, but from careful meditation on Scripture, listening to wise counsel, experience, observing the natural order, and learning the specialized skills which pertain to a particular craft or discipline.

There is a procedural fairness element to wisdom: a wise person does not believe the first report but hears both sides before reaching a conclusion (Prov 18:17). Wisdom can be manifested in being able to resolve "the obscurities of conflicting claims."[12] Wisdom involves being alert to the consequences of actions, such as how people respond to provocations (e.g., Prov 15:1), and acting accordingly.

As noted, Scripture describes certain skills as a form of wisdom. This is true of civil rule and lawmaking. By wisdom "kings reign, and rulers decree what is just" (Prov 8:15–16; see also 1 Kgs 3:28). Law is complex, and lawmaking is a highly specialized skill. As Edward Coke famously said, legal judgments "are not to be decided by natural reason but by the artificial reason and judgment of law, which law is an art which requires long study and experience, before that a man can attain to the cognisance of it."[13]

How should lawmakers enact laws consistently with wisdom? A great deal could be said; I offer a few brief thoughts. Wise lawmakers will understand the moral law and seek to work with, and not against, the grain of creation. Their laws will be consistent with the moral law, and they will promote those things that are good, such as human life, marriage, family, and property, and prevent those things that are evil. They will uphold justice and defend the oppressed and vulnerable. Wise lawmakers will not permit injustice to stand. They will recognize that they are accountable to God for the laws they enact.

Wise lawmakers will understand the people they are regulating, their habits and temper, and be alert to the consequences of their decisions. If a particular law is enacted, will the people accept that

---

12. Oliver O'Donovan, *The Ways of Judgment* (Grand Rapids: Eerdmans, 2008), 7, referring to 1 Kgs 3:16–28.

13. Prohibitions Del Roy (1607) 12 Co Rep 63.

law or rebel against it? Will it have the desired consequence? Wise lawmakers will recognize that there are limits to their power: civil law must promote the good and punish evil, but civil laws have limited power to effect change in the human heart. Wise lawmakers will take broad counsel from a range of advisers.

Wisdom is crucial for lawmaking. It is not enough to identify a moral or legal principle from Scripture or the natural law. Lawmaking requires wisdom to determine *how* to enact a moral or legal principle into civil law. I will give some examples later in the book to illustrate how this is so.

TRANSFORMATION AS A SPECTRUM

The principles of freedom and transformation may seem to be at odds with each other. One principle emphasizes the radically distinct nature of the Christian faith, while the other appears to emphasize the opposite. Nevertheless, it is better to see these principles as complementary rather than opposed to each other. It is true that a Christian view of law is radically different from a non-Christian view of law. It is also true that non-Christians can perceive moral truth and the principles of the natural law, which reflect the nature of reality.

This leads to the question: When ought we apply a transformative approach, and when are we in the realm of freedom? I suggest that the answer is through the lens of "Brunner's spectrum." In his book *Revelation and Reason*, theologian Emil Brunner wrote:

> No Christian theologian has maintained that our mathematical knowledge or our formal logic is affected by sin; on the other hand, all theologians are agreed that our knowledge of God is most deeply affected by sin. ... There is no "Christian mathematics" but there is a Christian theology and Christian anthropology. We cannot indicate the state of affairs by drawing a line of demarcation between them, but only by a proportional statement: The nearer anything lies to that centre of

existence where we are concerned with man's relation to God
and the being of the person, the greater is the disturbance of
rational knowledge by sin; the farther anything lies from this
centre, the less is the disturbance felt, and the less difference
there is between knowing as a believer or as an unbeliever.[14]

Brunner's point is that there is a spectrum of knowledge, with theology and anthropology at one end, and mathematics and formal logic at the other. "Anthropology" here means the nature of humans as beings created in God's image, not the study of other cultures. All fields of human knowledge and endeavor sit somewhere along the spectrum. Christian teaching makes a big difference to the content of theology and anthropology but little difference to the content of formal logic or mathematical knowledge.

The following table sketches a visual picture of this idea:

CHRISTIANITY'S DIFFERENTIAL IMPACT ON DISCIPLINES OF KNOWLEDGE

Disciplines where Christianity has a very high impact:	Disciplines where Christianity has a high impact:	Disciplines where Christianity has a moderate impact:	Disciplines where Christianity has little or no impact:
Theology Anthropology Ethics	Education Psychology Sociology Politics	History Literature Science Economics	Mathematics Formal logic Languages Engineering

At the left end of the spectrum are disciplines where Christianity makes a big difference to the content of that knowledge. These disciplines will be significantly impacted by Christianity. Obvious examples include theology, ethics, anthropology (including human rights

14. Emil Brunner, *Revelation and Reason: The Christian Doctrine of Faith and Knowledge*, trans. Olive Wyon (Philadelphia: Westminster, 1946), 383.

and sexuality), and a person's worldview. As discussed in greater detail later in this book, the Bible recognizes a pattern of creation which is applicable to all people and written on the heart. All people, therefore, have some instinctive knowledge of right and wrong, and of God's created order. Thus, non-believers are able to perceive these things, but sin has blinded their minds and seared their consciences. The impact of sin is much greater in these areas. As Brunner put it, "All theologians are agreed that our knowledge of God is most deeply affected by sin."

At the right end of the spectrum are those disciplines where Christianity makes the least difference, and where there are significant areas of common ground, especially mathematics and formal logic. The mathematical fact that $2+2=4$ holds true for all people everywhere; rational people accept this to be true, and it requires no special biblical insight.

Two caveats should be noted. First, the theological and philosophical ideas underlying one's conception of a discipline will vary widely. One person may believe that the universe is a random collection of atoms without meaning or purpose which happens to contain mathematical truths, while another believes that the universe was created by God and subject to a moral order. That is, Christianity will make a difference to one's conception of the underlying purpose or significance of the discipline. Second, Christianity will affect the manner in which a person undertakes work in a particular discipline and their reasons for doing so, whether honestly or dishonestly, or for their own glory or not.

Acknowledging these two caveats, the actual content of the discipline is not greatly affected by whether one is a Christian. All rational people accept that $2+2=4$, even if we may disagree on why this is the case and what significance attaches to it. As Brunner put it, "No Christian theologian has maintained that our mathematical knowledge or our formal logic is affected by sin."

In the middle are disciplines where Christianity has important influence but it is less pronounced, and there are significant areas of common ground. There is scope to disagree as to where, precisely, we position certain things—for example, some may disagree about where I have placed politics or economics. The point is not that everyone must agree with where everything has been placed, but it should not be controversial that there *is* a spectrum, or that Christianity makes more difference to some areas of knowledge than others.

How is this relevant to law? Law does not sit at any one place on the spectrum, but straddles the entire spectrum. This is because laws deal with almost the full range of human activities, from birth to marriage to death, regulating education, employment, business, property ownership, and many other things. This suggests that Christianity will affect different areas of law differently depending on their subject matter.

With regard to laws that deal with matters of the value of human life and sexuality, Christianity will make a big difference, and so it is not surprising that Christianity is at its most controversial in relation to laws concerning marriage and family, and questions such as abortion and euthanasia. However, where laws deal with matters closer to the other end, we can expect that Christianity will make much less difference to the way we think about those things. At this end of the spectrum, there will be greater scope for freedom for lawmakers in enacting civil law.

Christians often tend to focus on the controversial issues. But in my view, a large number of areas of law are at the "non-transformative" end of the spectrum. This includes large swathes of the law relating to contracts, property, torts, corporate law, competition (antitrust) law, public law, criminal law, and so on. This is not to say that the Bible has nothing to say on these matters, but it has much less to say about these areas than others. For many areas of civil law, lawmakers have significant freedom when enacting laws.

KEY ASPECTS OF
THE CHRISTIAN VIEW OF LAW

In what way is the Christian view of law distinct from non-Christian views of law? Many aspects of biblical teaching impact and shape the way Christians think about law. This section aims to briefly explore key aspects of Christian teaching and how it affects law. It is not intended to offer a comprehensive treatment of law or the Christian worldview, and some aspects are fleshed out in more detail in later chapters.

The Christian teaching about law is based on the fundamental truth that Jesus is Lord. The Bible teaches that God created the world and made humanity in his image (Gen 1:1, 26–28), and God's creation of the world implies his lordship over that creation. "There is no authority except from God" (Rom 13:1), and "from him and through him and to him are all things" (Rom 11:36). Jesus rules as the resurrected Messiah, and all authority in heaven and on earth has been given to him (Matt 28:18; Acts 2:31–36; Col 1:15–20).

Another fundamental aspect of biblical teaching concerning law is that there exists a divinely given moral law which applies to all people at all times. Protestant Christians often think about law as a requirement or command specifically given by God. However, the first revealed law was given at Mount Sinai in Exodus 20. And yet, as will be discussed in chapter 2, there was a clear recognition of sin and the applicability of moral requirements long before this. Scripture therefore recognizes the existence of a universally applicable moral law, which predated the giving of the law to Moses. To explain this, Christian theology has traditionally affirmed that this moral law was given at creation, implanted on Adam's mind or conscience, and applies to the entire human race.[15] That is, the moral law existed

---

15. See, e.g., *Westminster Confession of Faith*, ed. S. W. Carruthers (Presbyterian Church of England, 1946), IV.2; Anthony Burgess, *Vindiciæ Legis: or, a Vindication of the Morall Law and the Covenants*, 2nd ed. (London: Thomas Underhill, 1647), 115, 117–18.

prior to the giving of the revealed law in Scripture and prior to the entry of sin into the world.

Closely related to the moral law is the concept of moral order. Genesis 1 and 2 describe an order embedded within creation. God made men and women in his image and gave them dominion over the creation (Gen 1:27–28). Humans thus reflect God's image in their nature and character and in their role in exercising stewardship and dominion over creation. The command to "fill the earth and subdue it" (Gen 1:28) has often been called the "creation mandate," suggesting that the role of humanity is to engage in a wide range of cultural activities, building communities and uncovering the riches of God's world, and this includes establishing institutions of law and justice.

God put the man into the garden "to work it and keep it" (Gen 2:15), he created woman and thus marriage and sexual union (Gen 2:18–25), reflecting God's intent that men and women were to reproduce and fill the earth (Gen 1:28), and God rested on the seventh day to establish the pattern of a weekly day of rest (Gen 2:1–3). These patterns correspond to many of the precepts of the moral law as set out in the Decalogue. Therefore, the requirements of the moral law are not simply arbitrary commands but objective moral standards embedded in creation, reflecting the nature of that creation.

When God made humanity, he imposed a probationary test of obedience, known in the Reformed tradition as the covenant of works. Adam was commanded not to eat of the tree of the knowledge of good and evil (Gen 2:16–17), and his failure to keep this command brought sin into the world, including the subjection of the creation to corruption.[16] The entry of sin into the world has important implications for law. Although the moral law remains written on the heart (Rom 2:14–15) and remains the standard against which all people will be judged, the knowledge of this law is marred and distorted by sin (Rom 1:18–23; 8:7).

---

16. Gen 3:1–19; Rom 5:12–18; 8:19–23.

Scripture deals with the problem of sin in two main ways. The first is through the mechanisms of civil law and government. This can be traced back to the covenant with Noah, which repeats aspects of the creation mandate and includes a promise that God will preserve the regularity of the creation and the patterns of the seasons (Gen 8:20–9:17). The Noahic covenant has been described as a covenant of preservation, in which God committed to maintain and preserve the created order.[17] One important aspect of this is the provision made (in embryonic form) for civil law and government. God declared that:

> Whoever sheds the blood of man,
> > by man shall his blood be shed,
> for God made man in his own image.

This sets out a "general human responsibility to administer proportionate retributive justice,"[18] and its establishment as part of the covenant of preservation suggests that human civil law and government have an important role in maintaining earthly peace and stability in human society. This suggests also that civil law is universal, common to all people, and concerned with mitigating the effects of sin and preserving order in this world.[19] Indeed, in a fallen world, government and civil law are necessary as a means to restrain sin and provide a measure of order. Romans 13:4 describes the civil ruler as God's servant who bears the sword and who "carries out God's wrath on the wrongdoer."

This suggests both the benefits and limitations of civil law. Although civil laws cannot change the fundamental orientation of the human heart, through coercion and punishment they can

---

17. Randy Beck and David VanDrunen, "The Biblical Foundations of Law: Creation, Fall and the Patriarchs," in *Law and the Bible: Justice, Mercy and Legal Institutions*, ed. Robert F. Cochran Jr. and David VanDrunen (Downers Grove, IL: IVP Academic, 2013), 38–39.

18. VanDrunen, *Politics after Christendom*, 82.

19. VanDrunen, *Politics after Christendom*, 25–56.

restrain evil conduct. Civil law has limited power to prevent oppression and can only ever provide an approximation of justice in this world. Indeed, although civil laws and governments are good things, Scripture is profoundly ambivalent about civil rulers, who themselves are often a source of oppression, and warns us not to put our trust in princes (Pss 118:9; 146:3). Civil law is administered by imperfect human beings and cannot effectively deal with the problem of human sin.

Thus, secondly, God has revealed a plan to undo the effects of sin and bring about perfect justice. This plan of salvation includes the redemption of his people (Matt 1:21; John 6:39) and the restoration of the entirety of creation (Col 1:20). This was first foreshadowed in Genesis 3:15 with the promise that the woman's seed would crush the serpent's head, undoing the curse and effects of sin in this world, and subsequently expanded in the promise of land, blessing, and descendants made to Abraham (Gen 12:1–3), which typified a greater heavenly reality (Heb 11:16). The Messiah's victory will culminate in a new heaven and a new earth where the consequences of sin are entirely done away with (Rom 8:18–23; Rev 21:1–4).

The entry of the Israelites into the land was a partial temporal fulfillment of the promise made to Abraham. This promise was ultimately fulfilled through Jesus Christ, the son of Abraham and the son of David, who revealed a righteousness apart from the law (Rom 3:21). However, the new kingdom did not do away with law but rather fulfilled the perfect righteousness of that law, as the Messiah merited the salvation of his people through obedience to the law and offered a perfect sacrifice to remove the curse associated with breach of the law (Rom 5:18–19; 2 Cor 5:21; Gal 3:13). The cross is therefore the ultimate demonstration of both God's justice and his mercy (Rom 3:26). Christ did not "come to abolish the Law or the Prophets ... but to fulfill them" (Matt 5:17).

The resurrected Christ has been given all authority in heaven and on earth (Matt 28:18–20) and will reign "until he has put all his enemies under his feet" (1 Cor 15:25). He will return as the victorious king to judge the living and the dead (John 5:26–29; 2 Cor 5:10). Isaiah describes the Messiah's mission to "bring forth justice to the nations" (Isa 42:1):

> He will not grow faint or be discouraged
> till he has established justice in the earth;
> and the coastlands wait for his law. (Isa 42:4)

A day has been appointed when "God will bring every deed into judgment, with every secret thing, whether good or evil" (Eccl 12:14; see also Matt 12:36), and when perfect justice will finally be enacted. In the meantime, the last days are often characterized by conflict between the kingdom of God and earthly rulers, whose power has been disarmed.[20] The kingdom has come but has not yet been fully consummated. As Augustine wrote, the city of man and the city of God "are interwoven and intermixed in this era, and await separation at the last judgement."[21]

The existence of a universally applicable moral law and a created order entails that there are objective standards of justice, truth, and righteousness to which laws and governments should conform and for which they will give an account. This is not something confined to Christians or the church, but applies to all people. That universal standard, traditionally known as "natural law," provides (or ought to provide) the foundation for human civil laws, as well as a standard against which human laws may be evaluated.

The moral law was first given in revealed form to the Israelites in the context of their redemption from slavery in Egypt. At the heart of the law was the Ten Commandments or words, outlining the key requirements of the law (Exod 20:1–17; Deut 5:6–21), which contain a much clearer and more authoritative statement of the moral law than available through the law written on the heart. The Decalogue

---

20. Ps 2; Luke 12:11; 21:12; 1 Cor 2:6–8; Rev 17:12–14.
21. St. Augustine, *Concerning the City of God against the Pagans*, trans. Henry Bettenson (New York: Penguin Books, 1972), 46.

has often been seen as a summary of the moral law. The books of the Pentateuch contain detailed laws regulating the worship and life of ancient Israel, specifying how the Israelites were to live as God's redeemed people. The Mosaic laws can be understood as fleshing out the requirements of the moral law and applying them within the context of ancient Israel as God's covenant people.

God's lordship over his creation also implies that all those in authority are themselves under authority and that there is no absolute power in this world. As Jesus cautioned Pilate: "You would have no authority over me at all unless it had been given you from above" (John 19:11). Rulers are warned to be wise and "kiss the Son" (Ps 2:12), recognizing that they are subject to and must give an account to him.

One particular focus of law in Scripture is a concern for the weak and oppressed. Many of the Mosaic laws have as their object the protection of those who are poor or vulnerable, especially the alien, the widow, and the fatherless, with many laws containing provision for those in need or prohibitions on exploiting the vulnerable.[22] God's anger burns at injustice and oppression, and this is frequently a reason why judgment is exercised against the Israelites as well as other nations.[23] An important aim of civil law is to ensure justice and mercy are maintained.

Sometimes a tension has been thought to exist between the external, coercive nature of law and government, and the internal, voluntary, Spirit-led nature of the kingdom of Christ. Christian thinking has traditionally employed a series of institutional, eschatological, and theological distinctions to reconcile these things.

First, there is a distinction between different institutions and their powers. Although Christ rules over all things, he does not rule over all things in precisely the same way. Instead, there are differently constituted authorities with different roles and powers,

---

22. E.g., Exod 21:2–11; 22:22–27; 23:9; Lev 19:14, 33–34; 23:22; 25:23–55; Deut 10:17–19; 14:28–29; 15:7–15; 21:10–14; 24:17–22; 26:12–13; 27:19. See also Ps 82:3; 146:9; Isa 1:17; Jer 5:28; Zech 7:10; Mal 3:5.

23. E.g., Isa 10:1–2; Amos 1:13; 4:1; 8:4–6.

especially the family, church, and government.[24] While governments have coercive powers and are concerned to promote the good and restrain evil, the role of the church in its corporate sense does not possess legal or coercive power but exists for the purpose of teaching the word of God, carrying out public worship, making disciples of Christ, administering the sacraments, and exercising discipline. The existence of these institutions suggests mutual restraint on the powers and functions of the others. Whatever terminology we employ to express this, whether differentiated "spheres" or "kingdoms," there is an important difference between the role and powers of the civil and ecclesiastical structures.

Second, there is an eschatological distinction between the future kingdom and the present, secular age. The kingdom of Christ has broken into the present age, but the kingdom has not yet been fully consummated, and it exists alongside and intermingled with the concerns and affairs of the present world. The present age is marked by "corruption and temporality" and is governed in a preservative, political manner, while the future kingdom of Christ is restorative, pertaining to the life to come, aiming at nothing less "than the restoration of all things."[25] Civil government is legitimate, but also provisional and penultimate.[26]

Third, there is a distinction between the internal realm of the conscience and the external realm of law. In Christ, believers are free from the wrath of God and the curse of the law, and adopted as God's children. This freedom confers a status which cannot be touched by human hands: no human intermediary can come between the believer and Christ or affect the believer's standing. This both relativizes the believer's attachment to earthly authority and also limits

---

24. See Abraham Kuyper, *Lectures on Calvinism* (Grand Rapids: Eerdmans, 1931), 95–96 (arguing that there is a wide range of different spheres that exercise sovereignty, including trade unions and universities as well as the family, church, and state).

25. Matthew J. Tuininga, *Calvin's Political Theology and the Public Engagement of the Church: Christ's Two Kingdoms* (Cambridge: Cambridge University Press, 2017), 112, 140, 146, 151.

26. VanDrunen, *Politics after Christendom*, 25–56.

the claims of civil rulers. Christians can view civil laws with detach-
ment because they are free to obey laws—even unjust laws—without
compromising their fundamental status in Christ.[27]

Although the kingdom of Christ and civil law have very different
characters, they are not in contradiction to each other, but reflect
the institutional, eschatological, and theological differences between
family, church, and government, the kingdom of Christ and the present age, and the internal realm of freedom over against the external
realm of law.

The moral law is perfect and unchanging, expressing God's perfect will for humanity. Human law is temporal, penultimate, external,
coercive, liable to change, and reflects a passing order. The external, coercive, and temporal nature of the civil ruler's function suggests that we should have modest expectations for civil law. Laws
and governments are good things, even blessings, providing a measure of peace and safety which would be unlikely to exist otherwise.
Nevertheless, they cannot change the heart or directly advance the
kingdom of Christ.

THE IMPACT OF CHRISTIANITY
ON THE WESTERN VIEW OF LAW

There is a long tradition of Christian reflection on law, and
Christianity has had a deep influence on the Western legal tradition, especially in countries such as England, the United States, and
Australia. Another helpful way of developing a biblically informed
view of law is to consider the ways that Christianity has influenced
the Western view of law. As a very brief summary, the impact of
Christianity on Western law can be seen in the following areas.[28]

27. Martin Luther, "The Freedom of a Christian," trans W. A. Lambert, in *Selected
Writings of Martin Luther: 1520–1523*, ed. Theodore G. Tappert (Minneapolis: Fortress,
2007), 3, 20.

28. For more detail see John Witte Jr. and Frank S. Alexander, eds., *Christianity
and Law: An Introduction* (Cambridge: Cambridge University Press, 2008); Harold J.
Berman, *Law and Revolution: The Formation of the Western Legal Tradition* (Cambridge,
MA: Harvard University Press, 1983); Harold J. Berman, *Law and Revolution II: The*

The first is the idea of natural law—that is, that there exists a universally applicable moral law which provides an overriding standard to which human civil laws must conform. The history of natural law is complex, but there has been widespread agreement in the church that there exists a moral law, given by God, which is a model for human law. It is not sufficient that human laws pass the applicable process for acceptance as civil laws (such as being passed by the houses of the legislature); they must also conform to the natural law. Human civil law is not simply the product of the human will, but something that must conform to universal moral principles and an overriding standard of justice. The commitment to natural law has meant that within the West there has been a distinctive view of sexual morality, a high regard for the institution of marriage and the family, a high regard for human life, and respect for property.

This idea of a higher law remains very important in the West, despite the widespread rejection of Christianity. Its continuing influence can be seen in the idea of constitutionalism—that is, the idea of an overarching set of commitments to constitutional principles, often set out in a written text, which, among other things, establish limitations on government power. It can also be seen in the idea of human rights (discussed below).

A second important contribution is the idea of limited government—that is, that civil governments do not possess absolute power. Only God is sovereign, and the authority exercised by civil governments and lawmakers is a delegated authority, conferred for specific purposes. The existence of the church as an institution distinct from the state implies that church and state have different purposes, functions, and powers, each limiting the reach of the other. The biblical teaching regarding sin means that political power is often abused

Impact of the Protestant Reformations on the Western Legal Tradition (Cambridge, MA: Belknap Press, 2003); John Witte, *Law and Protestantism: The Legal Teachings of the Lutheran Reformation* (Cambridge: Cambridge University Press, 2002); John Witte, *The Reformation of Rights: Law, Religion, and Human Rights in Early Modern Calvinism* (Cambridge: Cambridge University Press, 2007).

and so its exercise must be limited and held to account.[29] Under the Mosaic law, no one officeholder held absolute power, but power was distributed among the offices of prophet, priest, and king.[30]

Several mechanisms for distributing power have been developed in the West. Under the principle of representation, public officials are elected, and therefore subject to regular accountability for their actions. The rule of law stipulates that everyone is subject to the law, including government officers, and no one is exempt from prosecution.[31] Another important doctrine is the separation of powers, which holds that power should not be concentrated in one set of hands but should be divided among different branches of government, which exercise mutual restraint on the actions of the others.

Under the principle of federalism, government powers are distributed among central and provincial levels of government, preserving both local autonomy and avoiding the concentration of power. A related principle is the principle of subsidiarity taught by the Roman Catholic Church:

> A community of a higher order should not interfere in the internal life of a community of a lower order, depriving the latter of its functions, but rather should support it in case of need and help to co-ordinate its activity with the activities of the rest of society, always with a view to the common good.[32]

Another important contribution that Christianity has made is the idea of human rights—that is, that all people possess inalienable and pre-political rights that cannot be infringed by civil law.

---

29. See, e.g., Deut 17:16–17, which sets out three key limits on Israel's kings.

30. See, e.g., Deut 17:8–20; 18:15–22; 2 Sam 12.

31. Deut 17:18–20 could be seen as a statement of this principle, stipulating that the king was subject to the law of God. See Barbara E. Armacost and Peter Enns, "Crying Out for Justice: Civil Law and the Prophets," in *Law and the Bible: Justice, Mercy and Legal Institutions*, ed. Robert F. Cochran Jr. and David VanDrunen (Downers Grove, IL: IVP Academic, 2013), 123.

32. *Catechism of the Catholic Church* (Staten Island: St Pauls Publishing, 1994), 460 [1883].

These rights exist by virtue of the creation of humans in the image of God, from the natural law, and from the obligations in the Decalogue relating to worship, life, marriage, and property.[33] That is, because the first commandment requires that all people must worship the one true God, this means that civil rulers may not prevent people from doing so. Because the eighth commandment forbids theft, this means that there must be some protection of property rights in law. The requirements of the moral law thus establish limits on the power of the civil ruler and civil law. There remains near-universal acceptance of human rights in modern Western views of law, being a set of internationally agreed standards against which to measure human law, despite the fact that Christianity is widely seen as harmful.[34]

The Christian tradition has also maintained that God alone is lord of the conscience, and so any encroachment on it by the civil ruler exceeds its lawful authority. Thus, the protection of the conscience from coercion is another very important contribution to the Western legal tradition. As Martin Luther wrote:

> The temporal government has laws which extend no further than to life and property and external affairs on earth, for God cannot and will not permit anyone but himself to rule over the soul. Therefore, where the temporal authority presumes to prescribe laws for the soul, it encroaches upon God's government and only misleads souls and destroys them.[35]

---

33. John Witte, *God's Joust, God's Justice: Law and Religion in the Western Tradition* (Grand Rapids: Eerdmans 2006), 31–49.

34. On Christianity as harmful, see, e.g., Richard Dawkins, *The God Delusion* (Boston: Houghton Mifflin Co., 2006); Megan C. Lytle et al., "Association of Religiosity with Sexual Minority Suicide Ideation and Attempt," *American Journal of Preventative Medicine* 54.5 (2018): 644; Kiwoong Park and Ning Hsieh, "A National Study on Religiosity and Suicide Risk by Sexual Orientation," *American Journal of Preventative Medicine* 64.2 (2023): 235; Douglas Ezzy et al., "LGBTQ+ Non-Discrimination and Religious Freedom in the Context of Government-Funded Faith-Based Education, Social Welfare, Health Care, and Aged Care," *Journal of Sociology* 58.3 (2022): 6–7; Carl R. Trueman, *The Rise and Triumph of the Modern Self: Cultural Amnesia, Expressive Individualism, and the Road to Sexual Revolution* (Wheaton, IL: Crossway, 2020), 155.

35. Martin Luther, "Temporal Authority: To What Extent It Should Be Obeyed," in *Selected Writings of Martin Luther: 1520–1523*, ed. Theodore G. Tappert (Minneapolis:

Reflecting this principle, contemporary international human rights
law and the laws of many countries protect the rights of conscience
(in theory, if not in practice) by providing that every person has the
right to freedom of religion, conscience, and belief, and has the freedom to adopt (or not) a religion of their choice, free from undue
influence from civil government.[36]

Another distinctive feature of the Western legal tradition is the
jurisdiction of equity. Sometimes strict adherence to the law would
cause injustice, perhaps because there is no legal remedy for a particular wrong, or because a situation has arisen which was not contemplated by the drafters of a law. The jurisdiction of equity evolved
to meet this type of situation, allowing a remedy to be granted where
adherence to the law would cause injustice. As one jurist famously
observed, "In some cases it is necessary to leave the words of the
law, and to follow that which reason and justice requires, and to that
intent equity is ordained; that is to say, to temper and mitigate the
rigor of the law."[37] Where human laws fail, an underlying commitment to the law of God meant that justice could be ensured.

Another fundamental feature of the Western view of law is a commitment to due process or procedural fairness. Whenever a government body (whether the courts or the executive) makes a decision
which adversely affects a person's rights, that decision must be made
following a fair process, including giving the person affected an
opportunity to be heard. This is a deeply rooted value which draws
from scriptural teaching. Genesis 3:9 records that, after Adam ate the
fruit of the tree of the knowledge of good and evil, God called to Adam,
"Where are you?" Early Christian jurists found in this a requirement

---

Fortress, 2007), 295.

36. General Assembly, Resolution 2200A (XXI), International Covenant on Civil
and Political Rights, Article 18 (December 16, 1966).

37. Christopher St. Germain, *The Doctor and Student: Or Dialogues between a Doctor
of Divinity and a Student in the Laws of England*, 16th ed. (London: S. Richardson and
C. Lintot, 1761), 45. See also Martin Luther, "Whether Soldiers, Too, Can Be Saved,"
trans. Charles M. Jacobs, in *Selected Writings of Martin Luther: 1523–1526*, ed. Theodore
G. Tappert (Minneapolis: Fortress, 2007), 442–43.

of due process, believing that this was intended to demonstrate "that every defendant must be summoned before he can be lawfully punished. It was a tenet of natural law that no person should be punished or deprived of his basic rights unless he had been summoned and given an adequate opportunity to speak on his own behalf."[38]

All government decisions must be based on a careful and impartial examination of the facts, with both sides having an opportunity to be heard, and an adverse finding should only be made against someone on the basis of reliable evidence.[39]

Although much more could be said, the final thing to be noted in this chapter is that civil government and law are good things, given by God for our blessing. Civil rulers are appointed by God and are God's servant for our good (Rom 13:1–7). Christians are to make prayers and even *thanksgivings* for those in authority (1 Tim 2:1–2). Civil laws restrain evil and promote the good, providing a level of peace and order and preventing society from descending into chaos. No legal system is perfect, but an imperfect legal system is preferable to none.[40]

This chapter has explored foundational principles for a Christian approach to law. In the next chapter, I aim to dive more deeply into the different types of law found in the Bible and how these might apply today.

---

38. R. H. Helmholz, "Natural Law and Christianity: A Brief History," in *Christianity and Natural Law: An Introduction*, ed. Norman Doe (Cambridge: Cambridge University Press, 2017), 7. See also Gen 18:21.

39. Relevant biblical texts include Deut 17:6; 19:15; Prov 18:17.

40. Judg 21:25; Robert F. Cochran Jr. and Zachary R. Calo, introduction to *Agape, Justice, and Law: How Might Christian Love Shape Law?*, ed. Robert F. Cochran Jr. and Zachary R. Calo (Cambridge: Cambridge University Press, 2017).

II

LAW *and the* BIBLE

A s I have already noted, the Bible contains a great deal of teaching about law. But modern people find much biblical law puzzling; it seems distant from modern life. For example, the Israelites were told not to "plow with an ox and a donkey together" and to avoid garments of mixed cloth (Deut 22:10–11). Other parts are downright offensive to modern sensibilities. For instance, the Mosaic law said that "no one whose testicles are crushed or whose male organ is cut off shall enter the assembly of the LORD" (Deut 23:1). And yet it is true that all Scripture is God-breathed and useful for the Christian life (2 Tim 3:16–17), which means that we do not have the right to pick and choose which bits of the Bible we think are relevant today.

If we can't simply ignore laws such as these, what are we to make of them? This chapter considers how Christians ought to understand law in the Bible and sets out principles for thinking through the relevance of the Old Testament law today.

NATURAL LAW

In thinking about law and the Bible, we need to start with the concept of natural law. While to some this might seem a strange place
to start given the checkered history of natural law (especially in
the Protestant tradition), we start here because the Bible clearly
affirms the existence of a moral law which predates the giving of
the revealed law to Israel. That is, Scripture teaches that there is
a universally applicable moral law which is knowable in principle
outside of Scripture. This has traditionally been termed "natural
law" in Christian theology, although other terms such as "creation
ethics" might be used. Natural law is necessary to understand scriptural teaching and also for explaining the relevance of biblical law
for today.

There has been resistance to the idea of natural law in the
Protestant tradition. This is primarily because Protestant Christians
are accustomed to think about questions of morality in scriptural
terms: sin is a breach of revealed law. The Protestant tradition
holds that Scripture is sufficient to be equipped for the Christian life
(2 Tim 3:17) and that no person has the authority to bind the conscience of another. The content of morality is something revealed
by Scripture, and so anything not expressly revealed in Scripture is
not a binding moral principle.

But this leads to a difficulty. The Ten Commandments are typically considered to be the perfect summary of the requirements
of the moral law, yet they were given after thousands of years of
human history, and only to the nation of Israel. There is no record
in Scripture of a moral law being given prior to the Decalogue, and no
other nation or people group has ever been subjected to its requirements. If morality is solely the transgression of written or revealed
law, this would logically entail that there were no moral requirements
prior to Moses and that no moral law applies outside the nation-
state of Israel.

The scriptural answer to this conundrum is that there is a universal moral standard applicable to all people at all times which is

knowable outside the revealed law, even if that knowledge is distorted by sin. This is evident from at least four groups of Scripture passages. First, there are passages which indicate an awareness of the moral requirements of the law by people who are outside the covenant community. Second, there are passages that reveal judgment upon non-Israelite nations, to whom the law has not been revealed, for breaching moral standards. Third, there is express reference to a law written on the hearts of those who have not received the law. Fourth, Scripture teaches that the world has been made according to a divinely imposed order. We will explore these in turn.

Awareness of the Law Outside the Covenant Community

First we will address those passages that indicate an awareness of the moral requirements of the law, and even use the terminology of sin, among people to whom the revealed law had not been given. Many passages in Genesis show an awareness of the requirements of the moral law long before the revelation of the law to Moses. In Genesis 4, the Lord looked with favor on Abel and his offering, but not on his brother Cain's offering (which may suggest something related to the second commandment), and Cain murdered Abel out of jealousy. God spoke to Cain: "What have you done? The voice of your brother's blood is crying to me from the ground. And now you are cursed from the ground, which has opened its mouth to receive your brother's blood from your hand" (Gen 4:11). This is a clear recognition of the sixth commandment, even though there is no record in Scripture that God had given an express command not to kill.

The last verse of the same chapter records that "at that time people began to call upon the name of the Lord" (Gen 4:26)—namely, they began to worship God—consistent with the requirements of the first commandment.[1] Genesis 9 records the episode of Noah drinking himself into a stupor and lying uncovered inside his

---

1. John Calvin, *Commentaries on the First Book of Moses called Genesis*, trans. John King (Grand Rapids: Baker Books, 2003), 223.

tent. His son Ham saw his father naked and told his two brothers, Shem and Japheth, who covered their father up, turning their faces the other way so that they would not see their father's nakedness. Noah responds by cursing Canaan (Ham's son) and blessing Shem and Japheth (Gen 9:20–27). The sin recognized here seems to be Ham's mocking and failing to honor his father, in breach of the fifth commandment.

A key theme of Genesis is the calling of the people of the covenant promise into what would later become the nation of Israel. One important aspect of the requirements of the moral law is that they apply to people groups who are not within the covenant family. Genesis 19 records the destruction of Sodom and Gomorrah for their great sinfulness, in violation of the seventh commandment, as "the outcry against its people has become great before the LORD, and the LORD has sent us to destroy it" (Gen 19:13).

In other passages, unbelieving nations and peoples show an awareness of right and wrong. In Genesis 20 Abimelech responded to Abraham's deception about his relationship with Sarah as follows: "What have you done to us? And how have I sinned against you, that you have brought on me and my kingdom a great sin? You have done to me things that ought not to be done" (Gen 20:9). While there was a sense in which Abraham told the truth (see Gen 19:12), he certainly intended to (and did) deceive Abimelech, contrary to the ninth commandment, and the passage employs the terminology of sin.

Therefore, we see many instances of a clear recognition of moral principles, in substance equivalent to certain of the Ten Commandments but existing prior to the delivery of the Ten Commandments at Mount Sinai.[2] There is a recognition of at least the first, fifth, sixth, seventh, and ninth commandments, likely also the second, and potentially others.

---

2. Other examples could be cited from Genesis, such as Gen 6:5–8; 11:1–9; 12:10–20; 34:1–31; 38:6–10.

In Deuteronomy 4 Moses said the law given to Israel was to be a witness to the surrounding nations, "who, when they hear all these statutes, will say, 'Surely this great nation is a wise and understanding people' " (Deut 4:6). This presupposes that the non-Israelite nations were able to perceive the inherent wisdom and reasonableness of the Mosaic laws, and that they had the capacity to do so, which suggests that they possessed some inbuilt knowledge of the requirements of the moral law. Similar logic underlies New Testament passages which urge Christians to live godly lives among their non-Christian neighbors, who will recognize their good works.[3]

JUDGMENT ON NATIONS OUTSIDE THE COVENANT

The second broad grouping of passages are those in which non-Israelite nations are judged for failing to conform to the principles of the moral law. This is significant because the moral law was revealed in written form only to Israel. To take one example, in Amos 1–2 God judges the pagan nations surrounding Israel for their brutality, while Israel is judged for breaching the law of the Lord (see Amos 2:4).[4] This, of course, only makes sense if there is a moral standard against which the non-Israelite nations were judged. How could they be judged for breaching a law which did not apply to them and of which they had no knowledge? The imposition of judgment on the non-Israelite nations therefore means that the moral law was applicable to those nations, and also implies that those nations had some ability to understand the requirements of that law, outside of the revealing of the written law.

---

3. 1 Thess 4:12; 1 Tim 3:7; Col 4:5; 1 Pet 2:12.
4. Other examples recorded in Scripture include Gen 19; Josh 6, 8, 10, 11; Isa 13–23; Jer 46–51; Ezek 25–32, 35, 38–39; Dan 4, 5; Zeph 2 and the books of Obadiah, Jonah, and Nahum.

THE LAW WRITTEN ON THE HEART

There are several classic New Testament passages which affirm the existence of natural law. In Romans 1 Paul states that what can be known about God is plain to all because God has revealed it in creation (Rom 1:18–20). This truth is suppressed in unrighteousness, but it is the suppression of what is known, not ignorance. Paul also expressly refers to the moral requirements of the law applicable to the gentiles and written on their hearts, despite their not having the written law:

> For when Gentiles, who do not have the law, by nature do what the law requires, they are a law to themselves, even though they do not have the law. They show that the work of the law is written on their hearts, while their conscience also bears witness, and their conflicting thoughts accuse or even excuse them. (Rom 2:14–15)

The only way to make sense of this biblical teaching is to recognize the existence of a moral law, which is applicable to all people and knowable separately from the delivery of the written law in the Decalogue. Scripture consistently assumes or asserts the validity of this moral law. For this reason, the church has affirmed the existence of a moral law written on the heart, which has been understood as the "natural law." Natural law is the moral law, applicable to all people at all times, equivalent in substance to the Ten Commandments, written on the heart and knowable through the conscience and reason.

THE CREATED ORDER

Another key aspect of the idea of natural law is that of a created order. Natural law is broader than simply a list of rules or commands but reflects the nature of creation as an ordered reality. Rules can help describe the nature of the natural law, but they do not exhaust its content. David VanDrunen gives a helpful illustration of this point: "'Do not commit adultery' is an important universal rule, but there is a lot more to a successful, lifelong marriage relationship and to training children toward responsible adulthood."[5]

The creation narrative in Genesis 1–2 describes the creation of man and woman and the establishment of an order that reflects key aspects of their nature. This narrative is not "neutral," but sets out patterns and structures which inform the logic and purpose of the law, including the creation of man and woman in the image of God, the creation of a companion for man, and God's resting on the seventh day. The creation of humans in God's image (Gen 1:26–28) underscores the preciousness of human life and that no person has the right to take that life away (Gen 9:6), which underlies the logic of the sixth commandment.

God declared that "it is not good for man to be alone" and so made Eve as a helper, establishing a sexual and marital union with the man (Gen 2:18–25). That this is intended to be a pattern for subsequent generations is evident from verse 24: "Therefore a man shall leave his father and his mother and hold fast to his wife, and they shall become one flesh." Paul applies the logic of this verse to warn against sexual immorality, as all sexual intercourse unites the participants as one flesh, which (for Christians) would amount to joining Christ's members to a prostitute (1 Cor 6:16–18).

God created the world in six days and rested on the seventh (Gen 2:1–3). God does not need rest (John 5:17) but did this to establish a pattern for creation, which is given as the rationale for the Sabbath in Deuteronomy 5:12–15. God placed the man in the garden to work and tend it and to have dominion over the earth (Gen 1:26–28; 2:15, 19–20). Thus, work and rest are part of the patterns established at creation.

The narrative provides clear evidence of patterns and structures embedded in creation, especially marriage, work, and the Sabbath, which are closely tied to the fourth, sixth, and

---

5. David VanDrunen, *Politics after Christendom: Political Theology in a Fractured World* (Grand Rapids: Zondervan, 2020), 135–36.

seventh commandments. This suggests, therefore, that the Ten
Commandments are not simply arbitrary rules, but reflect the
nature of creation and humanity's place within that creation. This
also explains their applicability to the non-Israelite nations: rather
than being simply divine laws given by God for the regulation of
Israel, the Ten Commandments reflect something universally applicable to all people.

If the substance of the Ten Commandments is knowable through
natural law, why did God give the law at Mount Sinai? Scripture recognizes that humans suppress the truth in unrighteousness (Isa 5:20;
Rom 1:18), and so our knowledge of the moral law is distorted and
corrupted by sin. Our "natural" knowledge is not a perfect or complete reflection of the moral law. The written law, including the Ten
Commandments and other parts of Scripture, explains the core precepts of the moral law with much greater clarity than could be known
through reason and the conscience.

An understanding of natural law also explains why the moral
law is relevant today. It is true that the law was given to the people
of Israel in the context of a covenant relationship with God after
their redemption from Egypt (Exod 19:5–6; 20:1–2). The law is
not addressed to any other people group, and no other nation state
stands in a similar relationship with God today. Nevertheless, the
relevance of the moral law derives from the fact that it expresses
God's unchanging moral requirements for all people.

CATEGORIZING BIBLICAL LAWS

The term "law" is used in different senses in Scripture. "Law" can be
the law written on the heart (Rom 2:14–15), the universally applicable moral law (Rom 3:19), the requirements of the Mosaic law (Gal
5:3), or it can mean simply "principle" or "animating power" (Rom
7:23).[6] There are different types of commands in Scripture, includ-

---

6. Douglas J. Moo, "'Law,' 'Works of the Law,' and Legalism in Paul," *Westminster Theological Journal* 45, no. 1 (Spring 1983): 73.

ing universal commands, commands addressed to people in particular positions such as civil rulers, parents, and husbands, and some
private commands to particular individuals, such as the command
to Abraham to sacrifice his son.[7] Not every command in Scripture
forms part of the "law." According to James Bannerman, to find out
whether a scriptural command or example is of permanent obligation, we should ask: "Was this command ... founded on moral
grounds, common to all men at all times, in all circumstances, or
on local and temporary grounds, peculiar to certain men in certain
circumstances, at some given time?"[8]

One key issue with regard to biblical law is how to treat the Mosaic
laws of the Pentateuch. What relevance do these laws have today?
The Christian tradition has customarily divided the Mosaic laws into
three categories: moral, ceremonial or ritual, and civil or judicial.[9]
One main purpose of this distinction is to explain the contemporary applicability of the Mosaic laws. The traditional view is that the
moral law continues to apply today; the ceremonial laws have been
repealed or fulfilled in Christ and are no longer binding; and the
judicial laws do not bind in their original form, but the underlying
moral principle encapsulated in those laws is applicable, although
they need careful translating into the New Testament context.

A number of writers have objected to this threefold distinction,
giving three main reasons. First, the labels "moral," "ceremonial,"
and "judicial" never appear in Scripture.[10] Second, there is no hard

---

7. Francis Turretin, *Institutes of Elenctic Theology*, ed. James T. Dennison Jr., trans.
George Musgrave Giger (Phillipsburg, NJ: P&R Publishing, 1992), 2:29.

8. James Bannerman, *The Church of Christ: A Treatise on the Nature, Powers, Ordinances,
Discipline, and Government of the Christian Church* (Edinburgh: Banner of Truth, 1960),
2:406.

9. E.g., Thomas Aquinas, *Summa Theologica* (London: R. & T. Washbourne, 1915),
IaIIae 99:2–4; *Thirty-* (1571), article 7; John Calvin, *Institutes of the Christian Religion*,
ed. John T. McNeill, trans. Ford Lewis Battles (Louisville: Westminster John Knox,
1960), 4.20.14; *Westminster Confession of Faith*, XIX.3–4; Herman Witsius, *Economy of
the Covenants between God and Man*, trans. William Crookshank (London: 1822), 2:162.

10. E.g., Gordon J. Wenham, *The Book of Leviticus* (Grand Rapids: Eerdmans, 1979),
32; Wayne Grudem, *Christian Ethics: An Introduction to Biblical Moral Reasoning* (Wheaton,

and fast distinction between the categories of laws, and there is dis-agreement as to how certain laws might be categorized. For example, the Old Testament contains a prohibition on eating meat with the blood in it. Since the command appears in Leviticus 19:26, it might be considered a law specific to Israel that is repealed in the New Testament. However, it was also given in the context of the Noahic covenant, which is not specific to Israel (Gen 9:4). Is this command moral or ceremonial? Finally, the distinction does not achieve its main purpose, which is to tell us whether the laws continue to apply.[11]

There is certainly force in these arguments. A Mosaic law may exhibit characteristics of more than one of the categories. The cer-emonial laws are sometimes framed in moral-sounding terms (for example, Lev 11:10–12, 20, 42), and the law sometimes imposes civil penalties for breaches of ceremonial or moral law (for example, Lev 19:8). Scripture does not neatly distinguish between the different categories, with many passages containing moral, ceremonial, and civil laws all together.[12] The judicial laws are applications of the moral law in particular circumstances, and so could be considered moral as well as civil. The New Testament treats some judicial laws as appli-cable in the church.[13]

Nevertheless, while the terms "moral," "ceremonial," and "judi-cial" are not employed in Scripture, as with doctrines such as the Trinity and infant baptism, a distinction of this nature is necessary to account for biblical teaching.

Consider first why it is important to have the moral law as a cat-egory. Except for the Sabbath, the New Testament expressly upholds the continuing validity of all of the Ten Commandments.[14] These

---

IL: Crossway, 2018), 250.

11. Joel McDurmon, *The Bounds of Love: An Introduction to God's Law of Liberty*, 2nd ed. (independently pub., 2019), 26–41.

12. For example, Lev 19:3–8, 17–26.

13. Matt 18:16; 2 Cor 13:1; 1 Tim 5:19.

14. First Commandment: Matt 4:10; Luke 4:8; Second Commandment: Acts 15:20; Third Commandment: Matt 5:33–37; Fifth Commandment: Matt 15:4; 19:19; Mark 10:19; Luke 18:20; Eph 6:1–3; Sixth Commandment: Matt 5:21–22; 19:18; Mark 10:19; Luke 18:20; Rom 13:9; Seventh Commandment: Matt 5:27–28; 19:18; Mark 10:5–12, 19; Luke

commands therefore continue to apply as binding for the Christian, and little "translation" or modification is needed to apply them to today's context. "You shall have no other gods before me" and "You shall not murder" are commands that still apply to the Christian (and indeed all people). That is, the Ten Commandments apply today in almost identical terms. It is useful to think of these as the "moral law," expressing God's unchanging moral requirements for humanity.

In contrast to this, there are many laws in the Pentateuch that do not express an unchanging moral principle and are expressly repealed or fulfilled in the New Testament, especially the food laws and the laws relating to the sacrificial system.[15] As discussed below, this does not mean they are now irrelevant, but it does mean they no longer have any obligatory force in their original form: we are no longer required to perform the rituals of the sacrificial system or adhere to the Mosaic dietary laws. These laws are therefore treated very differently from the moral law by the New Testament. "Ceremonial" is a convenient label for these laws.

It is also true that the Old Testament treats the ceremonial laws very differently from the moral law. Isaiah condemned the Israelites for bringing "vain offerings" and stated that God detested their rituals because of their injustice and oppression (Isa 1:12–14; 58:3–4; see also Isa 66:3–4). Hosea said that God desires "steadfast love and not sacrifice, the knowledge of God rather than burnt offerings" (Hos 6:6). Several passages of Scripture suggest that God takes no pleasure in sacrifices (Pss 40:6; 51:6; Heb 10:5–6). Samuel asked Saul:

> Has the LORD as great delight in burnt offerings and sacrifices,
>   as in obeying the voice of the LORD?
> Behold, to obey is better than sacrifice,
>   and to listen than the fat of rams.
>
> (1 Sam 15:22; see also Mic 6:6–8)

16:18; 18:20; Rom 13:9; Eighth Commandment: Matt 19:18; Mark 10:19; Luke 18:20; Rom 13:9; Eph 4:28; Ninth Commandment: Matt 19:18; Mark 10:19; Luke 18:20; Acts 5:3–4; Eph 4:25; Tenth Commandment: Luke 12:15; Rom 13:9.

15. Acts 10:9–15; 11:1–18; 15:1–29; Heb 8–10.

Jesus leveled similar judgments at the Pharisees of his day (Matt 23:25–26; Luke 11:39–41). There is something obnoxious in rigorously obeying the ritual observances of the Mosaic law but disobeying the moral law; the rituals must be undertaken within the context of a living covenant relationship with God. This suggests that there is a primacy to the requirements of the moral law, and that there are biblical grounds for distinguishing the moral and ceremonial law.

There is a third category of Mosaic laws which is different from the moral and the ceremonial; they are not binding in their original form and yet are not fulfilled or repealed. For instance, Deuteronomy 22:8 required the Israelites to build a parapet on their roof when building a new home. Almost no one would argue that this command is binding in precisely its original form, and yet almost everyone would agree that it applies in some way.[16] Leviticus 19:13 states that "the wages of a hired worker shall not remain with you all night until the morning." Applying this today would not literally require daily payment of employees, but its principle can be applied in other ways. Some Mosaic laws are expressly referenced in the New Testament but applied in very different ways from their original context (e.g., 1 Cor 5:13). Unlike the ceremonial laws, these laws have not been repealed, and unlike the moral laws, they are not applicable in precisely their original form. "Civil" or "judicial" is a convenient label for these laws.

Accordingly, while there may be uncertainty about the categorization of particular laws, and certain laws may fall into more than one category, the threefold distinction of the law remains helpful for thinking about how the Mosaic laws apply today. When considering a particular law in Scripture, we ought to consider whether the law gives effect to an underlying principle which remains valid today, and how that principle may be translated into today's context. How might we go about doing this?

---

16. Grudem, *Christian Ethics*, 251. I will return to this example later in this chapter.

THE MORAL LAW

The moral law is that law established by God at creation which is applicable to all people everywhere at all times and sets out the requirements and duties owed by all people to God, reflecting the order of that creation. As I mentioned above when speaking about the natural law, the moral law has been written on the hearts of all people and is knowable through the conscience, although that knowledge has been corrupted by sin, so that natural knowledge will always be imperfect. The content of this law is summarized in the Ten Commandments; its content is fleshed out in other parts of Scripture, especially the Pentateuch, and its underlying logic is authoritatively explained in the New Testament, especially in the Sermon on the Mount. This is the understanding of the moral law held by the Christian tradition.[17]

The moral law may be described as "natural law" because it is knowable in principle apart from special revelation and because it reflects the natural order which God has implanted on his creation. Natural law and biblical law are different means of knowing the moral law, and therefore they have essentially the same content. However, natural law and biblical law are not identical in every respect. Biblical law is much more detailed, is more authoritative, and has much greater clarity, being delivered in written and spoken form, and as a result its knowledge is not as easily distorted.

Are there moral commands and requirements of the natural law beyond the text of Scripture? The Roman Catholic Church, for instance, considers that the natural law imposes a range of requirements that are not contained in Scripture, such as a prohibition on the use of contraception.[18] Does a commitment to natural law entail acceptance of such requirements?

---

17. See, e.g., *Westminster Confession of Faith*, XIX.2; *Second Helvetic Confession, 1566*, ch. XII in *Reformed Confessions of the Sixteenth Century*, ed. Arthur C. Cochrane (Louisville: Westminster John Knox, 2003), 247–49.

18. *Catechism of the Catholic Church*, 570 [2369–70].

It should first be recognized that the requirements of the moral law are broader than the precise words of the Ten Commandments. For instance, the seventh commandment directly prohibits adultery but does not in its terms prohibit rape, a sin of surely at least equal seriousness to adultery. And yet expositors throughout history have recognized that rape is obviously and uncontroversially within the scope of sins prohibited by the seventh commandment.[19]

This illustrates a key point about the moral law—namely, that it is broader than the precise words of the Ten Commandments, although the Ten Commandments remain a perfect summary of that law. Earlier writers like the Reformed theologian Francis Turretin explained this point by describing the Ten Commandments as synecdoches, where the part represents the whole. That is, they are like the bullseye on a target: the statement that encapsulates the heart of what is required or prohibited in the moral requirement. And yet there is more to the target than just the bullseye; the reference to the bullseye is in fact intended to capture everything on the target. The Ten Commandments therefore refer synecdochally to a broader range of things than simply what is expressed in their narrow words.[20]

This can be seen in the exposition and fleshing out of the law in other parts of Scripture. Leviticus 19, for example, prohibits a wide range of sexual conduct, which provides greater detail for the scope of the seventh commandment. Although it only refers to "adultery," the seventh commandment has in view a broader range of sexual sins.

This raises the obvious question: How do we know what else is on the target? What things does the moral law apply to beyond the express words of the Ten Commandments? Caution is obviously required here given that Jesus condemned those who teach "as

---

19. *Westminster Larger Catechism*, 139; Turretin, *Institutes of Elenctic Theology*, 2:121; William Perkins, *A Discourse of Conscience* (Cambridge: University of Cambridge, 1596), 845; Lancelot Andrewes, *The Morall Law Expounded* (London: Sparke, Milbourne, Cotes, and Crooke, 1642), 762; William Ames, *The Marrow of Theology*, trans. John Dykstra Eusden (Grand Rapids: Baker Books, 1968), 320.

20. Turretin, *Institutes of Elenctic Theology*, 2:35.

doctrines the commandments of men," elevating their own opinions to the status of divine decrees (Matt 15:9; Mark 7:7). We ought therefore to be careful before going beyond the bounds of scriptural teaching lest we attempt to clothe our personal opinions with divine authority.

The remainder of the Mosaic law and the New Testament illuminate and provide authoritative guidance as to the true nature and scope of the moral law. Lutheran theologian Johann Gerhard wrote that the Decalogue is the foundation of all law, and that all other precepts "can be traced back to the Decalogue."[21] Many of the laws of the Pentateuch are "a particularization of the general precepts of the Decalogue" and an application of its principles to specific situations.[22] Therefore, it is helpful to understand the Mosaic laws as an exposition of the Ten Commandments, fleshing out their meaning and applying the law to concrete situations.

Another relevant principle is the principle of "good and necessary consequence," which states that some things can be properly deduced from scriptural teaching, and such deductions are as authoritative as the express words of Scripture themselves. To take an example, there is no direct prohibition of rape anywhere in the Bible. Instead, there are various judicial laws which apply the death penalty to any man found committing this sin (see, e.g., Deut 22:25). These laws help explain the true scope of what is contemplated by the seventh commandment.

Further, the New Testament, and especially the Sermon on the Mount, explains the deeper logic and rationale of certain parts of the law, especially the sixth, seventh, and ninth commandments (Matt 5:21–48). In particular, Jesus makes clear that the commandments

---

21. Johann Gerhard, *On the Law*, ed. Benjamin T. G. Mayes and Joshua J. Hayes, trans. Richard J. Dinda (St. Louis: Concordia Publishing House, 2015), 14, quoting Gabriel Biel; Heinrich Bullinger, *The Decades of Henry Bullinger*, ed. Thomas Harding (Grand Rapids: Reformation Heritage Books, 2004), 2:220.

22. Martin Chemnitz, *Loci Theologici*, trans. J. A. O. Preus (St. Louis: Concordia Publishing House, 1989), 619 (I have changed "Decalog" to "Decalogue"); Gerhard, *On the Law*, 282; Wenham, *Leviticus*, 35.

are not merely a matter of external obedience, but they demand an internal heart attitude of purity and are based on love for God and neighbor.

The Christian tradition has therefore affirmed that the content of the moral law is equivalent to the Ten Commandments, understood in light of the Mosaic law as a whole and the later elaboration of the law in the New Testament. Under the principle of good and necessary consequence, the law may apply in specific ways in situations which are not specifically stated in Scripture. Beyond this, Protestant churches have generally been reluctant to affirm the existence of morally binding principles which are not stated in or deducible from Scripture. The Roman Catholic tradition typically has a stronger conception of the normative nature of the created order and has been more willing to draw firm deductions from an understanding of natural law.[23]

Both the Old and the New Testaments bear witness to the law and mutually illuminate each other. To take an example, in the Sermon on the Mount, Jesus said, "You have heard that it was said, 'An eye for an eye and a tooth for a tooth.' But I say to you, Do not resist the one who is evil. But if anyone slaps you on the right cheek, turn to him the other also. And if anyone would sue you and take your tunic, let him have your cloak as well" (Matt 5:38–40). What does this require? Taken to an extreme, it could mean that Christians are not entitled to defend themselves, protect their families, or use any force whatsoever—which is an interpretation some Christians have adopted.[24] Understanding this verse in the light of the Mosaic law, however, helps to illuminate its purpose. Leviticus 19:18 says: "You shall not

---

23. *The Catechism of the Catholic Church* (Staten Island: St Pauls Publishing, 1994), 492 [2036], states that "the authority of the Magisterium extends also to the specific precepts of the natural law, because their observance, demanded by the Creator, is necessary for salvation. In recalling the prescriptions of the natural law, the Magisterium of the Church exercises an essential part of its prophetic office of proclaiming to men what they truly are and reminding them of what they should be before God."

24. Michael Sattler, "The Schleitheim Articles," in *The Radical Reformation*, ed. Michael G. Baylor (Cambridge: Cambridge University Press, 1991), 177–78.

take vengeance or bear a grudge against the sons of your own people, but you shall love your neighbor as yourself: I am the LORD." The law therefore evinces a preoccupation with vengefulness and bearing grudges. This can illuminate the meaning of Jesus's statements, and suggests that Matthew 5:38–40 is about revengeful anger rather than lawful and proportionate defense and protection of one's life.

Sometimes a radical contrast is thought to exist between the demands of the Old and New Testaments. This is misguided. Jesus summed up the entire law in two commandments: "You shall love the Lord your God with all your heart and with all your soul and with all your mind. This is the great and first commandment. And a second is like it: You shall love your neighbor as yourself. On these two commandments depend all the Law and the Prophets" (Matt 22:37–40). Both of these commandments were drawn from the Mosaic law (Deut 6:5; Lev 19:18).

Even some of the more radical demands laid upon Jesus's disciples have parallels in the Mosaic law. Jesus said: "I say to you, Love your enemies and pray for those who persecute you, so that you may be sons of your Father who is in heaven" (Matt 5:43–48). An example of love for enemies in the Mosaic law can be found in Exodus 23: "If you meet your enemy's ox or his donkey going astray, you shall bring it back to him. If you see the donkey of one who hates you lying down under its burden, you shall refrain from leaving him with it; you shall rescue it with him" (Exod 23:4–5). The underlying principle embodied in this law is very similar to Jesus's teaching.

Thus, there is substantial continuity between the law under the Old and New Testaments, but it is not identical in every respect. It would be accurate to say that Jesus intensifies the standards of the law and yet at the same time uncovers the deeper heart of the commandments (see especially Matt 5:21–48).

Although the moral law is unchanging, some aspects of the moral law were adapted to Israel, not to the church.[25] Under the Mosaic

---

25. Turretin, *Institutes of Elenctic Theology*, 2:8.

covenant, the moral law was accompanied by a series of promised temporal blessings and curses for obedience and disobedience (Deut 28). Those promises were tied to the land of Israel and are no longer applicable in the New Testament era. The fifth commandment states: "Honor your father and your mother, that your days may be long in the land that the LORD your God is giving you" (Exod 20:12). The promissory aspect of this commandment ("that your days may be long in the land that the LORD your God is giving you") is not applicable to the church in precisely the same way because the church is not a nation in the physical land of Israel. Nevertheless, the commandment is still directly relevant in the new covenant era, as evidenced by Paul quoting it in Ephesians 6:1–3.

Another example is the fourth commandment, which (as given in Deuteronomy) required Israel to observe the Sabbath day, remembering that the people of Israel were slaves in the land of Egypt (Deut 5:12–15). The Sabbath was therefore an opportunity to rest and reflect on God's deliverance. This rationale is not applicable in precisely its original form, although it is not difficult to translate this to the New Testament context, such that the Sabbath (now "the Lord's day"; see Rev 1:10) is an opportunity to rest and reflect on God's deliverance in Christ.

Can unbelievers know the moral law even when they have not been taught the Ten Commandments? The clear scriptural teaching is that they can. Romans 2:14–15 teaches that the work of the law is written on the hearts of gentiles, who do not have the written law. The judgments inflicted by God on unbelieving nations shows that they were punished for breaching a standard they knew, or ought to have known. The moral law is therefore knowable by all people. The failure to worship God, for instance, is to deny what is clearly revealed in the creation regarding God's eternal power and divine nature (Rom 1:20).

This explains why unbelievers can live outwardly moral lives, such as by being faithful to their spouses and being generally truthful. It also explains why unbelievers can understand the principles of justice—often more so than the church, given the frequent absence of natural justice from church courts. Indeed, sometimes non-Christians perceive the requirements of the moral law more clearly than Christians can, as things which would not be tolerated in the world are embraced in the church (see 1 Cor 5:1).

However, Scripture also recognizes that all people suppress the truth in unrighteousness (Rom 1:18). Our consciences can be seared, particularly by repeated suppression of its warnings. Therefore, unless instructed by Scripture, the knowledge of the moral law will always be incomplete and corrupted, and Scripture remains necessary as a much clearer statement of the standards of the moral law.

I will discuss whether the moral law is still binding at greater length later in this chapter. In short, the moral law remains binding as a rule of conduct even though Christians are not under the curse or condemnation of the law.

CEREMONIAL LAWS

The second category of law is the ritual or ceremonial laws. These laws regulated the worship and religious life of Israel and marked out the Israelites as distinct from the gentile nations. These laws have been expressly repealed by the New Testament. In Acts 10 the food laws were abolished, overturning the distinction between clean and unclean meats (Acts 10:15) and ending the separation between Jew and gentile (Gal 3:28). In Hebrews, the old covenant, which is associated with the ceremonial laws and priestly ministrations, has been declared to be "obsolete" and "ready to vanish away" (Heb 8:13).

The nature of the laws helps explain why they were abolished. Unlike the other categories of law, which express fundamental principles of morality and the application of those principles within a specific context, the ceremonial laws were symbolic and typical. As symbols, they portrayed spiritual truths in visible form; as types, they portrayed in embryonic form something that would later be fulfilled by Christ.[26] The New Testament describes the ceremonial system as shadows of a greater reality (Col 2:17; Heb 8:5).

Although these rituals appeared to be efficacious—the "clear understanding of Leviticus is that sacrifice did effect atonement"[27]— the book of Hebrews states that "it is impossible for the blood of bulls and goats to take away sins" (Heb 10:4), and so the rituals in and of themselves were not able to achieve that which they symbolized. The ceremonial system and laws are symbols and types which are fulfilled in Christ; given that we now have the reality which those laws pointed to, it would make no sense to return to that which was transitory and incomplete. As such, the ceremonial laws are not binding in their original form. However, this does not mean that they are simply to be discarded as irrelevant. All Scripture is God-breathed and useful (2 Tim 3:16). On the road to Emmaus Jesus rebuked the two disciples: "'O foolish ones, and slow of heart to believe all that the prophets have spoken! Was it not necessary that the Christ should suffer these things and enter into his glory?' And beginning with Moses and all the Prophets, he interpreted to them in all the Scriptures the things concerning himself" (Luke 24:25–27).

This suggests that it is not possible to understand the Messiah's mission without a good grasp of the Old Testament, including the Mosaic ceremonial laws. Indeed, there is much "ceremonial" imagery throughout the New Testament that describes important aspects of God's character, Jesus's atoning work, and the nature of the church. Gordon Wenham wrote that it was in terms of the Levitical sacrifices "that Jesus himself and the early church understood his atoning death."[28] Jesus is our prophet and high priest (Acts 3:22; Heb 5:5–6). When Jesus died the curtain of the temple was torn in two (Matt 27:51), and by means of his own blood Jesus "entered once for

---

26. Geerhardus Vos, *Biblical Theology: Old and New Testaments* (Edinburgh: Banner of Truth, 1975), 144.

27. William J. Dumbrell, *The Faith of Israel: A Theological Survey of the Old Testament*, 2nd ed. (Grand Rapids: Baker Academic, 2002), 42–43.

28. Wenham, *Leviticus*, 37.

all into the holy places" (Heb 9:12). Christ's atoning work purifies his people from all unrighteousness (Titus 2:14; 1 John 1:9), reminiscent of the purification offering discussed in Leviticus 4:1–5:13.

Paul tells us that "Christ, our Passover lamb, has been sacrificed. Let us therefore celebrate the festival, not with the old leaven, the leaven of malice and evil, but with the unleavened bread of sincerity and truth" (1 Cor 5:7–8). Jesus is "the firstfruits of those who have fallen asleep" (1 Cor 15:20). Christ described his body as a temple (John 2:19–21), and Paul describes the bodies of Christians as temples of the Holy Spirit (1 Cor 6:19–20). God's people "like living stones are being built up as a spiritual house, to be a holy priesthood, to offer spiritual sacrifices acceptable to God through Jesus Christ" (1 Pet 2:5). Jesus instituted the Lord's Supper during the Passover celebration, drawing heavily on Old Testament themes (Matt 26:26–29; 1 Cor 11:23–26).

All these statements can only be understood in light of the Mosaic ceremonial laws.[29] This suggests the continuing animating relevance of the principles embodied in the ceremonial law, even though we no longer carry out its rituals in the New Testament era. That is, notwithstanding that the ceremonial laws have been abrogated, the underlying principle or meaning embodied in those laws remains applicable.[30] For example, the Old Testament rites teach us that "without the shedding of blood there is no forgiveness of sins," pointing us to obtain forgiveness by means of the shed blood of Christ (Heb 9:22; 10:12). We are not bound by the rules set out in passages such as Deuteronomy 18 relating to tithing, but the principles of generous giving and provision for leaders remain applicable.[31]

---

29. See also Wenham, *Leviticus*, 101–2, 111–12.

30. John Calvin, *Commentary on the Harmony of the Evangelists, Matthew, Mark and Luke* (Grand Rapids: Baker, 2003), 1:278.

31. Luke 10:7; 1 Cor 9:3–14; 2 Cor 9:6–11; 1 Tim 5:17–18.

JUDICIAL LAWS

The third category of biblical law is the civil or judicial laws given to
Moses. The contemporary relevance of these laws has been controversial. Leviticus 20:9, for example, states that "anyone who curses
his father or his mother shall surely be put to death." Is this law
applicable today? Some argue that civil governments should indeed
enforce laws such as these in their civil law.[32] Others argue that "the
Mosaic law is completely abrogated in its entirety."[33]

It must first be recognized that the use of the terms "judicial" or
"civil" to describe these laws does not exactly line up with the modern
concept of judicial or civil laws. In today's thinking, we typically draw
a sharp distinction between moral laws and civil laws, even if we do
not use that terminology. A civil law is something enacted into law
by the legislature or determined by the courts, and it has some legal
sanction or consequence attached to it. Unless this has occurred,
a principle or standard is simply a rule of morality—it is not "law."
The Mosaic laws do not sharply distinguish between moral and civil
in this way, and laws that would typically be categorized as "judicial
laws" in the Old Testament include both civil laws as we understand
that term as well as personal moral obligations that have no judicially
enforceable sanction attached to their breach.

We should also recognize that the judicial laws are not an exhaustive code. They were not intended to regulate every aspect of Israel's
life; there are gaps, omissions, and situations that are not addressed.
For example, there is little or no teaching in Scripture regarding
inheritance, employment law, environmental law, public law, contracts, company law, insolvency law, mining law, and so on. As such,
it makes no sense to view the judicial laws of the Old Testament as
an exhaustive blueprint for society today. The judicial laws consist

32. E.g., Greg L. Bahnsen, *Theonomy in Christian Ethics*, 3rd ed. (n.p.: Covenant
Media Press, 2002), 254; Rousas John Rushdoony, *The Institutes of Biblical Law*
(Phillipsburg, NJ: Presbyterian and Reformed Publishing, 1973), 237.

33. Grudem, *Christian Ethics*, 250. Note that Grudem does state that the Mosaic
laws contain wisdom to guide us today.

mainly of case laws—that is, laws dealing with specific situations which apply the principles of the Ten Commandments to a particular context.

The judicial laws do not directly apply today but must be translated into our own context. This is for several reasons. The laws were given to Israel within a particular theological, social, and political context. Israel was an agricultural society and had very different beliefs from today, including an acceptance of the legitimacy of slavery, very different views about the respective roles of men and women, a very different state of technological development, and so on. The law was given within that context and in many ways reflects the prevailing beliefs and practices of the time. More than this, Israel was God's covenant people, redeemed from Egypt and called to be a holy nation (Exod 19:5–6). The law was specifically given to Israel as God's chosen people and was supposed to reflect that covenant relationship: Israel was to obey the law out of gratitude for God's deliverance. No other nation stands in a similar relationship, and the law was not addressed to any other nation.

In the New Testament era, the church is now the people of God (1 Pet 2:9), and the church is not a nation in a physical land. It is for these reasons that the church has consistently affirmed that the judicial laws have expired together with the ancient state of Israel and do not oblige further.[34] That is, the judicial laws of the Mosaic code, including the punishment and sanctions specified for various offenses, have no direct applicability under the New Testament era. They do not bind either church or state today.

However, this does not mean they are irrelevant. While they are not directly binding in their original form, the principles underlying the judicial case laws remain applicable. The concept of natural law explains why this is the case. As noted earlier, natural law is the scriptural teaching that there is a universally applicable moral law in substance identical to the Ten Commandments. The judicial laws are

---

34. See, e.g., *Westminster Confession of Faith*, XIX.4.

an exposition of the Ten Commandments and an application of them
to a particular context. They remain relevant by virtue of the universal applicability of the natural law—that is, the judicial laws of Moses
remain relevant insofar as they explain and apply the moral law.

As the *Westminster Confession of Faith* famously expressed it, the
Old Testament judicial laws have expired and do not now need to
be obeyed "further than the general equity thereof may require."[35]
That is, the laws do not bind in their precise form, but their "general equity" remains valid. "General equity" refers to the universally
applicable principles of the natural law which are embodied in the
judicial laws.

This has important consequences for the way we think about the
Old Testament civil laws. It shifts the debate from *whether* they are
relevant today to *how* they are relevant. This is consistent with other
parts of Scripture. If all Scripture is God-breathed and useful, necessary for the people of God to be thoroughly equipped (2 Tim 3:16–17),
then the Mosaic law must remain useful today.

Properly applying Scripture requires careful meditation on the
judicial laws in the light of the Ten Commandments to tease out their
underlying principles and discern what they reveal about the moral
law. Those principles then need to be re-articulated and applied in
the very different context of today.

How might we go about this? Sometimes the New Testament
expressly tells us how certain judicial laws apply today. For example, some of the Mosaic laws specified the death penalty for various
offenses. The rationale for this was to "purge the evil from your
midst";[36] that is, the purpose of the punishment was to ensure
the purity of God's people. Reflecting the fact that the church, not
Israel, is now God's people, Paul applies these verses in the New
Testament to the removal of an unrepentant sinner from the church,
directly quoting these texts: "For what have I to do with judging

---

35. *Westminster Confession of Faith*, XIX.4.
36. Deut 17:7, 12; 19:19; 21:21; 22:21, 22, 24; 24:7.

Law and the Bible   61

outsiders? Is it not those inside the church whom you are to judge?
God judges those outside. 'Purge the evil person from among you' "
(1 Cor 5:12–13).

In many other cases, the New Testament does not authoritatively
explain how various judicial laws are to be applied. For these laws, the
principles embodied in the law need to be discerned and re-articulated
in today's context.

Let us work through how this might be done in the context of
an example I mentioned earlier in this chapter: "When you build
a new house, you shall make a parapet for your roof, that you may
not bring the guilt of blood upon your house, if anyone should fall
from it" (Deut 22:8). This law reflects the fact that Israelites of the
time typically built houses with flat roofs and spent a lot of time on
those roofs. A parapet was necessary to prevent people falling off
and injuring or killing themselves.

I have suggested that we ought not to see judicial laws such as
these as directly binding in their original form. Thus, this law does
not require us today to build a parapet on our roof: in our time, houses
typically do not have flat roofs, we do not use them in the same way,
and in many cases building a parapet would be more unsafe than
not having a parapet. What is required is to discern the principle—
the aspect of the moral law as set forth in the Ten Commandments—
underlying the law and apply it to today's context. This parapet law is
an application of the sixth commandment. Its underlying principle
could be described as "love your neighbor" or, in more satisfying
terms (to me at least), as an obligation to take reasonable steps to
eliminate foreseeable risks over which you have control, which is
essentially the modern law of negligence.

How might this law apply today? We might be required to build
a balustrade or handrail on balconies and staircases or build fences
around swimming pools. The principle is also potentially applicable
in a wide range of scenarios, including gun regulation, food hygiene,
and occupational health and safety.

There is a civil and a personal aspect to this law. That is, it applies to people individually, requiring them to take reasonable steps to eliminate foreseeable risks. It also applies to lawmakers, who ought to enact laws requiring people to take reasonable steps to eliminate foreseeable risks and impose penalties if they do not. Pool owners should erect a fence around their pool. Civil lawmakers should enact a law requiring pool owners to erect a fence around their pools.

The civil and the personal nature of the obligation imposed here may not be identical. That is, the principle of this law may oblige me personally to stop and remove a rock from the middle of a road where it poses a risk of damage to traffic. However, it would not be feasible to impose a mandatory legal obligation to do so—it is not feasible to legislate to remove all risks whatsoever. The personal obligation is therefore a more exacting one.

One significant feature of the law is worth noting. The law applies only to persons who build a *new* house—it does not require people to "retrofit" a parapet on existing houses. Why? It may be that building a parapet on an existing house would have been too burdensome, expensive, or inconvenient given that the house was already built. This suggests that there are questions of wisdom and degree when interpreting the scope of judicial laws and considering how they might apply today.

That is, the law should not be interpreted so as to require the total elimination of every conceivable risk whatsoever because that would be excessively burdensome. Road accidents cause over thirty-eight thousand deaths every year in America. These deaths could easily be prevented by imposing a mandatory national speed limit of 18 mph. However, this would carry enormous inconvenience, and the benefit of such a law is not thought to be worth the cost. It would also very likely not be feasible to enforce such a law. What level of inconvenience is worth sacrificing for the sake of ensuring safety? There is no one-size-fits-all answer; this would depend on the circumstances of each issue, and there may be a range of legitimate

answers. What is necessary will also change as technology and circumstances change.

Accepting the rationale of the parapet law (people must take
reasonable steps to eliminate foreseeable risks over which they have
control, and lawmakers must legislate to ensure they do so) is only
the first step in a complex process of lawmaking. Considering what
laws are necessary to guard against identified risks raises a range of
policy questions. Should the laws be framed as a prescriptive system
of rules that mandate what steps must be taken? Or should the laws
be a more flexible, principles-based system? Should breaches be
punishable by criminal penalties, or should there be a civil right of
action to sue for loss or damage (or both)? Should the penalty be a
fine, compensation, or imprisonment (or all of these)? Should a reg-
ulator be established to enforce compliance, or should it be enforced
by the courts? Each of these models has strengths and weaknesses,
and there is not one correct answer to these questions.

There is legitimate scope for disagreement and divergence
in how to give effect to the principle behind the parapet law. In
Australia, drivers are permitted a maximum blood alcohol reading
of 0.05g/100ml. In Brazil, drivers are not permitted to drive with
any alcohol in their blood. Both of these laws reflect an intention to
prevent a foreseeable risk and are consistent with the biblical principle, but the legal standard in each country is very different. This
does not mean that one is right while the other is wrong.

Some Christians consider that for every conceivable question of
law, there is a binary choice between God's perfect standard revealed
in Scripture and humanity's autonomous, humanistic, ungodly standard. What this discussion of the parapet law demonstrates is that
questions of wisdom, judgment, and prudence are unavoidable.
There is not one simple way to enact this principle into civil law,
and there is legitimate room to disagree. Clearly, the principle rules
out some possibilities as wrong or unbiblical. But for many questions, there is not a simplistic binary choice between whether we
apply God's standard or man's standard, but a more nuanced and

complex process of uncovering the logic underlying the judicial laws and applying those principles wisely to the very different circumstances of today.

LAW AND THE CHRISTIAN TODAY

The law was given by Moses and was addressed to Israel, not the church, specifically in the context of the redemption of Israel from Egypt (Exod 20:2). What relevance does it have now? Few issues have caused greater controversy in the history of the church. Many parts of the New Testament appear to be profoundly negative about the law. The writer to the Hebrews speaks of the old covenant becoming "obsolete" and says that it will soon disappear (Heb 8:13). Paul said that Christians are "not under law, but under grace" (Rom 6:14–15). The law "kills" (2 Cor 3:6), held people captive before the coming of Christ (Gal 3:23), was "but a shadow of the good things to come" (Heb 10:1), and has now been set aside "because of its weakness and uselessness" (Heb 7:18).

It is therefore not surprising that a variety of views have been expressed in the history of the church regarding the place of the law in the Christian life. Some seem to think that true Christian maturity consists solely of law-keeping.[37] Others urge that the law has no relevance to the Christian life, or would argue that Christian discipleship should not be viewed in terms of obedience to the law.

Lutheran theologian Gerhard O. Forde argued that sanctification is "the art of getting used to the unconditional justification wrought by the grace of God for Jesus' sake."[38] For Forde, the doctrine of justification by faith alone which was recovered in the Reformation is an attack on the "ordinary scheme of morality and religion" whereby

---

37. In his foreword to Bahnsen, *Theonomy in Christian Ethics*, Rousas John Rushdoony wrote that "Salvation is by the grace of God through faith, and sanctification is by law" (xii).

38. Gerhard O. Forde, "The Lutheran View of Sanctification," in *The Essential Forde: Distinguishing Law and Gospel*, ed. Nicholas Hopman, Mark C. Mattes, and Steven D. Paulson (Minneapolis: Fortress, 2019), 83.

we attain merit through effort. Law did not prevent sin, it only made it worse, and so living a moral life, or seeking to obey the law, is a threat to the principle of grace alone.[39]

Now it is certainly true that sanctification can be seen as the out-working of the implications and logic of justification. If we have been *declared* righteous, then we should *be* righteous. As put by Timothy Keller, the gospel eats away at the "inner engines that drive sinful behavior," transforming the fundamental orientation of our hearts. Our failures in actual righteousness—living Christlike, godly lives—"come mainly from a lack of orientation to our justification."[40] It is therefore true that justification, not the law, is the ground and the impelling force of our sanctification.

Nevertheless, they are separate things: justification is the once-for-all act whereby a person's sins are forgiven and he is declared to be righteous,[41] while sanctification is the ongoing and always incomplete process of growth in godliness.[42] The New Testament speaks of sanctification as an active process, something that Christians work out with fear and trembling (Phil 2:12). Paul exhorted the Philippians to "press on toward the goal," "forgetting what lies behind and straining forward to what lies ahead" (Phil 3:13–14), and he urged the Corinthians to run so that they might obtain the prize (1 Cor 9:24–27). These descriptions hardly seem like a passive process of simply "getting used to" one's justification.

Does the law have a place in this ongoing process of sanctification? Within the Protestant tradition, there are two streams of

---

39. Forde, "Lutheran View of Sanctification," 89.

40. Timothy Keller, *Center Church: Doing Balanced, Gospel-Centered Ministry in Your City* (Grand Rapids: Zondervan, 2012), 69–71.

41. Rom 4:5; 8:1; Gal 2:16; Eph 2:8; Phil 3:9; Titus 3:7.

42. It is beyond the scope of this book to engage with this question in any detail, but it will be evident that I have little patience for the "New Perspective on Paul," which, among other things, redefines justification in ecclesiological rather than soteriological terms. The literature is voluminous; see, e.g., Guy P. Waters, *Justification and the New Perspectives on Paul* (Phillipsburg, NJ: P&R Publishing, 2004); Gary L. W. Johnson and Guy P. Waters, eds., *By Faith Alone: Answering the Challenges to the Doctrine of Justification* (Wheaton, IL: Crossway, 2007).

thought which argue that the law has little or no place in the Christian life. The first is that the primary function of the law is to convict people of their sin, and once it has served that purpose, it has no further applicability for believers.

Luther wrote that "Christ did not wield the sword, or give it a place in his kingdom. For he is a king over Christians and rules by his Holy Spirit alone, without law."[43] While the unrighteous are in need of external compulsion, in the form of the law, the righteous person willingly does good, and so "it is impossible that the temporal sword and law should find any work to do among Christians." Christians "are subject neither to law nor sword, and have need of neither."[44]

Lutheran theologian Philip Melanchthon argued that the radical, free grace of the gospel implies the abrogation of all law. Given that no one could keep the moral law perfectly, the law was deadly; the gospel proclaims the saving work of Christ and is nothing less than freedom from the law: "Those in whom Christ's Spirit dwells are entirely free from all law."[45]

These statements appear to suggest that the law has no place in the Christian life. For reasons such as these, some scholars have argued that Luther did not affirm the third use of the law (see below for this terminology).[46] However, Luther in his *Treatise on Good Works* wrote a detailed exposition of the Decalogue which explains the content of the good works required of believers, arguing that "there are no good works except those works God has command-ed."[47] He later wrote that "it is most surprising to me that anyone

---

43. Luther, "Temporal Authority," 283.

44. Luther, "Temporal Authority," 279, 281.

45. Philip Melanchthon, *Loci Communes*, in *Melanchthon and Bucer*, ed. Wilhelm Pauck (Philadelphia: Westminster, 1969), 126.

46. See Jeffrey G. Silcock and Christopher Boyd Brown, "Introduction to the Antinomian Disputations," in *Luther's Works: Disputations II*, ed. Jeffrey G. Silcock, trans. Jeffrey G. Silcock (St. Louis: Concordia Publishing House, 2020), 73:21–25; Todd R. Hains, *Luther and the Rule of Faith: Reading God's Word for God's People*, New Explorations in Theology (Downers Grove, IL: IVP Academic, 2022), 59.

47. Martin Luther, "Treatise on Good Works," trans. W. A. Lambert, in *Selected Writings of Martin Luther: 1517–1520*, ed. Theodore G. Tappert (Minneapolis: Fortress,

can claim that I reject the law or the Ten Commandments, since there is available, in more than one edition, my exposition of the Ten Commandments, which furthermore are daily preached and practiced in our churches."[48] Melanchthon emphasized that once regenerated, the Holy Spirit works within believers a will to do that which previously was commanded by the law: "Freedom does not consist in this, that we do not observe the law, but that we will and desire spontaneously from the heart what the law demands."[49]

Therefore, Luther and Melanchthon considered that believers willingly carry out God's will, which is in substance the same as the things required by the Ten Commandments. Luther wrote that "the righteous man of his own accord does all and more than the law demands,"[50] and Melanchthon wrote that the moral laws "are the eternal rule of the mind of God, they always sounded forth in the church, even before the time of Moses, and they shall remain in force forever and apply also to the Gentiles."[51] The *Book of Concord* affirms that although true Christians "are liberated and made free from the curse of the Law, yet they should daily exercise themselves in the Law of the Lord."[52]

A second stream of thought emphasizes that faithful discipleship according to the New Testament is not primarily obedience to the law, but being a faithful follower of Jesus. Jesus is the fulfillment of the law and the perfect example of an obedient, holy life, and the holiness demanded of Christians is to follow that example. Rather than a prescriptive code of law which characterized the Old Testament,

---

2007), 105–96.

48. Martin Luther, "Against the Antinomians," in *Martin Luther's Basic Theological Writings*, ed. William R. Russell, 3rd ed. (Minneapolis: Fortress, 2012), 177.

49. Melanchthon, *Loci Communes*, 123.

50. Luther, "Temporal Authority," 279.

51. Philip Melanchthon, *The Chief Theological Topics: Loci Praecipui Theologici 1559*, trans. J. A. O. Preus, 2nd ed. (St. Louis: Concordia Publishing House, 2011), 90–91.

52. *Book of Concord*, Solid Declaration, article 6.4.

we are presented with the example of Christ, the perfect man, and called to imitate him. As Octavius Winslow noted:

> There is no single practical truth in the Word of God on which the Spirit is more emphatic than the example which Christ has set for his followers to imitate. The church needed a perfect pattern, a flawless model. It wanted a living embodiment of those precepts of the gospel so strictly enjoined upon every believer, and God has graciously set before us our true model.[53]

It is certainly true that Christians are called to imitate Christ.[54] Does this mean that the law has no place? By no means; the New Testament expressly re-affirms the moral law in many places. Jesus said that he did not come to abolish the Law or the Prophets but to fulfill them, and continued:

> For truly, I say to you, until heaven and earth pass away, not an iota, not a dot, will pass from the Law until all is accomplished. Therefore whoever relaxes one of the least of these commandments and teaches others to do the same will be called least in the kingdom of heaven, but whoever does them and teaches them will be called great in the kingdom of heaven. (Matt 5:17–20)

By this statement, Christ confirms that "by his coming nothing is going to be taken away from the observance of the law."[55] In the Sermon on the Mount Jesus unpacked the true meaning of the Decalogue (Matt 5:21–48), treating it as continuing to bind his disciples. Paul said that faith does not nullify the law, but on the contrary upholds the law (Rom 3:31). Under the new covenant the law is written anew on the hearts of believers (Jer 31:33–34). The New Testament expressly affirms the Ten Commandments as well as the

---

53. Octavius Winslow, *The Glory of the Redeemer in His Person and Work* (London: John F. Shaw, 1844), 433.

54. 1 Cor 11:1; Phil 2:1–11; 1 Pet 2:21, 24.

55. Calvin, *Institutes*, 2.7.14.

two great commandments.[56] With the exception of the fourth commandment, each one of the Ten Commandments is treated as binding and is expressly affirmed in the New Testament.[57] (As argued in chapter 3, the fact that the fourth commandment is not expressly re-affirmed after the resurrection does not mean it is now obsolete). The New Testament writers condemn things which are forbidden by the Ten Commandments.[58] Christians are called to avoid sin (Rom 6:15; 1 John 2:1), which means transgression of the law (Rom 4:15; 1 John 3:4), and are told to keep Jesus's commandments (John 14:15).

Further, the New Testament expressly links sanctification with obedience to God's commands. Paul wrote that Christians ought to "bear one another's burdens, and so fulfill the law of Christ" (Gal 6:2) and that "neither circumcision counts for anything nor uncircumcision, but keeping the commandments of God" (1 Cor 7:19). He wrote to the Romans:

> Owe no one anything, except to love each other, for the one who loves another has fulfilled the law. For the commandments, "You shall not commit adultery, You shall not murder, You shall not steal, You shall not covet," and any other commandment, are summed up in this word: "You shall love your neighbor as yourself." Love does no wrong to a neighbor; therefore love is the fulfilling of the law. (Rom 13:8–10)

An understanding of natural law also helps to resolve these debates. As we have seen, the biblical teaching is that there is an eternal moral law, applicable to all people at all times, reflecting the

---

56. Lev 19:18; Deut 6:5; Matt 19:19; 22:36–40; Mark 12:28–31; Rom 13:9–10.

57. First Commandment: Matt 4:10; Luke 4:8; Second Commandment: Acts 15:20; Third Commandment: Matt 5:33–37; Fifth Commandment: Matt 15:4; 19:19; Mark 10:19; Luke 18:20; Eph 6:1–3; Sixth Commandment: Matt 5:21–22; 19:18; Mark 10:19; Luke 18:20; Rom 13:9; Seventh Commandment: Matt 5:27–28; 19:18; Mark 10:5–12, 19; Luke 16:18; 18:20; Rom 13:9; Eighth Commandment: Matt 19:18; Mark 10:19; Luke 18:20; Rom 13:9; Eph 4:28; Ninth Commandment: Matt 19:18; Mark 10:19; Luke 18:20; Acts 5:3–4; Eph 4:25; Tenth Commandment: Luke 12:15; Rom 13:9.

58. E.g., 1 Cor 6:9–10; Gal 6:19–21; Eph 4:25; 5:3–5; Col 3:5–9; 1 Pet 4:3.

order and structure of creation. If that is so, there is no reason to think the Christian should be exempt from that law or that it would be abrogated by the New Testament.

Christians are called to imitate Christ, but this does not mean that the law has no place in Christian discipleship or sanctification. The Holy Spirit guides the Christian and creates a willingness to be holy, but this remains imperfect until the resurrection (Rom 7; Gal 5:17). In the process of sanctification the Spirit works through the word of God, which includes the law and Jesus's commands (see, e.g., John 14:26; 17:17), and so the law is useful, and even necessary, because of indwelling sin which remains in believers.

For these reasons, the overwhelming view of the Christian tradition is that the moral law remains relevant to the Christian life as a rule of conduct, directing us how to live in a manner so as to please God.[59] The law assists in our sanctification, although the Christian life is not to be reduced to mere law-keeping.

How can this be reconciled with the New Testament's seemingly negative attitude toward the law? The apparent contradiction is resolved by considering the different senses in which the law applies. It can be considered first as a means of salvation (or, as earlier writers used to express it, as a covenant). As a means of salvation, the law requires absolute, perfect obedience in order to merit God's favor. Because of human sinfulness, no person is able to attain righteousness through the law, and the law brings only judgment and condemnation (Rom 3:9–20, 23; 8:7–8). The law is totally ineffective as a means of attaining salvation.

The gospel makes known a righteousness that is apart from the law, that comes through faith (Rom 3:21–22, 28). Christ bore our sins in his body on the cross (1 Pet 2:24) and removed the curse of the law that stood against us (Col 2:13–15). Obedience to the law plays no part in a sinner's attaining righteousness. When Paul says

---

59. *Westminster Confession of Faith*, XIX.6–7; Calvin, *Institutes*, 2.7.12; Turretin, *Institutes of Elenctic Theology*, 2:139–45.

that we are "not under law but under grace" (Rom 6:14–15; see also 1 Cor 9:20), he means that we are free from the need to obey the law as a means of obtaining righteousness, and free from the curse of the law as it condemns us for our sin.[60]

However, this does not mean that the law has no place in sanctification. Paul also wrote that we do not abolish or nullify the law but rather uphold it (Rom 3:31) and that he was not "outside the law of God but under the law of Christ" (1 Cor 9:21). The law remains relevant as a rule of conduct, and we obey willingly: "For this is the love of God, that we keep his commandments. And his commandments are not burdensome" (1 John 5:3).

This reflects the traditional teaching of the Protestant tradition that the moral law has three uses. The first (the pedagogical or theological use) is to bring an awareness of the knowledge of sin and expose us as condemned against God's righteous standard, so as to drive us to Christ for forgiveness (see Rom 3:20; 7:7–12). The second is the civil or political use of the law, whereby laws are enforced by civil governments to restrain sin and preserve peaceful society (Rom 13:1–5). The third use of the law (the moral or didactic) is to guide believers as to how to live to please God (Rom 3:31; 13:8).[61]

This chapter has examined the different types of law contained in Scripture and how the law is relevant today. As we will see in chapter 4, Christians have long held that civil law must be based on the principles of the moral law. As such, the next step as we consider how Christians should think about civil law is to ask, What is the content of the moral law? That is the subject of the next chapter, which examines the Ten Commandments.

---

60. Martin Luther, "The Freedom of a Christian," trans W. A. Lambert, in *Selected Writings of Martin Luther: 1520–1523*, ed. Theodore G. Tappert (Minneapolis: Fortress, 2007), 25–26.

61. Bullinger, *Decades*, 2:237–45; Chemnitz, *Loci Theologici*, 800–808; Gerhard, *On the Law*, 222–25; Calvin, *Institutes*, 2.7.6–13. Note that these writers all order the three uses of the law differently. I have followed that of Calvin.

III

THE TEN COMMANDMENTS
and CIVIL LAW

To think well about law from a Christian perspective requires a good understanding of the moral law. The Ten Commandments, which are widely considered to be one of the most important passages in Scripture, contain a summary of the moral law. This chapter contains an exposition of the Ten Commandments. It aims to unpack the key things commanded and prohibited in each of the commandments, and to explain something of the rationale of each commandment.

READING THE TEN COMMANDMENTS

The Ten Commandments (or "Words"; see Exod 34:28; Deut 4:13; 10:4) are given in two places in Scripture: Exodus 20 and Deuteronomy 5. These statements of the law are in largely the same terms, but there are some differences. There are differences of wording in the fifth and tenth commandments, and the rationales for the observance of

the Sabbath also differ. The first five commandments have rationales or promises attached, while the other commandments do not.
With the exception of the fifth, all the commandments are framed
in negative terms as prohibitions.

The Ten Commandments have traditionally been divided into
two tables. In the division of the law adopted by the Reformed tradition, the first four commandments set out our duty toward God,
and commandments five to ten express our duty toward our fellow
humans. Following Augustine, the Roman Catholic and Lutheran
churches combine the first two commandments and divide the tenth
commandment into two. According to this schema, our duty toward
God is set out in the first three commandments, with commandments four to ten expressing our duty to our fellow humans. In this
book I adopt the numbering of the commandments followed in the
Reformed tradition.[1]

The division of the law into two tables reflects Jesus's statement
that all the law can be summed up in two great commandments: "You
shall love the Lord your God with all your heart and with all your
soul and with all your mind" and "You shall love your neighbor as
yourself."[2] Closely related to the second great commandment is the
"golden rule"—namely, that we should do to others as we would wish
they would do to us, which Jesus considered to summarize the Law
and the Prophets (Matt 7:12; Luke 6:31).

This means that biblical law is ultimately about love—love for God
and love for our neighbor. Those who love God will seek to obey him
in the ways specified in the Ten Commandments. The second great
commandment follows from the first: if we love God, we will love our
neighbors who bear his image. Therefore, love is the fulfillment of
the law (Rom 13:10). The Ten Commandments must be understood
as giving effect to this imperative of loving God and neighbor and

---

1. Those who divide the tenth commandment into two almost without exception
analyze them as a compound whole. It therefore seems preferable to view this as a
single command.

2. Lev 19:18; Deut 6:4–9; Matt 22:36–40.

directing the way we express that love. This explains why the law has an internal as well as an external aspect. The law is not simply about external conformity, but also demands a heart response, and so it is not possible to truly fulfill the commandments without love. In both the Old and New Testaments there is a focus on the heart, and not merely outward obedience.[3]

The other books of the Pentateuch also contain many laws. It is common to understand these laws as a fleshing out of the Decalogue and as the application of it to particular situations. Deuteronomy is often seen as an extended commentary on the Decalogue, with chapters 6 to 26 expounding each of the Ten Commandments in turn:[4]

- First commandment: Deuteronomy 6:1–11:32
- Second commandment: Deuteronomy 12:1–32
- Third commandment: Deuteronomy 13:1–14:21
- Fourth commandment: Deuteronomy 14:22–16:17
- Fifth commandment: Deuteronomy 16:18–18:22
- Sixth commandment: Deuteronomy 19:1–22:8
- Seventh commandment: Deuteronomy 22:9–23:14
- Eighth commandment: Deuteronomy 23:15–24:7
- Ninth commandment: Deuteronomy 24:8–16
- Tenth commandment: Deuteronomy 24:17–26:19.[5]

The Decalogue encapsulates the heart of what is required or prohibited; it is not law in the modern technical sense, nor is it an

---

3. See, e.g., Deut 15:7–11; Zech 7:10.

4. John H. Walton, "Deuteronomy: An Exposition of the Spirit of the Law," *Grace Theological Journal* 8, no. 2 (1987): 213.

5. This adopts the division proposed by Alastair Roberts, "Deuteronomy: Chapter-by-Chapter Commentary," February 17, 2022, YouTube video, https://www.youtube.com/watch?v=xaoNjmTJjOo. See also John H. Walton, "The Decalogue Structure of the Deuteronomic Law," in *Interpreting Deuteronomy: Issues and Approaches*, ed. David G. Firth and Philip S. Johnston (Downers Grove, IL: IVP Academic, 2012).

exhaustive statement of what is comprehended by the law.[6] For example, the seventh commandment prohibits adultery. Leviticus 18 contains a wide range of additional prohibitions on sexual sin, which should be understood as fleshing out the seventh commandment and explaining the true reach of its prohibition. What is comprehended in the seventh commandment is broader than the narrow words of the commandment itself. Jesus also explains the true heart of the law in the Sermon on the Mount.[7]

Another illustration of this point is that a concern for the vulnerable and the poor is a key focus of the Mosaic law.[8] That is, the more detailed specification of the requirements of the Decalogue contained in the Pentateuch suggests that the moral law has a particular concern to prevent the vulnerable from being oppressed, although that would not be obvious from Exodus 20 and Deuteronomy 5 alone. Thus, the requirements of the law, especially the second table, are to be interpreted as having regard to this concern. All this suggests that there is more to the law than is apparent from a surface reading of the words, and it is therefore necessary to read the Ten Commandments in light of Scripture as a whole in order to understand their true reach.[9]

It is also important to see the law not as a series of arbitrary commands, but as consistent with human nature, the structure of creation, and with the character of God himself. God acts consistently with his character at all times, and so the giving of the Decalogue reflects his wisdom, truth, and goodness and is an image of God's righteousness and holiness.[10] The law was given by a God who is

---

6. Geerhardus Vos, *Biblical Theology: Old and New Testaments* (Edinburgh: Banner of Truth, 1975), 135.

7. Matt 5:21–37; 22:36–40.

8. E.g., Exod 21:2–11; 22:22–27; 23:9; Lev 19:14, 33–34; 23:22; 25:23–55; Deut 10:17–19; 14:28–29; 15:7–15; 24:17–22; 26:12–13; 27:19.

9. See Pierre Viret, *Exposition of the Ten Commandments*, trans. R. A. Sheats (Monticello: Psalm 78 Ministries, 2020), 34.

10. Johann Gerhard, *On the Law*, ed. Benjamin T. G. Mayes and Joshua J. Hayes, trans. Richard J. Dinda (St. Louis: Concordia Publishing House, 2015), 228.

loving, just, holy, and wise, and so we are bound to say that His law is loving, good, and wise. The law is "holy and righteous and good" (Rom 7:12) and is the perfect "law of liberty" (Jas 1:25). As put by Alan Cole, "The commandments are God's nature expressed in terms of moral imperatives."[11] For example, God is truth and hates lying, and so he forbids false witness (the ninth commandment). God does not wish his image to be destroyed, and so he prohibits murder (the sixth commandment).[12] As humans are made in God's image and endowed with reason, we can perceive the inherent wisdom and reasonableness embodied in the law (see Deut 4:6–8).

Although the Decalogue is framed almost entirely in negative terms, each commandment has a positive as well as a negative aspect. It is positive in the sense that it requires positive actions as well as simply refraining from conduct. For instance, having "no other gods before me" does not simply mean not worshiping Baal or Allah, it means worshiping the one true God with heart and mind. The law is also positive in the sense that it embodies what may be described as a positive vision for the good.

Christians have often fallen into the trap of believing that people are fundamentally thinkers and that the goal of our education, discipleship, and parenting is imparting knowledge. However, James K. A. Smith has argued that people are not primarily thinkers, but lovers. That is, we are not motivated primarily by ideas; instead, our orientation to the world is driven by what we love and desire. What we love is shaped by habits and patterns of behavior which embody a vision of the good life and which inscribe that vision on our hearts and character.[13] The implication of this is that, as well as developing better intellectual arguments and academic rigor, the church needs

---

11. R. Alan Cole, *Exodus: An Introduction and Commentary* (Downers Grove, IL: InterVarsity Press, 1973), 152.

12. Niels Hemmingsen, *On the Law of Nature: A Demonstrative Method*, trans. and ed. E. J. Hutchinson (Grand Rapids: CLP Academic, 2018), 101.

13. James K. A. Smith, *Desiring the Kingdom: Worship, Worldview, and Cultural Formation* (Grand Rapids: Baker Academic, 2009); James K. A. Smith, *Imagining the Kingdom: How Worship Works* (Grand Rapids: Baker Academic, 2013).

to work harder at articulating, and modeling, a winsome vision of the good, so as to re-orient our hearts as well as our minds toward that good.

Something of what I am getting at here can be illustrated as follows. The sixth commandment prohibits murder, which reflects the truth that life is precious. This is not simply a doctrine, but a reality reflected in the creation. There is something irresistibly winsome about a baby smiling. It is delightful to see a child take her first steps and tumble over, or hear her say her first words. The preciousness of life is reflected in its beauty, its very existence, at a deeper than merely intellectual level.

This beauty brings into stark relief those things that are contrary to the sixth commandment, which is not adequately captured by saying "murder is wrong." Taking away life destroys something of immense value and is a distortion of the right response to the value of creation. Murder is ugly and repulsive as well as morally wrong. This explains why, for example, the abortion industry does everything it can to prevent pictures of unborn children from being broadcast: the depiction of little fingers, tiny toes, and a heartbeat starkly shows the grotesqueness of abortion more powerfully than an intellectual argument ever could.

Something similar could be said about each of the commandments. This has significant implications for how we think about law. It is not sufficient to simply present the law as something true and obligatory; our hearts need to be oriented to see the law as something good and as a blessing. God's moral law is not repressive, impeding our happiness and the expression of our true selves. Rather, like the "rules" of music, it expresses the principles which direct us in a manner consistent with the way we have been made, and which lead to our flourishing. Simply bashing notes on a piano does not produce music. In a culture which despises God's commandments and calls them restrictive and harmful, it is necessary to reclaim their beauty, winsomeness, and goodness.

The law is not a static body of lifeless commands, like much of contemporary civil law. Rather, the law demands constant reading, repetition, and meditation, so that it is internalized (Deut 6:4–9). Psalm 1:1–2 commends the man whose "delight is in the law of the LORD" and who "meditates day and night" on that law. Psalm 19:7–11 describes the law in these terms:

> The law of the LORD is perfect,
>> reviving the soul;
> the testimony of the LORD is sure,
>> making wise the simple;
> the precepts of the LORD are right,
>> rejoicing the heart;
> the commandment of the LORD is pure,
>> enlightening the eyes;
> the fear of the LORD is clean,
>> enduring forever;
> the rules of the LORD are true,
>> and righteous altogether.
> More to be desired are they than gold,
>> even much fine gold;
> sweeter also than honey
>> and drippings of the honeycomb.
> Moreover, by them is your servant warned;
>> in keeping them there is great reward.

In summary, the way to read the Ten Commandments is to read them in light of the law as a whole as set out in the Pentateuch, understood through the lens of the unpacking of the nature of the law by Jesus. By reflecting and meditating on the law in the light of Scripture as a whole, together with the created order, we can uncover the deeper rationale underlying the commandments and see something of God's goodness and the beauty of his created order.

The *Westminster Larger Catechism* sets out a series of helpful rules for reading the Ten Commandments, including the following:

- The law is perfect and binds everyone to complete obedience; it requires the utmost perfection of every duty, and forbids the least degree of every sin.

- The law is spiritual and inward, and reaches the understanding, will, affections, and all other powers of the soul as well as words, works, and gestures.

- The same thing, in different respects, is required or forbidden in more than one commandment.

- Where a duty is commanded, the contrary sin is forbidden; and, where a sin is forbidden, the contrary duty is commanded.

- Where a sin is prohibited or a duty commanded, all sins and duties of the same kind are forbidden or commanded.[14]

PROLOGUE

The Decalogue opens with these words: "I am the LORD your God, who brought you out of the land of Egypt, out of the house of slavery" (Exod 20:2; Deut 5:6). The law was given within the context of an already existing covenant relationship between Israel and God. It was to be obeyed out of gratitude for God's deliverance of the people of Israel from Egypt; it was not a means of gaining God's favor or initiating a relationship with God. Israel was saved from bondage; the law now reveals how they are to live as God's redeemed people. As such, the moral law is not a means of attaining righteousness.

This suggests that the law demanded righteousness but not sinless perfection. King David was described as a man after God's own heart (1 Sam 13:14), notwithstanding that he committed major sins. Or perhaps more accurately, it could be said that the law *did* hold out a standard of sinless perfection, but it was not necessary (or possible) for God's people to attain that standard in order to be saved. Jesus Christ is the only one ever to have fulfilled the perfect requirements of the law (Matt 3:17; 17:5; Rom 5:19). Those who lived righteously and sought forgiveness for their sins, and who had faith in the coming Messiah, were saved.

As I have argued, the Ten Commandments are in substance identical to the universal moral law which applies to all people. The Ten Commandments are a restatement of the moral law with much greater clarity than the natural law, and indeed an amplification of the obligations of that law. Israel's deliverance from Egypt provided a strong reason and motivation for obedience over and above that which applied simply by virtue of its applicability as natural law.

The revelation of the law also brought a much greater level of obligation—and potentially condemnation—upon the Israelites. When the Israelites sinned, they were not just sinning against the natural law and conscience, but against the revealed requirements of the law (see Amos 2:4; 3:2).

THE FIRST TABLE:
"You Shall Love the Lord Your God with All Your Heart and with All Your Soul and with All Your Might"

FIRST COMMANDMENT
You shall have no other gods before me. (Exod 20:3; Deut 5:7)

The first commandment is the core commandment of the Decalogue. It is stated in negative terms as a prohibition. The commandment is elsewhere given in positive terms: "Hear, O Israel: The LORD our God, the LORD is one. You shall love the LORD your God with all your heart and with all your soul and with all your might" (Deut 6:4–5). Jesus repeats this commandment, describing it as "the great and first commandment" (Matt 22:37–40; see also Mark 12:29–31).

The first commandment requires that all people acknowledge the Lord as the one true God and worship and glorify him accordingly. It prohibits the worship of any other god or placing anything as more ultimate than him in our affections. It mandates true and inward love for God (Deut 6:4–5; 10:12–13). How can love be mandated by a command? If God is the perfection of beauty and goodness and has displayed undeserved mercy toward his people, even to the extent of not sparing his own Son, then the only proper response is adoration and worship (John 3:16; Rom 8:32).

A common theme in early Protestant writings on the law is that there is a close relationship between the first commandment and all the other commandments. This is because the first commandment is the foundation of the moral law. Luther wrote that faith and trust in God are the true fulfilling of the first commandment. And since all good works ultimately stem from faith, all other commandments stem from the first.[15] Similarly, a breach of another commandment ultimately stems from a breach of the first commandment: we commit sins such as lying, adultery, or theft because we make "something else more fundamental to our hope and joy and identity than God."[16] The link between knowing God and obedience is spelled out in Jeremiah 22:16, speaking of Josiah:

He judged the cause of the poor and needy;
    then it was well.
Is not this to know me?
    declares the LORD.

Given that God's eternal power and divine nature are evident in creation (Rom 1:20), it is possible to know that God exists and to know something of his power without Scripture. However, it is not possible to attain a saving knowledge of God or to understand the

---

15. Martin Luther, "Treatise on Good Works," trans. W. A. Lambert, in *Selected Writings of Martin Luther*, ed. Theodore G. Tappert (Minneapolis: Fortress, 2007), 112.

16. Timothy Keller, *Center Church: Doing Balanced, Gospel-Centered Ministry in Your City* (Grand Rapids: Zondervan, 2012), 70.

completeness of God's nature (especially such things as the Trinity) through natural law. The Bible contains a much more complete revelation of the nature of God than is possible to obtain through reason and nature.

The first commandment implies that there are clear limits on the role of the state and the civil law. Only God is ultimate, and so the civil government ought not to attempt to usurp God's position. The first commandment is about love for God, and it is not possible to mandate that love through civil law or coercion. The first commandment therefore suggests that there is a clear distinction between the moral law and the civil law, that not all sins should be crimes, and that not all things required by the moral law can be enforced in civil law.

Second Commandment

You shall not make for yourself a carved image, or any likeness
of anything that is in heaven above, or that is in the earth
beneath, or that is in the water under the earth. You shall not
bow down to them or serve them, for I the Lord your God am a
jealous God, visiting the iniquity of the fathers on the children
to the third and the fourth generation of those who hate me,
but showing steadfast love to thousands of those who love me
and keep my commandments. (Exod 20:4–6; Deut 5:8–10)

The first commandment concerns *who* we worship; the second concerns *how* we worship. The second commandment is about showing love for God by worshiping him in the manner he determines. It prohibits the making of images of God and the use of images in worship. The underlying logic of the second commandment is twofold. The first is that God, not humanity, determines the way he should be worshiped (see Deut 12:4–14, 31). Second, it is impossible to represent God visually because he is spirit, infinite and eternal.[17] As the Lutheran theologian Johann Gerhard wrote, "Because God

---

17. Deut 4:12–18; Isa 40:18; John 4:24; Acts 17:29; Rom 1:23.

is spirit and also His essence is invisible and infinite, He cannot be depicted in Himself nor as far as His essence is concerned."[18] The commandment is therefore concerned with accurately representing God's character and prohibiting anything that would amount to a false representation of him. Scripture draws a close analogy between idolatry and adultery, depicting the worship of idols as a type of spiritual adultery (e.g., Ezek 23:1–27; Hos 4:12–14).

From the commandment we can distinguish the following categories. The first is the use of images (whether of God or not) for worship. This is clearly prohibited by the second commandment. The second is the use of images other than God for purposes other than worship, such as statues or paintings of famous people. The second commandment does not prohibit this.

The third is the use of images of God for purposes other than worship, for example pictures of Christ in a story book. The second commandment certainly prohibits any attempt to depict the nature of God as spirit. But what about pictures of Christ? Given that Christ appeared in human form, it is sometimes thought to be legitimate to make depictions of Christ. A better view is that the second commandment prohibits any depiction of Christ, even for non-worship purposes.[19] The mere fact that God has manifested himself in visible form does not mean that it is lawful for us to make depictions of him.[20] There is no record of what Christ actually looked like, and so there is no way to ensure that a depiction of Christ accurately reflects his appearance on earth.

The second commandment reveals the limitations of natural law. The human desire for visual representations of the divine is such that any human-devised means of worshiping God always leads to error. The proper means of worshiping God is that which is revealed in Scripture.

---

18. Gerhard, *On the Law*, 71.

19. See *Westminster Larger Catechism*, 109.

20. Francis Turretin, *Institutes of Elenctic Theology*, ed. James T. Dennison Jr., trans. George Musgrave Giger (Phillipsburg, NJ: P&R Publishing, 1992), 2:65.

THIRD COMMANDMENT

You shall not take the name of the LORD your God
in vain, for the LORD will not hold him guiltless who
takes his name in vain. (Exod 20:7; Deut 5:11)

The third commandment is about showing love for God by rendering
the honor that is due to him and his name. The third commandment
has speech particularly in view, requiring that in our words we ought
to reverence his name, character, and word. It prohibits the misuse
of God's name such as by blaspheming, cursing, or swearing falsely
(Exod 22:28; Lev 19:12). In ancient Israel this sin merited the death
penalty (Lev 24:10–16). In addition, the failure of God's people to
live lives worthy of their calling can cause God to be dishonored
(Rom 2:24). Thus, the third commandment also demands that God's
people live a consistent, godly life to the glory of God. Luther wrote
that this commandment demands that we shun self-praise and not
seek honor for ourselves.[21]

FOURTH COMMANDMENT

Observe the Sabbath day, to keep it holy, as the LORD your
God commanded you. Six days you shall labor and do all
your work, but the seventh day is a Sabbath to the LORD your
God. On it you shall not do any work, you or your son or your
daughter or your male servant or your female servant, or your
ox or your donkey or any of your livestock, or the sojourner who
is within your gates, that your male servant and your female
servant may rest as well as you. (Deut 5:12–14; Exod 20:8–10)[22]

This commandment (note that the rationale has been omitted) is
about showing love for God by giving due time to rest and worship
him. The command is seemingly addressed to heads of households,

---

21. Luther, "Treatise on Good Works," 124, 131–32.
22. The version quoted here is from Deuteronomy, which is slightly more fulsome
than its counterpart in Exodus.

who were to ensure the observance of the Sabbath by all under their authority. The commandment guarantees a day of rest for all, including children, servants, sojourners, and animals. As noted previously, the fourth commandment is the only commandment that is not expressly reaffirmed in the New Testament, which has generated controversy as to whether it remains binding today.

Exodus and Deuteronomy contain different rationales for observing the Sabbath. In Exodus the rationale has to do with the pattern of creation: "In six days the LORD made heaven and earth, the sea, and all that is in them, and rested on the seventh day. Therefore the LORD blessed the Sabbath day and made it holy" (Exod 20:11). In Deuteronomy the rationale relates to God's deliverance of Israel from Egypt (Deut 5:15). The underlying rationale of the Sabbath therefore reflects both the pattern of one day's rest in seven established in creation (Gen 2:2–3) and also the redemption of God's people from slavery.

There are "ceremonial" or Israel-specific aspects of this commandment. The rationale of redemption from slavery given in Deuteronomy specifically refers to Israel's redemption. The rest contemplated is physical rest in the land of Israel. However, the fact that there are Israel-specific aspects of this commandment does not mean that there are no continuing moral aspects that apply today.

The twofold rationale given in Exodus 20 and Deuteronomy 5 suggests two things about the fourth commandment. The first is that it is something inherent in the order of creation and therefore binding or applicable until that order disappears; as such, the theological presumption ought to be that the principle of the Sabbath continues to oblige under the New Testament era. It is equally true that, given the significant changes between old and new covenants, the manner of observance of the Sabbath will have changed significantly. Accordingly, the historic teaching of the church has been that the underlying moral imperative remains, but that not every precise detail of its observance set out in the Old Testament continues. As B. B. Warfield put it, "Christ took the Sabbath into the grave with him and brought the Lord's Day out of the grave with him on the resurrection morn."[23]

How does the Sabbath relate to natural law? The *Westminster Confession of Faith* states that "it is the law of nature, that, in general, a due proportion of time be set apart for the worship of God."[24] That is, it is a requirement of morality grounded in the law of nature that all people should set aside some time for rest and worship, and apart from Scripture it is possible to deduce in general terms an obligation to worship the Creator.[25] However, the specific ordinance of the weekly Sabbath rest is something that had to be revealed in Scripture. The universal moral nature of the principle of rest and worship also supports the view that the obligation of the fourth commandment continues in the New Testament era.

The fourth commandment is often viewed as a burdensome and restrictive requirement. The Sabbath requirements of the Mosaic law certainly appear burdensome. The law deemed that lighting a fire or gathering wood was a breach of the fourth commandment (Exod 35:1–3; Num 15:32–36). However, reflecting on the biblical texts as a whole reveals a much richer picture of this law.[26]

The Pentateuch institutes a series of sacred festivals and assemblies which are expressly described as sabbaths and connected with the weekly Sabbath.[27] In the Sabbath Year all debts were to be canceled and slaves set free (Exod 21:2; Deut 15:1), and during the Jubilee Year (seven sabbaths of years) all transferred property was to be returned (Lev 25:13). In other feasts, the Israelites were to rejoice and celebrate God's goodness with thankfulness, showing generosity

---

23. Benjamin B. Warfield, "The Foundation of the Sabbath in the Word of God," in *Selected Shorter Writings of Benjamin B. Warfield*, ed. John E. Meeter (Phillipsburg, NJ: P&R Publishing, 1970), 1:319.

24. *Westminster Confession of Faith*, XXI.7.

25. See also *Catechism of the Catholic Church* (Staten Island: St Pauls Publishing, 1994), 525 [2176].

26. Exod 23:10–19; 31:12–18; 35:1–3; Lev 23, 25; Deut 14:22–16:17.

27. Lev 23:1–3; 25:1–8; Col 2:16.

toward others.[28] Themes of joy and communion with God are given
particular emphasis in these feasts.[29] The Sabbath informs all the
laws of the Pentateuch concerning festivals and is itself listed as a
feast day.[30] McGarvey and Pendleton note that "bountiful feasts on
the Sabbath day were common among the Jews."[31]

This presents quite a different perspective on the Sabbath than
one exclusively concerned with a list of do nots. It suggests that, in
addition to a weekly pattern established at creation, the principle
underlying the fourth commandment is based on the redemption
of the people of Israel from slavery and the fact that they had been
brought into a land of freedom and abundance, which should be
extended to all of the Israelite people. All of God's people were to
share in the blessings of the land and had a right to freedom.[32] As
the people had been redeemed from slavery, it would make little
sense for the Israelites to be enslaved to each other (Lev 25:42–43).

Jesus's mission is described in terms that evoke the Jubilee, which
is an extension of the Sabbath principle (Luke 4:18–19). Thus, Jesus
is presented as the ultimate fulfillment of the Sabbath, redeeming
his people from slavery to sin and bringing them into the perfect rest
of the new creation (Heb 4:8–11). Isaiah called the people of Israel
to "call the Sabbath a delight and the holy day of the LORD honorable"
(Isa 58:13). Thus, the fourth commandment should be seen not as a
legalistic and burdensome command, but as an opportunity for joyful
rest, thanksgiving for God's mercies, and sharing those blessings
with others through hospitality, fellowship, and good works, fore-
shadowing the eternal rest in the new heaven and new earth.

Laura Ingalls Wilder described what faithful Sabbath observance
was considered to be in parts of America in the late nineteenth

---

28. Lev 23:40; Deut 14:24–29; 15:26–29; 16:9–12, 13–15.

29. Deut 14:24–26; 16:11, 14–15.

30. Lev 23:1–3; Gordon J. Wenham, *The Book of Leviticus* (Grand Rapids: Eerdmans, 1979), 301.

31. J. W. McGarvey and Philip Y. Pendleton, *The Four-Fold Gospel* (n.p.: Standard Publishing Co., 1914), 492.

32. Exod 21:2–6; Lev 25:13, 23, 28, 42; Num 32; Josh 13ff.

century. The family stopped working and playing on Saturday night, and then:

> Sunday morning they ate a cold breakfast, because nothing could be cooked on Sunday. Then they all dressed in their best clothes and walked to church. They walked because hitching up the horses was work, and no work could be done on Sunday.
>
> They must walk slowly and solemnly, looking straight ahead. They must not joke or laugh, or even smile. Grandpa and his two brothers walked ahead, and their father and mother walked behind them.
>
> In church, Grandpa and his brothers must sit perfectly still for two long hours and listen to the sermon. They dared not fidget on the hard bench. They dared not swing their feet. They dared not turn their heads to look at the windows or the walls or the ceiling of the church. They must sit perfectly motionless, and never for one instant take their eyes from the preacher.
>
> When church was over, they walked slowly home. They might talk on the way, but they must not talk loudly and they must never laugh or smile. At home they ate a cold dinner which had been cooked the day before. Then all the long after-noon they must sit in a row on a bench and study their cate-chism, until at last the sun went down and Sunday was over.[33]

The last eleven words of this extract are telling. How different the picture of joyful rest and thankfulness given in the Bible is from such a joyless approach. The heart of the fourth commandment is not somber law-keeping but joyful and generous hospitality.

Observance of the Sabbath (now Lord's Day) may be even more important today than it has ever been. The twenty-first century is an age where everything is seen as a "form of instrumental making," where even the creation of life itself has become the technological

---

33. Laura Ingalls Wilder, *The Little House in the Big Woods* (New York: HarperTrophy, 1971), 87–89.

product of the human will. Observing the age-old ritual of one day's rest in seven in which "we lay aside our making and acting and doing in order to celebrate the completeness and integrity of God's making and acting and doing" bears witness to the God-givenness of time, and to the order of creation which stands outside the reach of human artifice.[34] A weekly rest can be a "disruptive witness" in a hyper-distracted age, a "day of protest against the servitude of work and the worship of money."[35]

THE SECOND TABLE:
"You Shall Love Your Neighbor as Yourself"

FIFTH COMMANDMENT

Honor your father and your mother, as the LORD your
God commanded you, that your days may be long, and
that it may go well with you in the land that the LORD
your God is giving you. (Deut 5:16; Exod 20:12)

The fifth commandment contains both vertical and horizontal aspects and so can be seen as transitioning from the first to the second table of the law. The commandment is particularly concerned with the parent-child relationship, but it is often interpreted more broadly than this. Francis Turretin wrote that "under the words 'parents' are understood all superiors—magistrates, masters, teachers, pastors."[36] That is, the traditional view is that the fifth commandment has a broader view than simply the parent-child relationship; it expresses love for neighbor by requiring us to respect those authorities that God has instituted.

Support for this broader interpretation can be found in the Mosaic law. As noted, Deuteronomy chapters 6 to 26 are an exposition of the

---

34. Oliver O'Donovan, *Begotten or Made?* (Oxford: Clarendon Press, 1984), 3, 12.

35. Alan Noble, *Disruptive Witness: Speaking Truth in a Distracted Age* (Downers Grove, IL: InterVarsity Press, 2018), 115–9; *Catechism of the Catholic Church*, 523 [2172].

36. Turretin, *Institutes of Elenctic Theology*, 2:35.

Decalogue. The section of Deuteronomy that expounds the fifth commandment is Deuteronomy 16:18–18:22. This includes sections on how the Israelites were to relate to the main authorities within Israel, namely law courts, the king, the priests and Levites, and prophets.[37] The Israelites were commanded to respect the decisions of the law courts (Deut 17:11–12).

Paul's command to the Romans to submit to the governing authorities (Rom 13:1–7) has been understood as an expression of the fifth commandment.[38] The New Testament stipulates that elders and pastors should be given honor and obedience (1 Tim 5:17; Heb 13:7), and the Mosaic law required Israelites to show respect for the elderly and rise in the presence of the aged (Lev 19:32).

As well as imposing obligations on children toward their parents, the commandment has been understood to impose duties on parents toward their children. The Mosaic law imposes clear restrictions on the power of parents (e.g., Lev 19:29), and the New Testament requires parents to provide for, teach, and not exasperate their children.[39] Sixteenth century Reformer Heinrich Bullinger wrote that parents were under a duty to nourish and feed their children, to teach and instruct them in the substance of the Christian faith, and to find them a suitable occupation.[40]

Thomas Aquinas wrote that "there is in man an inclination to certain more specific ends which he has by nature in common with other animals; and, according to this inclination, 'those things which nature has taught to all animals' are said to belong to the natural law, such as the union of male and female and the education of the young and similar things."[41] Thus, a broader understanding of the

37. Deut 17:8–20; 18:1–8, 14–22.

38. Simon P. Kennedy, "The Decalogue, Resistance, and Political Obedience in Early Protestant Thought," *Journal of Religious History* 46, no. 1 (March 2022): 143.

39. Eph 6:4; Col 3:21; 1 Tim 5:8.

40. Heinrich Bullinger, *The Decades of Henry Bullinger*, ed. Thomas Harding (Grand Rapids: Reformation Heritage Books, 2004), 1:291–4.

41. Thomas Aquinas, *Summa Theologica* IaIIae 94:2, in *Aquinas: Political Writings*, ed. R. W. Dyson (Cambridge: Cambridge University Press, 2020), 118.

fifth commandment is consistent with traditional understandings of
the natural law, including a parental obligation to educate children.

While it is not possible to directly enforce that children should
honor their parents, the broader concept of authority and obligation
that underlies the fifth commandment is essential for the proper
ordering of society. Without respect for civil law and civil government, society will quickly descend into anarchy.

It should also be noted that in Scripture human relationships
and loyalties are not absolute. Jesus said, "If anyone comes to me
and does not hate his own father and mother and wife and children
and brothers and sisters, yes, and even his own life, he cannot be
my disciple" (Luke 14:26). Likewise, as discussed in chapter 5, the
obedience owed to civil rulers is not absolute. We are to love God
with our whole heart, and this must take precedence over all human
ties of allegiance.

Sixth Commandment

You shall not murder. (Exod 20:13; Deut 5:17)

The sixth commandment demands that we show love for our neighbors by valuing their lives and respecting the image of God in them.
The rationale underlying this commandment is that humans are
made in the image of God, and only God has the right to give and
take away life (see, e.g., Gen 9:6). The commandment is tautologous,
given that "murder" means "unlawful killing," so the commandment
effectively says: you shall not do the killing which you shall not do.[42]
What, then, is the killing which we should not do?

The Scripture spells this out in other places. First, there is a
distinction between the intentional and unintentional killing of
another (Exod 21:12–14; Deut 19:4–7, 11–13); the commandment
clearly prohibits intentional murder. In addition, the commandment requires that reasonable care be taken to prevent injury and

---

42. Greg L. Bahnsen, *Theonomy in Christian Ethics*, 3rd. ed. (n.p.: Covenant Media
Press, 2002), 307.

remove risks to life (Exod 21:29; Lev 19:16; Deut 22:8). Not doing something to prevent injury or death is culpable, although not as culpable as intentional murder. The sixth commandment therefore prohibits the intentional, reckless, and negligent taking of life. The Christian tradition has maintained that the sixth commandment does not prevent lawful punishment by judicial authority, just war or killing a person in self-defense, although important limits are placed on these.[43]

There is an internal dimension to the command; Jesus made clear that the commandment prohibits hatred as well as murder (Matt 5:21–26), consistent with the requirement of the Mosaic law that the Israelites were not to hate their brothers or bear grudges (Lev 19:17–18).

Self-preservation is an obvious and universal feature of the created world; as such, it is not difficult to see how the sixth commandment is consistent with the natural law. Aquinas wrote that "inasmuch as every substance seeks the preservation of its own being according to its nature; and, according to this inclination, whatever is a means of preserving human life belongs to the natural law, and whatever impedes it is contrary to it."[44]

As noted above, Deuteronomy chapters 6 to 26 are an exposition of the Decalogue. The section that deals with the sixth commandment is Deuteronomy 19:1–22:8. These passages make clear that a concern for justice and fair process is connected with the sixth commandment, and that a failure to provide adequate institutions of justice renders Israel guilty of the blood of the innocent (Deut 19:1–13; 19:15–21). These chapters contain some surprising inclusions which do not appear to correspond with the sixth commandment (e.g., Deut 19:14; 21:18–21; 22:1–7). One possible interpretation is that the sixth commandment reveals a concern for the underlying causes of strife

---

43. Turretin, *Institutes of Elenctic Theology*, 2:112–15. See, e.g., Deut 20, which imposes limits on the Israelites when waging war.

44. Aquinas, *Summa Theologica* IaIIae 94:2, in Dyson, *Aquinas: Political Writings*, 118.

and enmity, and so overlaps with other commandments such as the fifth and eighth.

The sixth commandment underlies the proper role of civil law. Romans 13 describes the civil ruler as God's servant, who bears the sword and who "carries out God's wrath on the wrongdoer" (Rom 13:4). Perhaps the most fundamental role of civil government is to protect the people who are under the ruler's care and defend them from internal and external threats to their safety.[45] Civil law should define the situations in which the taking of life is unlawful and establish procedures and mechanisms for its punishment.

SEVENTH COMMANDMENT

You shall not commit adultery. (Exod 20:14; Deut 5:18)

Few areas of biblical teaching contrast more starkly with contemporary views than this teaching on sexuality. The law expounds on this commandment in Deuteronomy 22:13–30 and perhaps most comprehensively in Leviticus 18. It will be apparent from these passages that "adultery" is used in the seventh commandment as a placeholder or synecdoche for many other types of sexual sin, including sex outside of heterosexual marriage, divorce, incest, rape, bestiality, and polygamy. Jesus also makes clear that the command extends to sins of the heart—namely, lust (Matt 5:27–30).

The seventh commandment is framed in negative terms. It might be tempting, therefore, to reduce the teaching of this commandment to a list of forbidden fruits, as if the Bible's teaching on sex is purely a long list of do nots. It is common to present the Christian view as repressive and restrictive, even harmful—to the point of denying a person's fundamental identity.[46] The predominant view today is that the good life consists of sleeping with whom you want, when you

---

45. Luther, "Whether Soldiers, Too, Can Be Saved," 435–36.

46. See Carl R. Trueman, *The Rise and Triumph of the Modern Self: Cultural Amnesia, Expressive Individualism, and the Road to Sexual Revolution* (Wheaton, IL: Crossway, 2020).

want; the modern Western view insists on the removal of all external restrictions and reduces the entirety of sexual morality into a single principle, that of consent. The Christian ideal of insisting that sex is for marriage borders on ridiculous to the modern mindset and is thought to be the path of restriction, repression, and hypocrisy. As such, the seventh commandment brings into stark relief competing visions of the good life.

The Bible is not anti-sex; quite the contrary. Scripture contains many positive statements about the goodness of sex and marriage.[47] The positive side of biblical teaching about sex is found in places such as Proverbs 5:15–19:

> Drink water from your own cistern,
> > flowing water from your own well.
> Should your springs be scattered abroad,
> > streams of water in the streets?
> Let them be for yourself alone,
> > and not for strangers with you.
> Let your fountain be blessed,
> > and rejoice in the wife of your youth,
> > a lovely deer, a graceful doe.
> Let her breasts fill you at all times with delight;
> > be intoxicated always in her love.

The "union of male and female" has for centuries been seen as a feature of the natural law.[48] The biblical teaching about sex therefore reflects our created nature, and contravening it always has consequences. All sexual sin is, ultimately, destructive. The Bible contains many examples of the destructive consequences of the unbridled

---

47. E.g., Gen 2:24–25; Prov 5:15–19; Song 1:1–4; 2:3; 4:11–16; 5:1, 4–5; 7:6–13; Mark 10:6–9; 1 Cor 7:2–5; Eph 5:25–33; Heb 13:4.

48. Aquinas, *Summa Theologica* IaIIae 94.:2, in Dyson, *Aquinas: Political Writings*, 118; Franciscus Junius, *The Mosaic Polity*, ed. Andrew M. McGinnis, trans. Todd M. Rester (Grand Rapids: CLP Academic, 2015), 45–46.

sexual appetite (Gen 19; 2 Sam 11; 2 Sam 13). While sex is good, and
a blessing, it is necessary for it to be expressed within proper bounds.

Perhaps in relation to no other commandment is it so important to be reminded that we are lovers and not thinkers—that is, our
orientation to the world is defined primarily by what we love, not
what we think. It is necessary to recover the positive aspects of the
Bible's teaching on sex and present the beauty of the Bible's teaching
in a winsome way. The great challenge for the church therefore is
to present the biblical teaching on sexuality as something positive,
and to model faithful, happy unions.

The promise of the sexual revolution is freedom from outdated
shackles. This, however, has not eventuated in practice:

> A sexual revolution that set out to free women from unfair
> expectations of modesty hasn't levelled the playing field
> between the sexes at all. Instead, it's rolled out an aggressive,
> visual, low-intimacy, emotionally disconnected male-stan-
> dard sexuality for everyone, including women—to our con-
> siderable detriment.[49]

The fruit of denying the Christian teaching about sex is not
unbounded pleasure and freedom, but joyless casual encounters
and broken homes, with devastating consequences for men, women,
and children.[50] R. R. Reno has argued that the "moral deregulation"
of American society through the removal of traditional moral beliefs
has disproportionately impacted the poorer and lower classes, leading to high levels of crime, imprisonment, fatherlessness, addic-
tion, divorce, and financial stress, while having little impact on the

---

49. Mary Harrington, "How Sexual Empowerment Screws Women," *UnHerd*, August
19, 2020, https://unherd.com/2020/08/what-wap-gets-wrong-about-sex.

50. Patrick Parkinson, "For Kid's Sake: Repairing the Social Environment for
Australian Children and Young People," *The Australian Family* 32, no. 3 (2011): 23.

elites who were responsible for dismantling those beliefs.[51] Children raised in single-parent homes have:

- 77 percent greater risk of being physically abused;

- 87 percent greater risk of being harmed by physical neglect;

- 74 percent greater risk of suffering from emotional neglect;

- 120 percent greater risk of experiencing some type of maltreatment overall.[52]

How might the seventh commandment relate to civil law? Here it is necessary to note that not all sins should be crimes. Even if it were desirable, in today's climate it would be impossible to criminalize all sins comprehended by the seventh commandment, and the Mosaic law expressly accommodated sins such as polygamy and divorce (Deut 24:1–4; Matt 19:3–9; Mark 10:4–9). Nevertheless, the logic or principle of the seventh commandment ought to underlie civil law, and civil laws ought to promote and value marriage and discourage its dissolution.

EIGHTH COMMANDMENT
You shall not steal. (Exod 20:15; Deut 5:19)

It is true that we are not defined by our property or our possessions (Luke 12:15). It is also true that property is to some degree an extension of who we are. My house is not simply a structure which (mostly) keeps the elements out; it reflects the time, effort, and money my family has poured into it through building, repairing, and decorating

---

51. R. R. Reno, *Resurrecting the Idea of a Christian Society* (Washington, DC: Regnery Publishing, 2016).

52. Jill Goldman, Marsha K. Salus, Deborah Wolcott, and Kristie Y. Kennedy, *A Coordinated Response to Child Abuse and Neglect: The Foundation for Practice* (Washington, DC: U.S. Department of Health and Human Services, 2003), 31.

in order to provide a comfortable home and a place to show hospitality. To disrespect someone's property is to disrespect that person. As
noted, the second great commandment and the golden rule underlie
all the specific commands of the Decalogue. The eighth commandment is an expression of the requirement to love our neighbors by
respecting their property.[53]

Property rights are often thought of as a series of exclusive rights
in relation to something—for example, the right to possess land and
exclude others. The biblical view of property is quite different. As
with all the commandments, the Pentateuch considerably broadens
the logic of the eighth commandment into a wide range of obligations.
There is much more to the eighth commandment than simply not
taking someone else's property; the eighth commandment reflects a
broader principle of fairness, love, and generosity in dealings with
other people, especially those of the household of faith (cf. Gal 6:10).

In contrast to modern Western individualistic notions, property
ownership in Scripture is conceived as containing obligations toward
others, mandating an attitude of generosity, especially toward the
poor and needy. The Israelites were commanded not to take advan-
tage of each other, especially the poor and needy, in their dealings
(Lev 25:14–17; Deut 24:14–15) and were forbidden to use dishonest
weights (Lev 19:35–36; Deut 25:13–16). The law stipulated that pro-
ductive assets such as a millstone could not be taken as security for
a loan (Deut 24:6). Defrauding one's neighbor or withholding the
wages of a hired man amounted to stealing (Lev 19:13).

The Israelites were prohibited from gleaning to the edges of their
field, so that the poor were able to collect for their needs.[54] As I have
noted, the law exhibits a particular concern for the vulnerable
and the poor. Various specific laws of the Pentateuch that are connected with the eighth commandment require fair dealing with the

---

53. Bullinger, Decades, 2:41.

54. Lev 19:9–10; 23:22; Deut 24:19–22. The law also contained restrictions on
abuse of this right: Deut 23:24–25.

vulnerable.[55] Israelites were prohibited from charging interest on charitable loans to fellow Israelites (Lev 25:35–38; Deut 23:19–20). In these ways, the eighth commandment gives effect to the golden rule[56] and contrasts strongly with the classic liberal view of property. The Mosaic law even dictated the price to be paid when land was sold (Lev 25:15–16). Property "is not a thing but rather a relationship which one has with a thing," and "the law of property is not really about things but rather about people."[57]

There is a close connection in the Old Testament between the Sabbath and the eighth commandment. At the end of every seven years, all debts were to be cancelled and slaves set free (Exod 21:2; Deut 15:1); during the Jubilee Year, all land was to be returned to its original allocation (Lev 25:13). Freed slaves were to be furnished liberally from the flock, threshing floor, and winepress (Deut 15:12–15). The prohibition on charging interest appears in Leviticus in the chapter dealing with the Jubilee, connected with the Sabbath (Lev 25:35–38); the equivalent prohibition in Deuteronomy appears in connection with the eighth commandment (Deut 23:19–20). In Israel, Sabbath and property were therefore closely connected. The logic seems to be that, as God has blessed the people in redeeming them and giving them a stake in the land of Israel, each Israelite was to be generous so that all might share in the blessings of the land.

Together with the laws referred to in previous paragraphs, the Sabbath Year and Year of Jubilee were intended to make provision for the poor in an age without a welfare state. The modern context of mechanized agriculture is obviously very different to the subsistence farming of ancient Israel, but the clear point is that property

---

55. Exod 22:22–27; 23:9; Lev 19:13; 23:22; Deut 24:17–22.

56. Early Reformed writers often argued that the golden rule underlies the Ten Commandments: Bullinger, *Decades*, 2:41; Martin Bucer, *De Regno Christi*, in *Melanchthon and Bucer*, ed. Wilhelm Pauck (Louisville: Westminster John Knox, 1969), 360.

57. Kevin Gray and Susan Francis Gray, "The Idea of Property in Land," in *Land Law: Themes and Perspectives*, ed. S. Bright and J. Dewar (Oxford: Oxford University Press, 1998), 15; Kevin Gray and Susan F. Gray, *Elements of Land Law*, 5th ed. (Oxford: Oxford University Press, 2008), 4 (italics removed).

ownership carries obligations and responsibilities toward others, especially those in need. Property rights can never be conceived as absolute. What the Lord said of Israel is true of every person: all land is his, and we are but tenants and sojourners (Lev 25:23).[58]

There is a long Christian tradition of reflecting on property which is very different from modern individualistic notions. Medieval thinkers who reflected on issues of poverty and property came to what to modern eyes are startling conclusions. They considered that the rich have a natural obligation to feed the poor; one medieval text said that a "man who keeps more for himself than he needs is guilty of theft." Another said that not feeding the poor was tantamount to killing them. The poor person who took from the rich to feed himself could not be said to have stolen: he was merely taking what was his by natural right. While such an obligation could not be enforced in the courts, several writers argued that there existed a power of "evangelical denunciation" such that, where (for example) a rich man refused to provide for the poor, a bishop had power to compel him to do so.[59]

Early Reformed writers considered it to be the civil ruler's duty to provide for the poor, distinguishing between those in need and those who "either feign need or invite it by laziness and soft living."[60] The Roman Catholic Church holds that rich nations have a moral duty to give aid to poorer people and nations.[61] These approaches are considerably more open to the redistribution of wealth than many Christians would consider to be legitimate today. Rather than Scripture being *opposed* to government redistribution of wealth, the Christian tradition has often maintained that the eighth commandment *requires* such redistribution. The Pentateuch requires justice

---

58. See further Jonathan Burnside, *God, Justice, and Society: Aspects of Law and Legality in the Bible* (Oxford: Oxford University Press, 2011), 215–19; Jonathan Sacks, *Deuteronomy: Renewal of the Sinai Covenant* (New Haven, CT: Maggid Books, 2019), 135.

59. Brian Tierney, *The Idea of Natural Rights: Studies on Natural Rights, Natural Law, and Church Law, 1150–1625* (Grand Rapids: Eerdmans, 1997), 70–75.

60. Bucer, *De Regno Christi*, 308.

61. *Catechism of the Catholic Church*, 586 [2439–40].

"not only in how the law is applied, but also in how the means of exis-tence—wealth as God's blessing—are distributed."[62]

The legitimacy of private property has been controversial in the Christian tradition, with some writers arguing that under the natu-ral law all property is held in common. Against this, Aquinas argued that people will take greater care with that which is their own and so resources will be better managed under private ownership, which is a matter for human positive law.[63] John Locke famously argued that people have a right to the property they have created through their labor.[64] The communist experiments of the twentieth century suggest that where there is no private property, there is little incentive for people to work hard. Thus, private property rights are necessary for society to function. The better view, therefore, is that private prop-erty is not inconsistent with the natural law. Consistent with this, the eighth commandment can be seen as a foundation for private property rights: if "stealing" means the unlawful taking of something belonging to another person, then that would make little sense if the person did not own that something.[65]

Property rights are legitimate, and it is a reasonable infer-ence that they ought to be protected by law in some way. Property rights are of little value if there is no mechanism to enforce them. However, the eighth commandment does not prescribe a particular form these rights must have, or how they ought to be recognized in law. Throughout history there have been a wide variety of arrange-ments relating to property, from nomadic tribes, communal owner-ship, feudal tenure, state-enforced property rights, to the modern Torrens system of property registration. The scriptural command

---

62. Sacks, *Deuteronomy*, 132.

63. Aquinas, *Summa Theologica* IIaIIae 66:2, in Dyson, *Aquinas: Political Writings*, 207–9.

64. John Locke, *Two Treatises of Government*, ed. Peter Laslett (Cambridge: Cambridge University Press, 1960), II, § 27.

65. See also Philip Melanchthon, *The Chief Theological Topics: Loci Praecipui Theologici 1559*, trans. J. A. O. Preus, 2nd ed. (St. Louis: Concordia Publishing House, 2011), 129.

is compatible with a wide variety of arrangements relating to property ownership.

As with the sixth commandment, there is something tautologous in the eighth commandment: "You shall not do the taking of property which you shall not do." What amounts to the unlawful taking of someone's property will depend on the particular laws and customs in each time and place. A book by Andrew Naselli and J. D. Crowley provides an illustration of this point. While on mission in Cambodia, one of the book's authors planted a mango tree, and in the fourth year it produced a meager three mangoes. Before he had a chance to do so, a local friend picked and ate all three of the mangoes. In Western societies this would have constituted trespass and theft, and therefore a breach of the eighth commandment. However, in that culture, it was not considered theft to take produce from someone's field; the real wrong was the author's stinginess in not sharing.[66] Theft is wrong, but what is considered to be theft varies among different cultures. What constitutes property, what rights are conferred by property ownership, and when property rights are lost, are all matters that are determined by the positive civil laws of each jurisdiction.

The commandment therefore leaves a great deal to human wisdom in designing a system of laws that confer property rights. For example, should others have a legal right to access a person's land, such as for a thoroughfare (which is common in England) or to connect essential services? To what extent is it legitimate for councils to impose regulations relating to the use of land, such as planning and building controls, housing of livestock, and noise? Should governments have the power to compulsorily acquire property to build public infrastructure? What rights should an owner have in relation to a river that adjoins her land, and what obligations does she have to other users of that water? Should there be any rights in

---

66. Andrew David Naselli and J. D. Crowley, *Conscience: What It Is, How to Train It, and Loving Those Who Differ* (Wheaton, IL: Crossway, 2016), 118–9. There is a biblical parallel in Deut 23:24–25.

intellectual property, and if so, what counts as property and what rights should be conferred? Do I have any rights in the air above my home or the ground beneath? None of these questions are directly answered by Scripture, and so they are matters of wisdom rather than biblical prescription.

NINTH COMMANDMENT

You shall not bear false witness against your neighbor. (Exod 20:16; Deut 5:20)

By prohibiting the bearing of false witness, the ninth commandment requires us to love our neighbors by respecting their reputations and telling the truth about them. The ninth commandment has personal, social, and civil aspects. It uses the terminology of bearing false witness rather than lying, but it is to be interpreted as including all forms of lying as within its scope. God is truth (John 14:6; Rom 3:4; Titus 1:2), lies are devilish (John 8:44), and God's people should be committed to the truth, reflecting God's character (Eph 4:15, 25). The commandment also prohibits other forms of harmful speech such as gossip and slander (Lev 19:16).

There is an important social aspect to this commandment. Trust is essential for a well-functioning society; a society that lacks trust will find great difficulty in conducting business and engaging in the joint effort which is necessary to achieve almost anything worthwhile. And truthfulness is essential to trust: society "cannot easily survive without at least a general commitment to truthful speech."[67] Aquinas considered that one important element of the natural law was that "there is in man an inclination to a good specific to himself, belonging to his rational nature"; thus, according to Aquinas, "Man has a natural inclination to know the truth concerning God and to live in

---

67. Gilbert Meilaender, *Thy Will Be Done: The Ten Commandments and the Christian Life* (Grand Rapids: Baker Academic, 2020), 99.

society."[68] The ninth commandment reflects the fact that sociability and cooperation are important parts of man's rational nature.

The language of bearing witness used in this commandment is evocative of the courtroom, perhaps because a court is a forum where coercive determinations about guilt and innocence are made, and those determinations have the potential to destroy a person's liberty, reputation, or livelihood. Bearing witness about someone may have momentous consequences for that person. This suggests that one purpose of the ninth commandment is to protect the integrity of the institutions of justice, which depend on accurate and truthful information for just outcomes. A justice system is "dependent on being able to trust the word of a witness."[69] The misuse of legal institutions and procedures can lead to great injustice (see, e.g., 1 Kgs 21).

Scripture reveals a broader concern for justice and truthfulness which goes well beyond simply not uttering falsehoods. The Israelites are commanded not to do injustice in court (Lev 19:15). It is a breach of the ninth commandment for a person to fail to speak up when a public charge has been made about which she has knowledge (Lev 5:1). Judges must administer justice impartially, and all people are entitled to fair treatment in law, regardless of their social or economic status (Exod 23:1–3, 6–8; Lev 19:15; 24:22). Justice must take place openly, not in secret (Deut 17:5). The commandment therefore has important legal implications, requiring open, impartial, fair, and proportionate justice (Deut 16:19–20; 19:15–21; 24:16). While it is not possible to eradicate lying by law, the principle underlying the commandment could find legal expression in laws prohibiting perjury, providing a remedy for defamation, and a prohibition on false and misleading conduct in business dealings.

Deuteronomy 16 commands the Israelites to appoint judges in all their towns, and it states: "You shall not pervert justice. You shall not show partiality, and you shall not accept a bribe, for a bribe blinds the

---

68. Aquinas, *Summa Theologica* IaIIae 94:2, in Dyson, *Aquinas: Political Writings*, 118.
69. Walton, "Deuteronomy," 213, 222.

eyes of the wise and subverts the cause of the righteous. Justice, and only justice, you shall follow, that you may live and inherit the land that the LORD your God is giving you" (Deut 16:18–20). This appears in the section of Deuteronomy dealing with the fifth commandment. Similar principles apply in relation to the ninth commandment.[70] There is, therefore, a connection between the fifth and the ninth commandments, suggesting that the proper exercise of authority is closely connected to truth and justice.

Also connected with this commandment is the question of how we attain truth in a world of sin and falsehood. A commitment to truth demands a commitment to due process both personally and in official decision-making. This is because no human person has perfect knowledge; people lie, tell part of the truth, understand and recollect things imperfectly, and often further their own agendas when presenting their views. Therefore, the Mosaic law required judges to investigate accusations thoroughly, and an accused person could only be convicted on the testimony of two or three witnesses.[71] This commitment to truth extends well beyond the courtroom: "The one who states his case first seems right, until the other comes and examines him" (Prov 18:17). A wise person, a wise parent, a wise judge, and a wise church court will carefully and impartially consider all sides of an issue before reaching a decision.[72] Indeed, due process is a required feature of judicial and administrative decision-making in Western legal systems: in Australia, it is unlawful for governments to make decisions without following procedural fairness.

---

70. E.g., Deut 24:14–18.
71. Num 35:30; Deut 13:12–14; 17:4–7; 19:15–21.
72. Matt 18:16; 2 Cor 13:1; 1 Tim 5:19. James 3:17 connects wisdom with impartiality.

Tenth Commandment

You shall not covet your neighbor's wife. And you shall
not desire your neighbor's house, his field, or his male
servant, or his female servant, his ox, or his donkey, or
anything that is your neighbor's. (Deut 5:21; Exod 20:17)

The tenth commandment prohibits coveting that which belongs
to another person. It can be seen as corresponding to the inward
aspects of other commandments, especially the sixth, seventh, and
eighth. The positive virtues which correspond to the prohibition
include contentment and thankfulness, as well as generosity toward
those in need, remembering the Lord's mercy and goodness (see
Deut 26:1–15). Love for neighbor demands generosity toward others,
not coveting what is theirs.

Coveting may seem a relatively benign sin—after all, coveting of
itself does not directly affect another, and may not even be visible
to others. Why, then, is it singled out in the Decalogue? One reason
is that coveting is indeed serious, being "a root of all kinds of evils,"
and left unrestrained may lead to greater evils such as theft, murder,
or adultery.[73] As powerfully illustrated in the story of David and
Bathsheba (2 Sam 11), envy is an attack on the dignity of other people,
seeking to supplant them and occupy their place in the world.[74]

A second reason is that covetousness is idolatry (Col 3:5), the
inverse of thankfulness and contentment, and leads to greater sin
(see Rom 1:21–23). The first and tenth commandments therefore act
as bookends for the Decalogue, with the first commanding love and
worship of the one true God, and the tenth warning us to beware of
that lack of contentment which so easily leads us into excessive love
for other things.

---

73. 1 Tim 6:10; Jas 4:1–2; see 2 Sam 11; 1 Kgs 21.

74. I owe this point to Alastair Roberts, "Deuteronomy 5: Biblical Reading and
Reflections," Alastair's Adversaria, May 4, 2020, https://audio.alastairadversaria.com
/sermons/10098/deuteronomy-5-biblical-reading-and-reflections.

In this chapter I have examined the content of the Decalogue, a perfect summary of the moral law, and provided some general guidance on how each commandment might apply to civil law. In the next chapter, I will go into much greater detail on how the moral law should affect civil law today, especially regarding how far modern-day lawmakers' freedom should extend.

IV

MORAL LAW and CIVIL LAW

T he typical approach to civil law today is legal positivism, which
   states in short that whatever is determined to be law by the lawmaker is law. This leads to a classic dilemma in legal philosophy:
Would a law, for example, that stated that all blue-eyed babies must
be murdered at birth be a valid law?[1] Now, it might be that a sane
legislature would never pass such a law, and a sane citizenry would
never accept such a law, but the point remains. Could such an enactment be considered a law?

   This chapter considers civil law—namely, laws enacted by civil
governments and lawmakers. The historic Christian view is that
civil law must be based on the universal principles of the moral law.
Christian thinkers have long considered that civil law is subject to a
higher law—namely, the universally applicable moral law (or natural law)—and ought to be the application of the principles of that law

---

1. Leslie Stephen, *The Science of Ethics* (London: Smith, Elder & Co, 1882), 143;
A. V. Dicey, *Introduction to the Study of the Law of the Constitution*, 6th ed. (London:
MacMillan, 1902), 78.

to the changing circumstances of human existence. Christians have
traditionally held that laws which do not conform to natural law are
not laws. Augustine said that "a law which is not just does not seem
to me to be a law."[2] Aquinas said that if at any point a human law "is
in any respect at odds with the law of nature, it will then no longer
be law, but a corruption of law."[3] Human laws derive their validity
from their conformity to the natural law.

As I argued in chapter 1, subject to overall consistency with the
natural law, lawmakers have considerable freedom in enacting civil
laws. This chapter considers how lawmakers ought to go about building on the foundation of the moral law to enact civil laws.

THE ROLE OF THE CIVIL GOVERNMENT

As this is a book specifically about law, we cannot discuss the role of
the government at length.[4] But it is necessary to address the question,
What is the scope of the civil ruler's role in making laws?

First, it is important to appreciate the distinction between the
prescriptive and the providential will of God. Based on passages
such as Deuteronomy 29:29, theologians have drawn a distinction
between the prescriptive, or preceptive, will of God (the revealed
requirements of the moral law that God's people are expected to obey)
and his providential or decretive will (God's secret will whereby he
ordains all that comes to pass).[5] For the most part, when thinking
about law and civil government, Christians are accustomed to think
in prescriptive terms: What would a biblically faithful form of civil

---

2. Augustine, *De Libero Arbitrio*, trans. Dom Mark Pontifex (London: Longmans,
Green and Co, 1955), 1.5.11.

3. Thomas Aquinas, *Summa Theologica* IaIIae 95:2, in *Aquinas: Political Writings*, ed.
R. W. Dyson (Cambridge: Cambridge University Press, 2020), 130.

4. See, e.g., John Calvin, *Institutes of the Christian Religion*, ed. John T. McNeill,
trans. Ford Lewis Battles (Louisville: Westminster John Knox, 1960), 4.20; Johannes
Althusius, *Politica*, trans. Frederick S. Carney (Indianapolis: Liberty Fund, 1995); David
C. Innes, *Christ and the Kingdoms of Men: Foundations of Political Life* (Phillipsburg, NJ:
P&R Publishing, 2019).

5. See, e.g., Herman Bavinck, *Reformed Dogmatics*, ed. John Bolt, trans. John Vriend
(Grand Rapids: Baker Academic, 2003–2008), 2:242–45.

government look like? What laws should a ruler enact to be faithful to Scripture?

However, the Bible does not answer this question in comprehensive detail. The overwhelming view of the Christian tradition is that the Bible outlines the moral principles and standards that apply to all people at all times, but it does not lay out a detailed blueprint for what a biblically faithful form of civil government would look like, or a comprehensive code for civil law.

Further, while it is true that God wills *preceptively* that all people obey his moral law, God does not will *decretively* that all people will do so. This means that the tasks of governing and lawmaking take place in the messy reality of a sinful world. As I will argue below, it is necessary for civil governments and civil laws to take account of fallen and sinful people, and so an ideally perfect form of civil law is an illusion. This complicates the question of what God's will is for modern civil law.

It is nevertheless true that the Bible does have much to say that is relevant. Some of this teaching has been explored in earlier chapters. The Old Testament outlines the moral law and applies those principles within the specific context of the Israelite nation in books such as Leviticus and Deuteronomy. In so doing, it both gives a perfect example of how to apply the unchanging principles of the moral law within a specific context and further fleshes out the logic of the law. The New Testament further expounds and amplifies the principles of the moral law, including by exposing the inward nature of the law.[6]

The few passages in the New Testament that address the civil ruler are tantalizingly brief and are in providential rather than preceptive terms. That is, the New Testament writers assume that the rulers that exist have been placed there by God, and they are much more concerned with ensuring a godly personal response from Christians than with telling rulers how to enact laws. As an example, when told about Pilate's slaughter of Galilean worshipers, Jesus did not waste a

---

6. See, e.g., Matt 5:21–32; Rom 13:9–10.

single word condemning the injustice but rather warned his hearers to repent, lest they also perish (Luke 13:1–3).

In Romans 13—the classic New Testament passage regarding the civil ruler—Paul describes the civil ruler as "God's servant for your good" and as "an avenger who carries out God's wrath on the wrong-doer" (Rom 13:4), which suggests something of the core function of the civil government. However, Paul's point in this chapter is not to define the proper limits of the ruler's function, but to commend him as a servant of God and command the Christian to submit to his authority (Rom 13:1–7). Christians are to make prayers and suppli-cations "for kings and all who are in high positions, that we may lead a peaceful and quiet life, godly and dignified in every way" (1 Tim 2:1–2). When asked whether it was lawful to pay taxes to Caesar, Jesus famously replied: "Render to Caesar the things that are Caesar's, and to God the things that are God's" (Matt 22:15–22; Mark 12:13–17; Luke 20:20–26).

The Bible outlines in detail the moral principles to which we are subject and contains many principles which are relevant to civil law, but it does not comprehensively explain what a biblically faithful form of civil government would look like, or what laws civil rulers should enact. As this book has emphasized, Scripture leaves consid-erable room for wisdom in deciding these matters. The Bible con-tains many principles of law and morality which remain applicable today; it tells us some of the things civil rulers should *not* do (such as allow oppression or injustice), and it gives an example of a legal system in a particular context (the Mosaic law). However, it is not an exhaustive blueprint for civil law for all time.

Of course, this is not to suggest that there is anything deficient in the Bible or the Mosaic law. Theologians have often described the Mosaic law as an adaptation of the principles of natural law to the polity of Israel.[7] It is simply to say that it is not, and was never

---

7. See, e.g., Franciscus Junius, *The Mosaic Polity*, ed. Andrew M. McGinnis, trans. Todd M. Rester (Grand Rapids: CLP Academic, 2015), 60–64.

intended to be, an exhaustive blueprint for the laws of every human society throughout history.

Paul's description of the civil ruler as God's servant to carry out God's wrath on the wrongdoer (Rom 13:4) suggests that the primary and core function of the civil ruler is to promote the good, suppress evil, and punish the evildoer,[8] and so civil laws should be directed primarily to that end. From this passage Oliver O'Donovan argues that the practice of judgment, "the discipline of enacting right against wrong" and maintaining the distinction "between the just and the unjust," is the core function of government.[9]

However, while the core of the civil ruler's role is clear, Scripture does not exhaustively define its outer limits. Modern legal systems contain detailed bodies of law that go well beyond anything in the Bible. There is nothing in principle illegitimate about this: the complexity of modern society, as well as technological and social developments, have necessitated the enactment of laws governing those developments.

Civil government and civil law are good things. Civil rulers are God's servants, and, difficult though this might often be, we are to give thanks for them (1 Tim 2:1–2). However, Scripture's teaching about civil government is not all positive.

LAW AND TENSION

Scripture also teaches that the civil government is often in conflict with the church and Christianity. Although the state has, from time to time, been brought under subjection to Christ, the mechanisms of the state are often employed to attempt to bring Christ and his followers under subjection. This is entirely consistent with what the New Testament leads us to expect. Jesus warns his disciples to expect persecution (John 15:20), telling them that they will be brought before "the synagogues and the rulers and the authorities"

---

8. John Murray, *The Epistle to the Romans* (Grand Rapids: Eerdmans, 1965), 2:151–52.

9. Oliver O'Donovan, *The Ways of Judgment* (Grand Rapids: Eerdmans, 2008), 3–5.

(Luke 12:11). Psalm 2 describes the plotting of earthly rulers against the Lord and his anointed, seeking to cast off their bonds. In Acts 4 the apostles directly applied this psalm to the persecution of the church by earthly rulers (Acts 4:23–28), and many examples of persecution are recorded in subsequent chapters of the book of Acts.[10]

The Bible therefore leads us to expect that there will be tension between Christianity and civil government. Indeed, there is warrant for thinking that this ought to be our ordinary expectation, as witnessed abundantly throughout the history of the church, and all the more so now that the days of Christendom are long gone. Even where a Christian makes it into a position of leadership, non-Christian thought today is so widely suffused throughout society and cultural institutions in the West that one single leader often makes little difference.

This is not to suggest that there can never be change for good or that we ought to give up attempting to influence government. It is not the case that there will only ever be tension between Christians and the government. Nevertheless, Christians ought to expect tension and conflict with civil government. This tension might take the form of active resistance to Christianity, where rulers persecute Christians or enact laws hostile to Christianity. In our age law is used, and will increasingly be used, as a means of suppressing Christian beliefs, especially the public manifestation of Christian teaching. There is an increasingly vehement view that traditional Christian doctrine—especially biblical teaching about sexuality—is not only outdated but actually harmful and therefore must be eradicated from the public square. The works of man "always seem attractive and good," and the works of God "are always unattractive and appear evil."[11]

There can also be tension even where there is no active hostility. One reason for this is that the church and the government have

---

10. E.g., Acts 5:17–42; 6:8–8:3; 12:1–19; 16:16–40; 17:1–9; 21:27–26:32.

11. Martin Luther, "Heidelberg Disputation," trans. Harold J. Grimm, in *Selected Writings of Martin Luther: 1517–1520*, ed. Theodore G. Tappert (Minneapolis: Fortress, 2007), 65.

very different goals and purposes: the church exists to proclaim the gospel while the government exists to punish the evildoer. Some of the things the government seeks, which in themselves may be good things, can be inimical to Christianity. For example, civil governments typically wish to promote safety and prosperity for their people. However, prosperity is not usually conducive to zeal for Christ's kingdom (see Matt 19:22–24; Mark 10:23–25). It is a good thing for the holders of political power to be accountable to the people and for the people to have a say in the creation of their laws. Nevertheless, democracy often results in bad laws and may encourage the idea that the people are subject to no higher authority.[12]

Even where a government does seek to support and promote Christianity or the church, the result may not be a happy one. A church that relies on patronage, money, or coercion from the government will be tempted not to be overly zealous; a church that is too closely aligned with the authorities will find it difficult to call those authorities to account or present the claims of the gospel with forthrightness. Although the story is not all bad, the church under Christendom often tended toward hypocrisy, laziness, and corruption. Thus, even where the government actively supports Christianity or the church, the kingdom of Christ does not always benefit.

Therefore, while it is most natural to expect tension where governments are actively hostile to Christianity, different sorts of tensions may arise even where governments are supportive of Christianity. Often it is the case that there is tension between Christians and civil law, which means that Christians should have modest expectations about their ability to have a transformative impact on governments and civil law. Of course, this does not mean that all laws within a given legal system will be in tension with Christianity. However, our

---

12. See D. A. Carson, *Christ and Culture Revisited* (Grand Rapids: Eerdmans, 2008), 122–39; and David T. Koyzis, *Political Visions & Illusions: A Survey & Christian Critique of Contemporary Ideologies,* 2nd ed. (Downers Grove, IL: IVP Academic, 2019), 124–52.

ordinary expectation ought to be that there will be at least some areas
of tension.

HOW LAWS ARE MADE

It is necessary to make some remarks about how laws are made
because this has important implications for how we think about
law. By this I am not referring to the procedure by which a bill is
drafted and passed through the houses of the legislature. Rather, I
am speaking of the two things that drive the creation of laws: circumstances and values.[13] Law is the product of the intersection of
these two things.

Laws must be adapted to the circumstances of the society being
regulated, and law reform is often triggered by changing circumstances. As new circumstances arise, law may need to respond to
those changes, whether they be societal trends, evidence of harmful behavior, a crisis, new technologies, environmental degradation,
and so on. An example of new technology which necessitated a regulatory response is the automobile, which has required lawmakers
to implement speed limits and other rules to ensure safety on roads.
Such rules did not exist before the twentieth century because they
were not needed.

Circumstances vary widely across time as well as between countries. England (a densely populated country with a very small land
mass) has much stricter laws regulating land use than Australia (a
sparsely populated country with a very large land mass). In Australia,
local councils require property owners in fire-prone areas to keep
their grass no higher than 10 cm during the summer months in order
to minimize the risk of fire. Such laws would be unnecessary in other
countries.

---

13. Iain Benson has argued that "values" talk is inherently subjective and under-
mines the objective nature of moral truth: Iain T. Benson, "Do 'Values' Mean Anything
at All? Implications for Law, Education and Society," *Journal for Juridical Science* 33
(2008): 117. I sympathize with this argument, but no other word seems to quite capture
my meaning here.

Developments such as new technologies, forms of communication and transportation, the creation of new types of property such as intellectual property, the development of new materials, environmental crises, the internet, social media, artificial intelligence, big data, facial recognition, pandemics, nuclear energy, IVF, advances in gene science and technology, driverless cars, electronic payments and transactions, blockchain, bitcoin, and cryptocurrency—all these and more present unique regulatory challenges which demand a response.

In addition, underlying the creation of all laws is a particular set of values—philosophical and ethical commitments, even if unarticulated, that could be secular or religious, left wing or right wing, wise or misguided. These commitments will shape what is considered to be an appropriate response to society's circumstances. Some (thankfully few) think it would be preferable for things like road safety to be worked out through market forces rather than government regulation. When faced with differences in wealth within a population, some wish to even the scales through taxation and wealth redistribution while others emphasize personal initiative and responsibility. Laws are driven by values, and just as changes in circumstances can trigger law reform, changes in values can also trigger changes to the laws. Changes in beliefs about sexuality have effected hugely significant changes in law, such as laws facilitating no-fault divorce, the decriminalization of abortion and homosexual activity, and, more recently, laws permitting same-sex marriage.

This variation in values among societies has implications for law and what is thought to be the proper role of the government. Up until 2015 in France, an edict required bakeries in Paris to remain open during the summer to ensure that there was bread available. The law was originally enacted in the late eighteenth century when the lack of fresh bread led to riots: such is the French love of real bread that the lack of its availability became a social and political issue. In other countries, it would not be thought the proper role of government to be regulating when businesses can and cannot take their holidays, and many people are content with mass-produced bread, so the inability to buy bread from a bakery would not pose a danger of unrest.

Given that, as this book has emphasized, the principles of the moral law are universally applicable and unchanging, Christians have sometimes seen changes in society's moral beliefs as a departure for the worse. However, it is also true that values can change in a more benign and less ultimate sense without challenging the principles of the moral law. For example, in earlier times children were expected to be seen and not heard; this is no longer the case. Early books of etiquette suggested that it was not "a very fine habit" to pick up excrement in the street and hold it up for another to smell, which presumably was a common enough occurrence to warrant mentioning.[14] In Australia in the 1920s it was not considered respectable to eat garlic, and "God-fearing, good Christian families did not chew gum."[15]

Even among Christians who hold to traditional views of sexuality, there is now a much greater degree of openness about sex. Some married couples of a particular generation never saw each other naked. In earlier times, men did little housework and were not even allowed to be present during childbirth; there is now an expectation that men ought to be much more actively involved in the raising of their children. There have been huge changes in the role of women, as well as changes in standards relating to manners, hygiene, clothing, food, sport, and many other areas of life.

It is therefore inescapably true that there is a fluidity to cultural values. Even where we agree strongly on ultimate values or beliefs, less ultimate values can change, often significantly. And it is not the case that these values are necessarily more correct than others. It was not "wrong" for society to consider in the 1800s that children should be seen and not heard, and it is not "right" for society

---

14. Charles Taylor, *A Secular Age* (Cambridge, MA: Belknap Press, 2007), 138.

15. Kathleen McArthur, *Bread and Dripping Days: An Australian Growing Up in the 20s* (n.p.: Kangaroo Press, 1981), 10, 22.

to think otherwise now. Some changes in values have occurred as a result of greater knowledge: for instance, cultural practices relating to hygiene have resulted from a better understanding of infection. It would not have been wrong for a doctor to perform a medical procedure in the 1800s with unwashed hands, but it would be negligent for a doctor to do so now. Killing a tiger or giraffe would have been praised as a sporting achievement in the 1800s; now that they are endangered, it is considered wrong.

Now, many changes in values reflect unbiblical views or are the direct outworking of anti-Christian beliefs. However, many other changes are good and welcome developments and do not challenge the principles of the moral law. Many examples could be listed. One is that there is a much greater emphasis on accountability for holders of public office, with freedom of information and mechanisms of review now available. Another example is changed attitudes toward people with disabilities. The earlier attitude toward people with disabilities was very paternalistic, whereby others would decide what is in a disabled person's best interests. Current thinking gives much greater emphasis to promoting the person's autonomy and participation in society. A final example is the modern law of privacy, which reflects a fundamentally different conception of the appropriate boundaries of behavior and interaction from that considered acceptable in earlier times.[16] All these examples of changes in values are good things.

These changes have not been driven by the church or Christians, although they may unwittingly be an outworking of Christian views about the dignity of humans and the need to hold rulers accountable for the exercise of their power. These developments have occurred with little input from the church, and Christians have largely fallen in step with developments driven by the secular world. It may be uncomfortable to think of the world being ahead of the church in reforming values for the better and securing their embodiment in

---

16. See, e.g., Taylor, *A Secular Age*, 136–42.

law. But it is true that, often, rather than the church transforming the state, it is the other way around.

Many changes in values and circumstances have implications for law. It would be unlawful for surgeons not to wash their hands or wear sterile gloves before performing an operation, where previously this was not the case; it is now illegal to kill endangered species, when this would not have been the case when those species were not endangered. There is now a legal right for citizens to obtain information from government departments; corporations and other organizations have a legal obligation to respect privacy.

Law, therefore, is both reactive and proactive: it reacts to changes in circumstances and is driven by underlying ethical commitments and values. While the principles of the moral law do not change, values and cultural assumptions change, and inescapably so.

This has two significant implications. The first is that law is continually changing, and indeed it is necessary and desirable that this be so. Many lament the "incessant stream of lawmaking" emanating from our governments,[17] which is impossible for any person to keep abreast of. However unwelcome a ceaseless flow of legislation may be, if what I have written is correct, it is undesirable as well as impossible to stop continual reform and adjustment of laws. Circumstances are continually changing, as are society's values. We cannot predict the circumstances or the values of the future, and so we cannot foretell what laws will be necessary in times to come.

The second implication is that it is not possible to create a detailed blueprint for the laws needed in a society. At best, a political theory can provide foundational principles to guide lawmakers, but it cannot tell us specifically what laws will be necessary, or the detail of those laws. How the principles of morality apply in informing the drafting of laws will depend on the circumstances of the time. Enacting laws for a society involves the application of the principles

---

17.   Oliver O'Donovan, "Government as Judgment," *First T,* April 1999, https://www.firstthings.com/article/1999/04/government-as-judgment.

of the moral law to the particular circumstances of the time, which will vary from society to society and from age to age. Even countries which share a common legal heritage (such as Britain, the United States, Canada, and Australia) have diverged significantly due to the different circumstances prevailing in each country, their different values, and varying historical developments.

TWO CONFLICTING PRINCIPLES

There are two additional principles that bear on the manner in which civil laws are enacted, which are in tension with one another. The first is that the lawmaker has a directive power for the good. Romans 13:4 describes civil rulers as "God's servant for your good" and as "an avenger who carries out God's wrath on the wrongdoer," which implies that civil rulers have power to promote the good and suppress evil. Civil law should be based on the moral law, and laws which do not conform to the moral law are not truly laws. If necessary, human laws must cut against the grain of human behavior by prohibiting and punishing evil in order to promote the good.

James Davison Hunter argued in *To Change the World* that culture is not simply the aggregation of individual choices and values (which he describes as the standard evangelical view), but something driven by elite institutions and networks, who have much greater power to effect enduring cultural change.[18] Lawmakers can play a significant role in shaping the values of a society.[19] There is a place for law in helping people to "establish and preserve a virtuous character"— namely, by such things as "preventing the (further) self-corruption which follows from acting out a choice to indulge in immoral conduct"

---

18. James Davison Hunter, *To Change the World: The Irony, Tragedy, and Possibility of Christianity in the Late Modern World* (New York: Oxford University Press, 2010).

19. This is illustrated well in Darel E. Paul, *From Tolerance to Equality: How Elites Brought America to Same-Sex Marriage* (Waco, TX: Baylor University Press, 2018).

and "educating people about moral right and wrong."[20] Law can legislate morality, at least to some degree.

Civil law ought to promote the good and suppress evil, and it ought to play a directive role in encouraging society toward that good. However, there are clear limitations to the lawmaker's directive power. The Bible teaches that the heart is the wellspring of life—that is, all human actions ultimately spring from heart motivations (Prov 4:23; Matt 15:10–20). The jurisdiction of the civil ruler is coercive and external and cannot bring about heart change; only the Holy Spirit can work faith and repentance in a sinner's heart (1 Cor 12:3). Attempting to force people to be good or behave in Christian ways is unlikely to be a successful strategy long term.

A legal system ultimately relies to some degree on the character of the people as the motivating power for obeying the law or doing good. It is impossible to detect and punish every breach of law. If society is not generally "good," then people will seek to evade the law, avoid being caught, and look for loopholes so as not to obey. If the only reason people obey the law is out of fear of punishment and not any regard for the welfare of others, then it will be necessary to enact ever more detailed and prescriptive laws regulating ever more aspects of society, so as to ensure that people act for the common good—which is precisely what is happening in modern Western societies.[21]

As John Stuart Mill put it, speaking of the state of European morality in 1848:

> Conjoint action is possible just in proportion as human beings can rely on each other. There are countries in Europe, of first-rate industrial capabilities, where the most serious impediment to conducting business concerns on a large scale,

---

20. Robert P. George, *Making Men Moral: Civil Liberties and Public Morality* (Oxford: Clarendon Press, 1993), 1.

21. See, e.g., Ross Grantham, *The Law and Practice of Corporate Governance* (London: LexisNexis Butterworths, 2020), 469.

is the rarity of persons who are supposed fit to be trusted with the receipt and expenditure of large sums of money.[22]

Civil law relies on the willingness of citizens to obey the law, but civil law cannot inculcate the virtue it relies on to ensure obedience.[23]

The distinction between the preceptive and decretive will of God is also relevant here. It is true that God wills preceptively that all people repent and obey the law (Acts 17:30). And yet it is not the case that God wills decretively that all people will in fact do so. Therefore, there is no guarantee that the majority of people in any society will be Christian or virtuous. That is, there is no expectation that the conditions necessary to ensure obedience to civil laws will exist. This suggests that, while civil rulers and civil laws ought to promote the good, there may need to be modest expectations about their power to actually achieve this.

The second principle is the "hardness of heart" principle. Many biblical laws applicable to ancient Israel assumed the existence of certain social and cultural practices, permitting and regulating some things that are wrong without expressly prohibiting them. The law regulating divorce in Deuteronomy 24:1–4 is one example. In Matthew's Gospel, Jesus explained that divorce was permitted in Israel because of the people's "hardness of heart" but noted that "from the beginning it was not so" (Matt 19:8; see also Mark 10:5). That is, divorce was against God's plan for marriage, but it was permitted as an allowance for the people. The Mosaic laws were accommodated to Israel's sinfulness, permitting undesirable and sinful practices without either condoning or prohibiting them.

The typical function of the laws in those contexts is, while permitting their continuance, to regulate some aspects of those practices to mitigate their harshness or to prevent a greater evil. As Girolamo

---

22. John Stuart Mill, *Principles of Political Economy* (Amherst: Prometheus Books, 2004), I.VII.5.

23. See Ulrich Zwingli, *Commentary on True and False Religion*, ed. Samuel M. Jackson and Clarence N. Heller (Eugene, OR: Wipf & Stock, 2015), 295.

Zanchi noted in relation to the permission of divorce, God "prefers to yield to the husband's hard heart than to permit more serious evils"[24]—that is, the purpose of the law is to prevent a wife-hater from becoming a wife-killer.

The following passage provides another illustration of this point:

> When a man sells his daughter as a slave, she shall not go out as the male slaves do. If she does not please her master, who has designated her for himself, then he shall let her be redeemed. He shall have no right to sell her to a foreign people, since he has broken faith with her. If he designates her for his son, he shall deal with her as with a daughter. If he takes another wife to himself, he shall not diminish her food, her clothing, or her marital rights. And if he does not do these three things for her, she shall go out for nothing, without payment of money. (Exod 21:7–11)

The context here is a father selling his daughter to be the wife of another man or his son, presumably more well-to-do than the girl's father. The passage assumes the existence of a particular cultural and social practice that existed in ancient Israel but is unthinkable today, and also the existence of an accepted body of social norms which applied to that practice. The practice is not prohibited, nor is it condoned. Instead, the law intervenes to regulate some aspects of it by requiring that there be some protection for the daughter, who would have been in a particularly vulnerable position, by ensuring that her food, clothing, and marital rights are not diminished. The Mosaic law does not comprehensively regulate this particular practice but selectively intervenes in specific ways to prevent the vulnerable from being exploited.[25]

If allowances were made for people's sinfulness in the theocratic nation-state of Israel, which was to be a holy nation set apart for God

---

24. Girolamo Zanchi, *On the Law in General*, trans. Jeffrey J. Veenstra (Grand Rapids: Christian's Library Press, 2013), 95.

25. Another example of this is Deut 21:10–14.

(Exod 19:5–6), that principle applies all the more in secular nation-states, which are not God's people. The rationale is that if the laws of a nation set unreasonable expectations, or mandate something the people will not accept, the long-term result will be a weakening of respect for civil law. Applying this biblical principle means that civil laws must allow departures from biblical standards to accommodate human weakness and sin in some situations.

Thus, even where there is a clear and applicable *moral* principle, this does not always translate to clarity about the applicable *legal* standard, or to what extent the moral principle ought to receive recognition in law. Not everything that is sinful should be unlawful. Divorce was morally wrong under the Mosaic law, but legally permitted. Men selling their daughters into slavery was also permitted. This raises some unsettling questions. If civil rulers ought to accommodate their laws to the sinful practices of the people, which practices should be permitted? Should abortion, adultery, euthanasia, bestiality, and polygamy be permitted under this principle?

Both the principle of the lawmaker's directive power for the good and the "hardness of heart" principle have some scriptural warrant, but they do not sit easily together, and they raise difficult questions. Lawmakers ought to employ their power to direct society toward the good, but they must also recognize that ultimately they have limited power to achieve that. Lawmakers will need to accommodate human sinfulness but regulate evil practices so as to prevent oppression of the vulnerable.

How do we know when to apply each principle? In other words, when should rulers permit sinful practices, and when should they employ their directive power for the good? When should they seek to stamp out evil practices, and when should they accept the limitations of their powers?

It is not possible to give one-size-fits-all answers to these questions; much will depend on context, the circumstances, and the habits and temper of the people, which will vary over time and place. Charting a course between the Scylla of permissiveness and the Charybdis of futile compulsion requires a considerable degree of wisdom. That is, in seeking to be faithful to the multifaceted and complex task of lawmaking, much depends on wisdom applied to the context, and there is a level of freedom accorded to the lawmaker in deciding these things. In the early seventeenth century, Calvinist jurist and political philosopher Johannes Althusius rightly said that good rule must "consist in political prudence, in which no administration of a magistrate ought to be lacking."[26]

WHICH COMMANDMENTS OUGHT TO BE ENFORCEABLE BY LAW?

If the Ten Commandments express the universal principles of right and wrong, and civil laws ought to be based on the moral law, then should civil rulers enforce the Ten Commandments in law? If so, which of the commandments? It should first be noted that not everything that is a sin should be punishable as a crime—many aspects of the Ten Commandments are not susceptible to legal enforcement. It would be impossible to enforce the tenth commandment ("Do not covet") as a crime. Although the moral law underlies civil law, not every commandment ought to be enforced by the civil ruler.

Most Christians today would agree that the sixth to ninth commandments should receive recognition in civil law. That is, although it is not possible to enforce every sin that contravenes the second table of the Decalogue, the civil ruler should protect life, marriage, property, and establish institutions of civil justice premised on procedural fairness, consistent with those commandments. The respect for authority which is the basis of the fifth commandment is also necessary for any stable legal order.

The earlier Christian view was that the civil ruler ought to enforce both tables of the law—namely, the duties owed to God as well as those owed to other people. That is, the lawmaker should prevent breaches of the first four commandments. For example, the

---

26. Althusius, *Politica*, 136.

Westminster Confession of Faith states that, while the civil ruler may
not assume "the administration of the Word and sacraments, or the
power of the keys of the kingdom of heaven," his role includes the
following:

> He has authority, and it is his duty, to take order, that unity
> and peace be preserved in the Church, that the truth of God
> be kept pure and entire; that all blasphemies and heresies be
> suppressed; all corruptions and abuses in worship and disci-
> pline prevented or reformed; and all the ordinances of God
> duly settled, administered, and observed.[27]

This is no longer the dominant view. Most Christians today take the
view that the civil ruler ought not to enforce the first table of the law,
and so, even though breaches of the first four commandments are
sins, they ought not to be crimes or prohibited by law. As Charles
Hodge argued, "The proper sphere of civil government is the civil
and social relations of men, and their temporal welfare; conscience,
and of course religion, are beyond its jurisdiction, except so far as the
best interests of civil society are necessarily connected with them."[28]

The distinctions referred to in chapter 1 help explain why this
is the case. As noted there, a series of institutional, eschatological,
and theological distinctions have traditionally been employed to
explain the full nature of the Bible's teaching. Considered from an
institutional perspective, the lawmaker's role is coercive; eschato-
logically, civil law is connected with this passing age and so is provisional, temporary, and passing away; and theologically, lawmakers
can only regulate the outer person and cannot touch the internal
realm of the conscience.

Attempting to enforce the first four commandments would be
inconsistent with the true nature of the lawmaker's role, given that

---

27. *Westminster Confession of Faith*, XXIII.3.
28. Charles Hodge, *A Commentary on Romans* (Edinburgh: Banner of Truth, 1972),
414.

the magistrate has only external tools of compulsion. The first commandment demands the sincere worship of the one true God, which is not possible to enforce in law: true worship and love for God must come from Spirit-worked heart change. Faith "is a free act, to which no one can be forced."[29] Similar comments could be made about the second, third, and fourth commandments. Enforcing outward obedience to commandments would simply turn people into hypocrites. As Francisco de Victoria wrote, "To come to the mysteries and sacraments of Christ merely out of servile fear would be sacrilege."[30] The view that the civil ruler ought to enforce the first table of the Decalogue is premised on a particular set of historical conditions that no longer apply—namely, a society where the overwhelming majority of people were Christian. For these reasons, attempting to enforce the first table in law is not today typically considered to be a wise approach.

Nevertheless, there is a case for arguing that some aspects of the first four commandments may receive recognition in civil law. Oliver O'Donovan has argued that Christendom—that is, the idea of a confessionally Christian government (which was a historical reality for much of the history of the West)—can be seen as the response to mission, the secular power becoming obedient to Christ.[31] Where there is widespread belief in Christianity, it would not be wrong to have some corporate recognition of this in a public founding document or constitution. The Australian Constitution, for example, states that the federating colonies agreed to unite in one indissoluble Federal Commonwealth "humbly relying on the blessing of Almighty God."[32] This reflected widely held views in the 1890s (when the Constitution

---

29. Martin Luther, "Temporal Authority: To What Extent It Should Be Obeyed," in *Selected Writings of Martin Luther: 1520–1523*, ed. Theodore G. Tappert (Minneapolis: Fortress, 2007), 298, 304.

30. Francisco de Vitoria, "On the American Indians," in *Political Writings*, ed. Anthony Pagden (Cambridge: Cambridge University Press, 1991), 272.

31. Oliver O'Donovan, *The Desire of the Nations: Rediscovering the Roots of Political Theology* (Cambridge: Cambridge University Press, 1996), 195.

32. Preamble to the Australian Constitution.

was drafted) that Christian teaching provided the foundations of civilization and morality and ought to permeate society and underlie public institutions.[33]

Second, in a society where God was widely recognized to be the one true God, it may be considered legitimate to prohibit open blasphemy or images of God, in breach of the second and third commandments. Prior to the nineteenth century, English and American law held that Christianity was part of the common law, and so blasphemy was considered to dissolve the bonds of civil society and was punishable as a criminal offense.[34] These offenses were seen as analogous to idolatry in ancient Israel (see Deut 13).

Third, a case could be made for the recognition of the Sabbath principle in law. Historically, Sunday observance was mandatory in some Western legal systems. While Sunday laws have been seen as an infringement of the consciences of those who disagree with the principle of the Sabbath, this is not how they were viewed in earlier times. Pope Leo XIII argued in his encyclical *Rerum Novarum* that Sunday observance laws were justified as a guaranteed day of rest for workers who were vulnerable to exploitation in an age before labor rights.[35] That is, Sunday observance laws were seen not as an intolerant imposition on minorities but as a much-needed guarantee of rest.

But the principle of the Sabbath could have broader application. As noted, the Sabbath has both creational and redemptive rationales. The creational logic of the Sabbath reflects the obvious truth that finite creatures need regular times of rest. Reflecting this principle, civil laws should protect people from crushing work which destroys both soul and body and so may (for example) prohibit slavery, child labor, and oppressive work practices. Southern theologians such

---

33. Stephen A. Chavura, John Gascoigne, and Ian Tregenza, *Reason, Religion and the Australian Polity: A Secular State?* (New York: Routledge, 2019).

34. Stuart Banner, "When Christianity Was Part of the Common Law," *Law and History Review* 16, no. 1 (Spring 1998): 27.

35. Pope Leo XIII, "Rerum Novarum: Encyclical of Pope Leo XIII on Capital and Labor," in *Makers of Modern Christian Social Thought: Leo XIII and Abraham Kuyper on the Social Question*, ed. Jordan J. Ballor (Grand Rapids: Acton Institute, 2016), 41–42.

as Robert L. Dabney insisted on "detailed and excessively rigorous observance of the weekly sabbath" while defending race-based slavery with no provision for slaves to earn their freedom; as put by James Jordan, such theologians "strained at sabbatical gnats and swallowed a sabbatical camel."[36]

I am not arguing that all societies everywhere should enact laws such as these, but simply that it would be legitimate to do so where there is widespread commitment to the Christian religion within a society (which was the case historically in many nations). Attempting to compel outward conformity to piety in civil law is a recipe for hypocrisy. The Ten Commandments provide the foundational principles for morality and justice that ought to underlie civil laws, but it is not the case that a lawmaker must enact them into law word for word.

Finally, civil laws and governments cannot save souls or change a person's heart, but they may indirectly assist the ministry and mission of the institutional church. John Calvin considered that it was the duty of the civil ruler to provide "a public manifestation of religion" among Christians.[37] In some countries civil law today can (and does) support the church through such things as education, beneficial tax treatment, conferring legal status on church entities so that they may hold property (and be subject to regulation), and affording a measure of institutional autonomy to church entities. In these ways civil law may indirectly assist the ministry of the church and provide "a public manifestation of religion."

PRIORITIES FOR LAW TODAY

We are now in a position to discuss how lawmakers ought to go about making law. As noted, Christian thinkers have long considered that civil law ought to be the application of the unchanging principles of the moral law to the circumstances of human society. Unfortunately,

---

36. James B. Jordan, *The Law of the Covenant: An Exposition of Exodus 21–23* (Tyler, TX: Institute for Christian Economics, 1984), 91.

37. Calvin, *Institutes*, 4.20.3.

there is no formula for going about this task. Applying the principles of the moral law to a concrete situation requires taking into account all of the principles discussed in this chapter.

When confronted with a problem that requires legislative intervention, lawmakers ought to recognize that they are under authority: they are not a law unto themselves but are constrained by the moral law. Natural law, the universally applicable moral law, provides the foundation for the civil laws enacted by lawmakers. Recognizing this requires identification of the applicable moral principles, which should be sought from a careful examination of Scripture and natural law.

Lawmakers ought to reflect on nature and the common good, considering what ought to be promoted in law and how that good may be promoted. For example, the Ten Commandments suggest particular concern to value and protect life, marriage and the family, respect for authority, respect for property, and the integrity of systems of justice. Other parts of Scripture give clear indication of the need to protect the oppressed. Just laws and legal systems will seek to protect and give effect to these principles. They are not only for the church and Christian nations; they are the expression of universally applicable moral standards which are for the good of all people. It is true as a general principle that righteousness exalts a nation (Prov 14:34; 16:12).

There is a distinction between the moral and the legal, and identifying a moral principle does not always lead to a clear legal principle. It will typically be necessary to accommodate human laws to human sinfulness, and some things that are immoral may need to be tolerated. An outright prohibition may be counterproductive. Further, the moral law speaks at a high level of generality, giving foundational principles rather than detailed guidance about the precise form of laws to be enacted. Lawmakers have a directive power and ought to promote the good and suppress evil; however, there are limitations to this power.

It is also necessary to give careful consideration to the circumstances of the people and consider how the principles of the moral law might apply in today's circumstances, which are very different from those of biblical times. While the standards of the moral law and justice are not fallible and do not vary, how they apply to particular, concrete circumstances by fallible human rulers does vary.

There is no doubt that the erosion of Christian values in contemporary societies is a cause for deep concern. But lawmaking is a much more complex process than simply enacting the Ten Commandments or the Mosaic laws into legislation, requiring considerable wisdom and prudence. Attempting to turn issues of law into binary questions of right and wrong is more often than not an example of a "quest for illegitimate religious certainty," namely, seeking greater certainty than Scripture itself provides.[38]

This, of course, is not to descend into total relativism, or to suggest that there are no biblical priorities for civil law. There is much that extended meditation on Scripture and the natural law tradition can tell us about law and justice. Where should we begin in addressing the crisis in law from the perspective of Scripture and the natural law tradition? Priorities for civil law today include the following, which is not intended to be exhaustive.

First, a fundamental priority for civil law is to establish, defend, and promote the natural order of creation, which has been established by God for our good, especially by protecting human life, marriage, and the family, and also property and the institutions of justice. This is all the more important in light of the redefinition of gender, sexuality, and marriage in the West today, which poses a huge threat to society, families, and the church. The predominant view today is a fundamentally plastic view of humans, free from any objective constraints or metaphysically determined nature, and therefore subject to technological manipulation to achieve human ends.

---

38. Chapter 2 in R. Scott Clark, *Recovering the Reformed Confession: Our Theology, Piety, and Practice* (Phillipsburg, NJ: P&R Publishing, 2008).

Second, there are many indications in Scripture that God is concerned for the poor, the widow, the fatherless, the orphan, and the stranger, and his anger burns at oppression.[39] Another biblical priority is the protection and care of the vulnerable, and defending them from oppression. Civil rulers ought to identify who are vulnerable in their societies, such as the unborn, refugees, children, women, the elderly, and disabled, and take steps (including by enacting laws) to protect them.

Third, in Scripture Christians are told to pray for those in authority, "that we may lead a peaceful and quiet life, godly and dignified in every way" (1 Tim 2:2). Lawmakers therefore ought to promote peace and order. In addition, this text suggests that religious freedom is an important priority; that is, lawmakers ought to create the conditions in which the gospel may flourish and go forward.

A very significant challenge for humanity today is surveillance capitalism—namely, the capture and rendering into data, without consent, of every aspect of our daily lives to predict and manipulate our behavior for commercial gain—and its associated concentration of wealth, knowledge, and power.[40] A crucial priority for lawmakers today is surely to address the intrusion into privacy and other evils which are associated with surveillance capitalism.

A fifth priority is the challenge to the functioning of civil government and civil law posed by technocracy—that is, the wielding of power by technical experts who are not democratically elected. This was graphically illustrated during the coronavirus pandemic, where unelected public health experts made many significant decisions which had huge impacts on people's lives. While some may think it is a good thing for decisions to be made by experts rather than politicians, the dynamic created by technocracy is a problem for several reasons.

---

39. E.g., Exod 22:21–27; Deut 24:17; Ps 82:3; Prov 14:31; Zech 7:10; Matt 25:40.

40. Shoshana Zuboff, *The Age of Surveillance Capitalism: The Fight for a Human Future at the New Frontier of Power* (New York: Public Affairs, 2019).

First, as they are not elected, technocrats are not subject to democratic accountability. Appealing to technical experts is a means for governments to shield themselves from accountability. Second, many of the decisions made by experts are not in fact technical questions, but political and social questions. For instance, public health experts can tell us how much a society-wide lockdown will slow the spread of a disease during a pandemic with (perhaps) a reasonable level of accuracy. But they cannot tell us whether the benefits of doing so are worth the social, economic, and other costs that will result. These are social and political, not technical, questions. Finally, a technocratic approach to lawmaking dovetails with a technological view of humanity as fundamentally plastic, which in practice recognizes few limits on the power of lawmakers.

Sixth, there is increasing intolerance in the West for the claims of conscience—that is, a realm beyond the reach of civil law. There is little recognition today that there is a real evil in forcing someone to act in a manner they consider to be wrong or harmful, and laws are routinely enacted which do just this. It seems to me that there are two reasons for this. First, as just noted, many problems of public policy are seen as technical problems for experts (such as public health experts) to solve; in order to solve whatever the problem happens to be, unconditional obedience to those experts is considered necessary. Second, there is an increasing view that Christian beliefs relating to sexuality are actively harmful, and so it is seen as legitimate to suppress them. If women are considered to have a right to abort an unborn child, then doctors should be forced either to perform the abortion or to refer the woman to another practitioner, regardless of the doctor's personal views. In my view, there is a real need to recover conscience as an area which is not subject to coercion from civil law.

A seventh priority relates to the complexity and volume of legislation. Western governments are engaged in an incessant stream of lawmaking, amounting to hundreds and thousands of pages of legislation and executive orders every year. It is now virtually impossible for the expert, let alone the non-lawyer, to comprehend their legal obligations, and ignorance of the law does not excuse a person from breaking the law. One reason why this is occurring is the loss of a shared belief in moral standards, which results in the need to enact ever more detailed and prescriptive laws regulating ever more aspects of society.[41] The loss of any sense of an objective, shared morality means that the law must fill the void: if we cannot rely on a virtuous citizenry, we must enact ever more detailed regulations to influence behavior. This is a threat to the nature of law itself: "The very impulse to turn everything into law can be prejudicial to law, for then the rules become so vast, multiform, and changeable that no one can learn them, much less grasp what they mean."[42]

Another priority is the environment. Soil degradation is at unsustainable levels, and there will be more plastic in the oceans than fish by 2050. The rapacious extraction of economic value from animals and the earth, regardless of the environmental cost, is both a betrayal of the creation mandate and has increasingly negative consequences for people's health and livelihoods. If, as I argued in chapter 3, property and land are not really about things but about people, then lawmakers and civil governments need to take steps to protect the environment.

In modern Western cultures the primary punishment imposed for crime is imprisonment. Prison, however, is typically only imposed for very serious offenses, and restitution or compensation orders are rarely made. This means that in practice there is little effective punishment for crimes that are moderately serious, such as theft, assault, fraud, and domestic violence, but where a judge is unwilling to impose a prison sentence. The biblical approach is very different, being based on the twin principles of restitution and punishment

---

41. Harold J. Berman, *Law and Revolution: The Formation of the Western Legal Tradition* (Cambridge, MA: Harvard University Press, 1983), 34–35; Grantham, *Law and Practice*, 469.

42. J. Budziszewski, *Companion to the Commentary* (Cambridge: Cambridge University Press, 2014), 87.

proportionate to the offense.[43] It could be that following these principles more closely would lead to more effective punishment and a
reduction in crime, and (for example) provide greater protection for
women who suffer violence and abuse at the hands of their partners.

Finally, a Christian view of law will also offer a meaningful attempt
to address the challenges posed by non-Christian approaches to law.
Two contradictory approaches underlie much thinking about law
today. The first, as I mentioned at the beginning of this chapter, is
legal positivism, the view that a law is no more or less than something
that has passed through the relevant process within a jurisdiction
for the making of a law, such as passage through both houses of the
legislature. On this account, law is simply a product of politics, and
there is no "higher" law which has any impact on the validity of a law.[44]

A second widely held view is that law is subject to the dictates of
human rights, that law ought to be consistent with rights, and that
any law that infringes the precepts of human rights (or, more accurately, modern, Western, progressive notions of rights) is wrong.
Paradoxically, there *is* a sort of higher law to which ordinary laws
must conform.[45]

In principle, a focus on rights can be compatible with Christianity,
and Christianity has had a significant impact on our understanding
of human rights.[46] The difficulty is that what is mandated by modern,
Western, progressive notions of rights is constantly changing. The
classic modern statements of human rights penned in the mid-twen-
tieth century such as the Universal Declaration on Human Rights are

---

43. See, e.g., Gordon J. Wenham, *The Book of Leviticus* (Grand Rapids: Eerdmans,
1979), 312.

44. The leading articulation of legal positivism is H. L. A. Hart, *The Concept of Law*
(Oxford: Clarendon Press, 1961).

45. On the history of human rights, see Micheline Ishay, *The History of Human
Rights: From Ancient Times to the Globalization Era* (Berkeley: University of California
Press, 2008).

46. John Witte and Frank Alexander, eds., *Christianity and Human Rights: An
Introduction* (Cambridge: Cambridge University Press, 2011).

now considered outdated and in need of supplementation.[47] The problem with this, of course, is that the purpose of human rights is to be a universally accepted standard against which to hold ordinary law accountable, and so they must be above the political process. However, if rights are constantly redefined with the vagaries of changing opinion, then they are simply another product of the political process, not above it. Therefore, rights cannot serve as a universally accepted benchmark. Missing from many contemporary views of law is any sense of an objective order to which civil law must conform, and a Christian account of law can provide this standard.

TWO CASE STUDIES

How do the principles articulated in this book apply in the context of real-world situations? I have argued in this book that the moral law is relatively indeterminate and that lawmakers have a large degree of freedom when enacting laws. But is it not the case that the moral law is in fact quite clear on many issues? The concluding section of this chapter takes two case studies to illustrate how the principles set out in this book might apply. It should be noted that the purpose of the discussion below is not to lay out a legal blueprint for these issues but to discuss the applicable principles and how lawmakers might go about thinking about these issues from a Christian perspective.

GUN CONTROL

In light of the argument of this book, how should Christians think about gun control laws? A right to own guns is typically justified based on the right to self-defense. It is certainly true that all people have a right to self-defense—that is, the proportionate use of force

---

47. This can be seen, for example, in the drawing up of additional human rights documents such as the "Yogyakarta Principles" compiled in 2006, and the "Additional Principles and State Obligations on the Application of International Human Rights Law in Relation to Sexual Orientation, Gender Identity, Gender Expression and Sex Characteristics to Complement the Yogyakarta Principles" compiled in 2017. Available at https://yogyakartaprinciples.org.

to defend oneself. Aquinas said that "whatever is a means of preserving human life belongs to the natural law, and whatever impedes
it is contrary to it."[48] Based on this principle of the value of human
life, it is widely held that all people have a right to proportionate
self-defense under the natural law.[49] Some have argued that, from
this, there is a right to keep and bear arms.[50]

The Old Testament presupposes a right of self-defense in passages such as Exodus 22:2–3, which sets out what was to happen when
a homeowner defended his home against an intruder. This passage stipulated that if the thief broke in at night and was struck in
self-defense and died, there was no bloodguilt for the death, presumably because of the difficulty in seeing what was happening. If the
fatal blow occurred during daylight, then there was to be bloodguilt.
Thus, the exercise of force in self-defense must be proportionate to
the circumstances and not more than what is needed. Jesus said that
the time is coming when he who had no sword would sell his cloak
and buy one, implying that the use of force could be legitimate in
some situations (Luke 22:36).

A second important principle is that it is the government, not
individuals, that has the primary responsibility for ensuring public
order and safety. This is for two reasons. First, if this were not the
case, then the use of force in self-defense would be entirely a matter
for each individual. The strongest man and quickest gun would prevail. Second, it is an important principle of natural justice that no
person should be judge in her own cause (*nemo judex in causa sua*);
that is, no person can judge a case in which they have a personal
interest.

---

48. Aquinas, *Summa Theologica* IaIIae 94:2, in Dyson, *Aquinas: Political Writings*, 118.

49. Suzanne Uniacke, "Self-Defense and Natural Law," *America* 36, no. 1 (1991):
73; George Gillespie, *A Dispute Against the English Popish Ceremonies Obtruded upon the
Church of Scotland*, ed. Chris Coldwell (Dallas: Naphtali Press, 2013), 361.

50. E.g., Timothy Hsiao, "Bearing Arms in Self Defense: A Natural Law Perspective,"
Journal on Firearms & Public Policy 25 (2013): 120.

This means that the government has the right to determine whether the use of force in a particular instance was proportionate; if this were not so, then a person who exercises force in self-defense would essentially be acting as judge in her own cause, in violation of the *nemo judex* principle. Consistent with Exodus 22:3, the government may punish a person who uses excessive force when defending himself. The right to self-defense is subject to the overriding government interest in and power over public order and safety.

Therefore, the right to self-defense is not unlimited but is subject to important limitations, including that any force used must be proportionate to the threat posed. The civil ruler has the right and power to determine what is, and what is not, a legitimate use of force. And this means that, while there is a right to the use of force in self-defense, there is no absolute moral right to gun ownership, but this right can be qualified and limited in various ways in law.

The overriding government interest in public safety means that it would be entirely legitimate for lawmakers to pass laws limiting who has access to firearms (e.g., preventing violent criminals, minors, and mentally handicapped people from possessing guns), limiting the types of weapons that people may possess, restricting the purposes for which firearms may be possessed, requiring gun owners to obtain a firearms license, imposing requirements on gun owners relating to secure storage and access, or requiring gun owners to be trained in the use of their weapons. A lawmaker may stipulate that it is disproportionate to use certain types of weapons for the purpose of self-defense.

One key question for lawmakers is whether regulating access to guns will lead to increased safety and a reduction in violent crime. I think it unlikely that widespread gun ownership will tend to lead to a safer society, but there is probably not a single universally true answer. Much will depend on the circumstances, and what is right in one time and place may not be suitable in another time and place. For instance, guns were necessary in nineteenth-century America to protect settlers against threats from wild animals and hostile people.

By contrast, modern Western democracies such as Australia are comparatively safe, and widespread gun ownership may only lead to an escalation in violence.

Also relevant is the political culture of the people and what the likely response to any proposed gun regulation is. Australians are on the whole a very compliant people, and rates of compliance with gun laws are high. Americans, by contrast, have a much stronger tradition of resisting government, and there is a vocal and powerful gun lobby, which means that it is difficult to implement gun regulation.

In my view, gun regulation is somewhere in the middle of the transformative spectrum laid out in chapter 1. According to Scripture, Christians should be inclined to peacefulness and be willing to suffer wrong (Prov 25:21–22; Matt 5:39; Rom 12:17–19). Jesus said: "Blessed are the peacemakers, for they shall be called sons of God" (Matt 5:9), and so Christians ought to be uncomfortable with gun violence and culture. However, there is no absolute prohibition on the use of force, and there are many passages of Scripture in which force is not simply a necessary evil, but recognized to be legitimate (e.g., 1 Sam 17). Beyond this, there is not a great deal of teaching in Scripture concerning self-defense, and many of the principles involved are not specifically "Christian" principles but principles of reason and natural law. Christians could legitimately disagree on aspects of gun regulation, and there is likely not a one-size-fits-all approach.

There is no reason in principle why lawmakers cannot enact laws that regulate gun ownership. Whether they should do so in a particular context will depend on such things as whether the regulation will decrease violent crime, whether there is a legitimate need for people to own guns, and the likely response of the people to gun regulation.

ABORTION

Abortion is likewise an issue requiring great wisdom and sensitivity. I have argued in this book that the moral law is relatively indeterminate, leaving freedom to lawmakers in enacting civil law. I have also argued that sometimes lawmakers may need to accommodate civil laws to human sinfulness, based on the example of Scripture (Matt 19:8; Mark 10:5). How would these principles apply in the case of abortion?

Let us first identify the relevant principles. The sixth commandment prohibits all murder and unlawful killing. Scripture clearly recognizes that unborn children are people made in the image of God and places a high value on human life.[51] Abortion is not an issue where the moral law is indeterminate but is very much at the "transformative" end of the spectrum referred to in chapter 1. Only God has the right to give and take away life. There is a distinct Christian view of abortion—namely, that abortion is clearly contrary to the moral law.

Second, the fundamental role of civil government is to protect the innocent and punish the wrongdoer. Romans 13:1–4 describes the civil ruler as God's servant who bears the sword and "an avenger who carries out God's wrath on the wrongdoer," and similar teaching can be found in other biblical texts (Gen 9:5–6; Ps 82:3–4; 1 Pet 2:13–14). I have noted throughout this book that civil governments ought to protect the vulnerable, and there are none more vulnerable than unborn children.

The moral principle is clear, and its implications for civil law are also clear. The Christian view, therefore, would seem to be that civil governments should criminalize abortion except where necessary to save the life of the mother. Nevertheless, there are matters which are contestable, and there are questions of wisdom and judgment involved in the question of abortion. This is so in the following ways.

First, the goal of abortion policy is not to criminalize abortion. Rather, the goal is to eliminate, or minimize as far as possible, the abortions that occur within a jurisdiction. Recognizing this shifts the emphasis somewhat. While criminalizing abortion is an obvious way of achieving this goal, it means that questions of effectiveness and consequences cannot be ignored.

---

51. Gen 9:6; Exod 21:22–25; Ps 139:13–16; Jer 1:5; Luke 1:41–44.

Second, we might agree that abortion should be criminalized, but there is a question as to who is deemed to have committed a criminal offense when an abortion occurs. One obvious candidate is the person who carried out the abortion. The approach taken in America prior to *Roe v. Wade* was to target the abortionist.[52] In addition, many women are pressured into abortions by partners or parents; they then could be considered complicit. However, this would be a very difficult exercise to prove in court, effectively requiring the woman to testify against her loved ones. There may, therefore, be little point in attempting to attribute responsibility to partners or parents.

A third possibility is the woman herself, given that she is the one who has final say over her body and so bears ultimate responsibility as to the commission of an abortion. However, this is not the path that has traditionally been taken, at least in the United States. Clarke Forsythe has argued that prior to *Roe v. Wade*, nearly all American states "treated the woman as a victim and never prosecuted the woman as a principal or accomplice to abortion."[53] This was for evidential reasons, which meant that successful convictions could only be obtained against abortionists if women were not treated as accomplices.

Third, there is the question of what offense is committed. Although the Christian tradition has uniformly condemned abortion as a sin, theologians and writers have differed as to precisely what sin is committed. Many within the Protestant tradition have considered abortion as equivalent to murder.[54] Others, including well into the seventeenth century, argued that "ensoulment did not take

52. Roe v. Wade, 410 US 113 (1973); Clarke Forsythe, *Abuse of Discretion: The Inside Story of Roe v Wade* (New York: Encounter Books, 2013), 85.

53. Forsythe, *Abuse of Discretion*, 111. Examples of these statutes are collected in Dobbs v. Jackson Women's Health Organization, 597 US __ (2022), 79–108.

54. John Calvin, *Commentaries on the Last Four Books of Moses*, trans. Charles Bingham (Grand Rapids: Baker Books, 2003), 3:41–42 (commentary on Exod 21:22); Martin Chemnitz, *Loci Theologici*, trans. J. A. O. Preus (St. Louis: Concordia Publishing House, 1989), 738; Samuel Bolton, *The True Bounds of Christian Freedom* (Edinburgh: Banner of Truth, 1964), 132; Thomas Watson, *A Body of Practical Divinity* (London: Thomas Parkhurst, 1692), 360.

place at conception," and so abortion of an "unformed" fetus, while a sin, was not equivalent to murder.[55] Writing in the late eighteenth century, eminent jurist William Blackstone noted that English law did not treat the killing of an unborn child as equivalent to homicide, "though it remains a very heinous misdemeanor."[56] Thus, there are differences within the Christian tradition as to the seriousness of abortion.

Finally, the occurrence of abortion is closely connected with the social circumstances and moral beliefs prevalent in a particular culture. There is a widespread belief today that women should have autonomy over their bodies, including the right to abort an unwanted child. For those in desperate poverty, abortion may seem the only option.[57] Abortion policy cannot ignore those broader circumstances and beliefs.

Therefore, even for an issue where the moral and legal issues are very clear, there are difficult questions about effectiveness, responsibility, evidence, proof, and how best to implement legal changes having regard to surrounding circumstances and beliefs. There is also scope for legitimate differences of opinion on a relatively small number of issues connected with abortion, and so there is a need for lawmakers to exercise wisdom when regulating abortion, especially where there are bitterly held divisions such as exist today.

This chapter has examined the role of civil law and civil government, and how the moral law relates to human civil law. Wise lawmakers will seek to apply the unchanging principles of the moral law

---

55. John T. Noonan Jr., "Abortion and the Catholic Church: A Summary History," *Natural Law Forum* 12 (1967): 85, 101; Wolfgang P. Müller, *The Criminalization of Abortion in the West: Its Origins in Medieval Law* (Ithaca: Cornell University Press, 2016), 24–25. Examples of Protestant writers taking this position include John R. Weemes, *An Exposition of the Second Table of the Morall Law* (London: John Bellamie, 1632), 95–99; Gabriel Towerson, *An Explication of the Catechism of the Church of England* (London: J. Macock, 1685), 346–47.

56. Sir William Blackstone, *Commentaries on the Laws of England*, 9th ed. (Oxford: Oxford University Press, 2016 [1783]), 1:88.

57. This is horrifically illustrated in Jennifer Worth, *Shadows of the Workhouse* (London: Orion, 2008).

to the changing circumstances of human societies, and I have considered in the case studies above how lawmakers might go about applying the moral law to two particularly difficult contemporary issues.

But what about where lawmakers are not concerned to apply the moral law? How should Christians who live in societies which are deeply influenced by non-christian approaches view the laws of their country?

V

OBEDIENCE *and* DISOBEDIENCE

Now that we have seen how civil law ideally ought to relate to the moral law, this chapter addresses the issue of how Christians ought to respond to the laws that have been made by their lawmakers. In our day, most lawmakers are not Christians and so will not enact laws seeking to be obedient to Christ. Since this is the case, our ordinary expectation should be that there will be areas of tension between Christianity and law. In most societies there are a wide range of laws, including laws that are just and good as well as laws that are not.

Just laws raise no difficulty—Christians ought to obey them (Rom 13:1–7). But what about unjust laws? Does the requirement to obey civil rulers in Romans 13 mean that we should obey immoral laws? And how do we define just laws?

In many cases, it is straightforward to discern whether a law is just. Most countries require drivers to drive under a mandated speed limit and be licensed to drive. As a means of protecting life, these laws should not be particularly controversial. In other cases, it is straightforward for a Christian who wants to obey the moral law to discern when a law is unjust. The law in many countries allows terminally ill people to end their lives through "assisted dying." It is not particularly controversial for most Christians that such laws are wrong.

Between these extremes, though, there is a wide range of laws. Where I live, for example, there is a council ordinance which limits how many pets or animals I am allowed to keep on my property. Is that an illegitimate interference with my property rights? Can I disobey that law?

OBEDIENCE TO CIVIL GOVERNMENT

In order to answer this question, we should first look at some classic New Testament passages on obedience to civil authority. I mentioned Romans 13 above; there Paul wrote:

> Let every person be subject to the governing authorities. For there is no authority except from God, and those that exist have been instituted by God. ... Therefore one must be in subjection, not only to avoid God's wrath but also for the sake of conscience. ... Pay to all what is owed to them: taxes to whom taxes are owed, revenue to whom revenue is owed, respect to whom respect is owed, honor to whom honor is owed. (Rom 13:1–7)

Paul wrote in similar fashion to Titus, enjoining him to remind his congregation "to be submissive to rulers and authorities, to be obedient, to be ready for every good work" (Titus 3:1). Peter wrote to similar effect:

> Be subject for the Lord's sake to every human institution, whether it be to the emperor as supreme, or to governors as sent by him to punish those who do evil and to praise those who do good. For this is the will of God, that by doing good you should put to silence the ignorance of foolish people. Live as people who are free, not using your freedom as a cover-up for

evil, but living as servants of God. Honor everyone. Love the brotherhood. Fear God. Honor the emperor. (1 Pet 2:13–17)

We can see from these texts that, as a general principle, Christians are to submit to the governing authorities and obey their laws.

But some argue that passages such as Romans 13 and 1 Peter 2 only require Christians to obey laws that are consistent with the moral law and that all other laws are outside their scope. James M. Willson, for example, says that "no immoral civil power can demand ... the conscientious allegiance and subjection of the citizen."[1] However, this is not consistent with the teaching of the New Testament. Christians are not to resist evil; they are to "turn the other cheek" and "go the second mile" (see Matt 5:38–42). That is, we are called to submit even to unjust treatment and not stand upon our rights. This includes how we relate to civil law. After exhorting his hearers to "be subject for the Lord's sake to every human institution," Peter urged servants to

be subject to your masters with all respect, not only to the good and gentle but also to the unjust. For this is a gracious thing, when, mindful of God, one endures sorrows while suffering unjustly. For what credit is it if, when you sin and are beaten for it, you endure? But if when you do good and suffer for it you endure, this is a gracious thing in the sight of God. (1 Pet 2:18–20)

Peter's message is that all Christians under authority must suffer and bear up patiently under trial, following Christ's example, and must submit to unjustly exercised authority as well as justly exercised authority.[2] That is, Christians should obey their rulers, even when

---

1. James M. Willson, *Civil Government: An Exposition of Romans XIII:1–7* (Philadelphia: William S. Young, 1863), 110.

2. 1 Pet 2:18–25; 3:8–17; 4:12–19.

they are unjust. And this means that there are unjust or wrong laws which we ought to submit to.[3]

While unjust laws are wrong and ought not even to be considered as laws, obeying unjust rulers and their laws can be an important gospel imperative and a way in which Christians demonstrate that they belong to Christ. In doing so, we follow the example of Christ, the only truly innocent man who has ever lived, who patiently endured unjust suffering and the shameful death of the cross (1 Pet 2:21–23). As Martin Bucer wrote:

> [Christ] wills that his own also should obey from the heart not only the true kings and just princes of this world, but also very iniquitous lords and terrible tyrants to whom public power has been given (1 Peter 2:13–17), not only to pay legitimate taxes, but to observe their edicts with a patient spirit, acquiesce to their unjust judgments, and studiously meet all personal obligations to the State.[4]

Many writers in the Christian tradition have taken a similar view. Calvin considered that "the correction of unbridled despotism is the Lord's to avenge," and that no command has been given to God's people "except to obey and suffer."[5] Aquinas argued that unjust laws could be obeyed "in order to avoid scandal or disturbance, for which cause a man should even yield his right."[6]

The better view, therefore, is that there are some unjust laws that Christians should obey. However, this expectation of obedience is not absolute. It is not the case that Christians should obey all unjust

3. See also Charles Hodge, *A Commentary on Romans* (Edinburgh: Banner of Truth, 1972 [1835]), 406.

4. Bucer, *De Regno Christi*, in *Melanchthon and Bucer*, ed. Wilhelm Pauck (Louisville: Westminster John Knox, 1969), 186.

5. John Calvin, *Institutes of the Christian Religion*, ed. John T. McNeill, trans. Ford Lewis Battles (Louisville: Westminster John Knox, 1960), 4.20.31.

6. Thomas Aquinas, *Summa Theologica* IaIIae 96:4, in *Aquinas: Political Writings*, ed. R. W. Dyson (Cambridge: Cambridge University Press, 2020), 144. See also IIaIIae 104:6.

laws. As discussed below, some passages of Scripture commend God's people for disobeying the evil commands of rulers. It is legitimate in some circumstances to disobey wrong or unbiblical laws.

Therefore, in some circumstances, Christians ought to disobey unjust laws, and in other circumstances, Christians ought to obey unjust laws. This means that the question of whether a law is just or unjust is separate from the question of whether a Christian should obey that law. Even where a law is unjust or ungodly, it may be wise or right to obey that law.

CIVIL LAW AND CIVIL GOVERNMENT

But we must make another important distinction. Many discussions of civil disobedience focus on the question of obedience to "the state," or the government. That is, they ask whether an unjust government or tyrannical ruler should be obeyed. For example, Francis Schaeffer wrote that "at a certain point there is not only the right, but the duty, to disobey the state."[7] I suggest that this is an unhelpful focus. Instead, the focus should be on civil *law* rather than civil *government*. The question of obedience relates not to whether we should obey "the government" as a whole, but whether we should obey a particular civil law.

There are at least two reasons for this. First, in our day, there is a much clearer distinction between different types of governmental power, which was not the case in earlier times. Most laws are made by the legislature, not "the government." There are usually many civil laws in existence in a particular jurisdiction. Some of these laws will be good, others bad. The government holding office at any one time is not responsible for all the laws on the statute books: laws are enacted over a long period of time, by good legislators (relatively speaking) and bad. The question of whether we should obey "the

---

7. Francis Schaeffer, *A Christian Manifesto*, in *The Complete Works of Francis Schaeffer* (Carlisle: Paternoster, 1982), 5:469.

government" is too blunt. It is better to focus on particular laws and consider whether we should obey those laws.

Second, even legislators whose political views or character are repugnant may perceive moral truth and pass good laws. The requirement of obedience expected of Christians applies even to ungodly rulers such as Caesar (Rom 13:1–7) and the Cretan authorities (Titus 3:1), and so the fact that a lawmaker is immoral does not determine whether a Christian ought to obey the laws passed by the lawmaker. Legislatures usually consist of a wide variety of people with a wide range of views. Therefore, the personal morality or political views of the lawmaker are irrelevant to the requirement to obey. So, when considering whether a law is valid, the focus should be on the law, not the lawmaker or the government as a whole.

WHAT IS A JUST LAW?

There are further questions we should ask when trying to determine whether Christians should obey particular laws. One is, What makes a law just or legitimate? There are two basic requirements: First, a just law must implement the principles of the moral law and must not infringe those principles. A law which contravenes the moral law is not a just law (see, e.g., Isa 10:1–2).

In addition, a law must comply with positive law, by which I mean the civil law of a particular country or state. This means that a law must be enacted by the relevant lawmaker (such as Congress or Parliament) and be constitutionally valid. If a law does not comply with that positive law, then it has no legal validity and may be struck down as constitutionally invalid. For example, a law passed in the United States that infringes the First Amendment of the United States Constitution is invalid.

In considering laws enacted by non-Christian rulers, it is helpful to bear in mind the principles of freedom, contextualization, and wisdom. I noted in chapter 1 that the moral law is relatively indeterminate.[8] That is, it gives general principles and requirements but not detailed specifics as to the laws that should be enacted. While the moral law does not change, what it requires in specific contexts will change depending on the circumstances. The moral law can be reflected in civil law in a variety of ways. This means that lawmakers have a degree of freedom when enacting civil law.

The principles of natural law and common grace are also relevant. Christians are not the only ones able to perceive truth: although distorted by sin, unbelievers are able to perceive moral truth and the principles of justice—indeed, sometimes they can perceive it more clearly than Christians can (see, e.g., 1 Cor 5:1). It should not surprise us, therefore, that unbelieving civil rulers are able to appreciate, and give effect to, moral truth and the principles of justice when enacting laws, even if imperfectly.

Calvin understood this, writing that "if we regard the Spirit of God as the sole fountain of truth, we shall neither reject the truth itself, nor despise it wherever it shall appear, unless we wish to dishonor the Spirit of God."[9] Many laws on the statute books represent the considered application of reason and natural law by experienced non-Christian lawmakers, and Christians ought to be willing to recognize the wisdom embodied in them, regardless of their source. The blatantly unjust law is the exception, not the norm.

I argued in chapter 1 that many legal questions are not binary issues of faithfulness to Scripture, but much is in the realm of wisdom. This arises from the intentionally limited scope of God's revelation in Scripture. The Bible tells us much, but it is not an encyclopedia of human knowledge and does not set out a comprehensive code of politics and law. The Mosaic laws are detailed, but they are not exhaustive. Thus, while we can affirm with authority that God exists, that God is Triune, and that idolatry, murder, adultery, theft,

8. See David VanDrunen, *Politics after Christendom: Political Theology in a Fractured World* (Grand Rapids: Zondervan, 2020), 135–36.

9. Calvin, *Institutes*, 2.2.15.

and false witness are morally wrong, there are many other things which are not in the realm of certainty, but in the realm of fallible human wisdom. This is because Scripture does not give us the answer to those questions, whether directly or by good and necessary consequence. There may be only one correct answer to the many questions of law, politics, and civil government, but we do not have an infallible guide as to what that answer may be. Our answers are often provisional and subject to revision.

This ties in with the idea of the spectrum of knowledge introduced in chapter 1: there are areas of knowledge which are strongly impacted by Christianity, but many other areas are much less strongly impacted. The defined scope of scriptural teaching means that we cannot obtain the same level of certainty about matters that are not clearly addressed in Scripture. Attempting to have that level of certainty on every question is a distortion of Scripture and a misappropriation of the authority of God for merely human opinions.

And yet, the lack of divine certainty does not excuse people from the need to come to definite positions on these questions. There is a wide range of things on which Scripture is silent but which are necessary to resolve in some way—for example, which side of the road we should drive on or whether a presidential or parliamentary system of government is preferable. On these matters, citizens, governments, and lawmakers have freedom to decide what is best for their country, and there is not one correct answer.

If we fail to recognize these limitations of human knowledge, we risk turning all questions of law and politics into questions of biblical faithfulness. A better view is that they are often matters of wisdom. This does not mean that Scripture has *nothing* to say about questions of law—clearly, it does. The gospel has important social and political implications. But it does not tell us *everything*. And that means that much that relates to law is in the realm of wisdom.

Another uncomfortable reality is that many of the things we hold to be infallible truths are in fact more culturally determined than we like to admit. Two controversial examples will illustrate this point:

universal healthcare and firearm regulation. In Australia we have a system of national government healthcare, funded by taxation, that provides free emergency healthcare and subsidized medical care and pharmaceuticals for citizens and residents. Undoubtedly there are many deficiencies with this system, but overall it leads to a reasonably equitable and effective healthcare system which all Australians can benefit from. After the Port Arthur massacre in 1996, an extensive system of gun control regulation was introduced nationally, which requires all persons to hold a license in order to possess or use a firearm and limits the ability to obtain a gun license.

In the United States, a proposed universal government-funded healthcare system has been very controversial, and many Christians are strongly opposed to gun control, believing it infringes their God-given rights.[10] By contrast, Christians in Australia overwhelmingly submit happily to the laws which establish gun regulation and government healthcare, recognizing their benefits. Protecting life and public health have long been recognized to be part of the role of civil government, and there is nothing in Scripture that expressly rules these things out as illegitimate. As a generalization, Australia is a very safe place to live, with Australia's two largest cities among the world's safest cities, despite (or because of?) the lack of ready access to guns.

Thus, issues that are highly controversial for Christians in one country are cheerfully accepted in another as the price of living together—and even something to be thankful for. What this suggests is that we are significantly shaped by our culture and that some things we hold to be infallible truths are much more subjective than we like to admit.

The implications for law are clear. Many—perhaps even most—matters of law are not matters of absolute certainty for which the Bible determines a clear outcome. Even where the Bible sets out a

---

10. Andrew L. Whitehead, Landon Schnabel, and Samuel L. Perry, "Gun Control in the Crosshairs: Christian Nationalism and Opposition to Stricter Gun Laws," *Socius: Sociological Research for a Dynamic World* 4 (2018): 1.

clear *moral* principle about something, this does not always translate to a clear *legal* principle. And even where we *can* deduce a clear
legal principle, this does not tell us how a law should be drafted to
give effect to that principle.

It is true that "all authority is of God. No man has any rightful
power over other men, which is not derived from God. All human
power is delegated and ministerial."[11] As Francis Schaeffer said,
"God has ordained the state as a *delegated* authority; it is not autonomous."[12] However, God has not exhaustively prescribed all the laws
necessary for all governments throughout all times. Many issues of
law are matters of human wisdom in which lawmakers have a level
of freedom in making laws, and in which we are called to obey our
lawmakers, regardless of our own personal opinions. We may consider that universal healthcare is an expensive, inefficient system
and that restrictions on gun ownership are an infringement of liberty—and both those views are to some degree correct. As citizens,
we are perfectly entitled to agitate, protest, lobby, vote, donate,
write opinion pieces, and form groups to enshrine our views in law.
However, if such laws are lawfully enacted despite our opposition,
we are required to submit to them.

To take some examples, it is not unjust for governments to require
their people to obtain a driver's license, register and insure their
vehicles, and obey road rules. It is not unjust for governments to
require people to wear a mask to prevent infection during a pandemic (even if their effectiveness in doing so is limited). It is not
unjust for governments to mandate planning permission to renovate
or extend a church building and impose conditions on that reno-
vation. It is not unjust for governments to institute a system of gun
control, limiting who has access to firearms and what types of firearms are available. These can be reasonable regulations imposed by

---

11. Hodge, *A Commentary on Romans*, 406.
12. Schaeffer, *A Christian Manifesto*, 5:468.

governments to achieve goals that are within their competence, such as protecting life and ensuring the safety of their citizens.

Now that we've established what is a just law, how do we know the difference between a just law and an unjust law?

WHAT IS AN UNJUST LAW?

Scripture gives examples of people disobeying unjust laws, although it is more concerned with the question of obedience than with defining what is an unjust law. The Hebrew midwives, for example, refused to obey Pharoah's command to kill all male Hebrew children (Exod 1:15–21). Daniel and his friends refused to obey the Babylonian king's command to worship the ninety-foot golden image (Dan 3), and Daniel persisted in praying to God in defiance of the Babylonian law (Dan 6). Peter and John's reply when told not to teach in the name of Jesus clearly implies that the Sanhedrin exceeded their authority: "Whether it is right in the sight of God to listen to you rather than to God, you must judge, for we cannot but speak of what we have seen and heard" (Acts 4:19–20).

These passages suggest that there are two categories of laws which Scripture recognizes as illegitimate. First, a law which requires a person personally to sin or do evil is an unjust or immoral law, as evident from passages such as Exodus 1:15–21 and Daniel 3. Second, a law which attempts to prevent a person from obeying a biblical mandate or duty such as praying or speaking the gospel (see Dan 6; Acts 4:19–20) is unjust and wrong.

These seem to be the only categories of laws which are expressly considered illegitimate by Scripture. Nevertheless, there are good grounds for thinking that there are additional categories of laws which are unjust. I suggest there are six such categories.

Laws That Are Inconsistent with the Moral Law

The first category concerns laws that are not consistent with the moral law—that is, laws that command or permit something evil, such as the killing of unborn children, even if they do not require a person to do evil. The Christian tradition has long held that laws depend for their validity on their conformity to the moral law. Laws which do not conform to fundamental moral principles have no right to be considered laws.[13] Law is not simply the product of the human will, but something which must reflect the created order and the moral law, which provides an overriding standard to which human positive law must conform.

This category should not be read too narrowly. For example, medical practitioners who are Christians will rightly object on grounds of conscience to performing abortions. In the state of Victoria in Australia, the law requires such doctors to refer a person seeking an abortion to another medical practitioner who is prepared to conduct the abortion. Although there is no biblical command which precisely addresses this issue, this law effectively requires medical practitioners to participate in something that is morally repugnant— namely, the taking of an innocent life. The law is therefore contrary to the moral law.

LAWS THAT DO NOT MEET THE DEFINITION OF A LAW

The second category of unjust law arises from the definition of law. In order for something to be obeyed as a law, it must actually meet the definition of a law. If it does not, then it could not be considered a law. What, then, is a valid law? A widely accepted definition is that of Thomas Aquinas, who defined a law as an "ordinance of reason for the common good, made and promulgated by him who has care of the community."[14]

This definition sets out four criteria for a valid law. In order to be considered valid, the law must meet *all four* of the following requirements:

---

13. See, e.g., Augustine, *De Libero Arbitrio*, trans. Dom Mark Pontifex (London: Longmans, Green and Co., 1955), 1.5.11; Aquinas, *Summa Theologica* IaIIae 95:2, in Dyson, *Aquinas: Political Writings*, 130.

14. Aquinas, *Summa Theologica*, IaIIae 90:4, in Dyson, *Aquinas: Political Writings*, 82–83.

1. The law must be an ordinance of reason. That is, a law is not merely the arbitrary will of the lawmaker, but a reasoned response to a particular problem.

2. The law must be for the common good—that is, the good of the community, not the private benefit of the ruler.

3. The law must be made by him who has care of the community—that is, the legislator, or a person to whom law-making authority has been delegated.

4. The law must be promulgated, so that people are able to ascertain their legal obligations and comply with them.

If a purported law fails to meet any one of these requirements, it fails to be a proper law and is not truly a law. A requirement made by the local citizens' group or tennis club is not passed by "him who has care of the community" and so has no claim to be a law. A law passed in secret and not made known to anyone has not been promulgated, and so it is not binding. A "law" that is arbitrary is not an ordinance of reason, and so it is not a true law.

To take an example, during the coronavirus pandemic, the Victorian State government in Australia imposed "social distancing" mandates, requiring people to maintain a distance of 1.5m from each other in social gatherings, and forcibly closed gyms, bars, restaurants, and public houses. However, during some of the lockdowns it allowed brothels to remain open. Leaving aside the obvious question as to how the government envisaged that social distancing would be maintained, allowing brothels to remain open but closing gyms and pubs is totally arbitrary, lacking any obvious public health rationale. As such, it is difficult to describe this mandate as an ordinance of reason, and it comes close to being denied the status of a law.

LAWS THAT ATTEMPT TO REGULATE THE CONSCIENCE

A third category of unjust law is laws which attempt to regulate the conscience. The Christian tradition has consistently maintained that God alone is lord of the conscience, and so any encroachment on it by the civil ruler exceeds its lawful authority. As Martin Luther wrote,

The Crisis of Civil Law

The temporal government has laws which extend no further than to life and property and external affairs on earth, for God cannot and will not permit anyone but himself to rule over the soul. Therefore, where the temporal authority presumes to prescribe laws for the soul, it encroaches upon God's government and only misleads souls and destroys them.[15]

The realm of conscience and belief cannot be touched or regulated by civil law. Conscience refers to two things: a person's beliefs and her views of right and wrong. Civil laws may not attempt to prescribe or regulate a person's fundamental beliefs, as this is a matter between each person and God. Further, civil laws may not attempt to force a person to do or participate in doing something that the person considers morally wrong, because that would contravene the person's conscience.[16]

This principle is recognized by contemporary human rights law. The International Covenant on Civil and Political Rights states that "everyone shall have the right to freedom of thought, conscience and religion," and that "no one shall be subject to coercion which would impair his freedom to have or to adopt a religion or belief of his choice."[17] Unlike other rights, which may be limited in some circumstances, the right to adopt a religious belief or not is absolute and must not be coerced in any way. Despite this, conscience is increasingly under threat in the West today.[18]

---

15. Martin Luther, "Temporal Authority: To What Extent It Should Be Obeyed," in *Selected Writings of Martin Luther: 1520–1523*, ed. Theodore G. Tappert (Minneapolis: Fortress, 2007), 295.

16. Pope Paul VI, *Dignitatis Humanae*, December 7, 1965, [2].

17. International Covenant on Civil and Political Rights articles 18.1 and 18.2.

18. See, e.g., Thomas M. Messner, "From Culture Wars to Conscience Wars: Emerging Threats to Conscience," *Backgrounder* 2543 (The Heritage Foundation, April 13, 2011).

Laws That Are in Breach of the Laws of the Land

A fourth category of unjust laws is laws that are in breach of the laws of the land. To be valid, a law must comply with any requirements which exist in that jurisdiction relating to the enactment of laws. In the Westminster system of parliamentary government, a law must be passed by both Houses of Parliament and receive royal assent. If a law does not comply with requirements such as these, then it is not a law—it has no legal validity. Lawmaking power may also be conferred by legislation on executive agencies, who may make subordinate legislation and rules.

Further, in order to enact a valid law, the government must possess the authority to do so and must not exceed the authority conferred on it. In this regard, governments are precisely the opposite of individuals. It is a basic principle of civil law that individual people can do whatever they want, provided it is not unlawful. Conversely, governments are only entitled to do things (such as make laws) they are expressly empowered to do. Many constitutions limit the powers of governments and lawmakers, and many constitutions guarantee various rights which cannot be infringed. Where a lawmaker passes a law which exceeds the limits of its authority, that law is beyond power and has no legal validity.

However, a word of caution is necessary. Constitutional law is complex and is difficult for non-specialists to understand. Non-expert views about the constitutional validity of various laws abound, and most are incorrect. Constitutional law (especially American constitutional law) is notoriously uncertain and can take unexpected turns. It can be difficult to predict what will be deemed constitutionally invalid and what will not. In a real sense, it could be said that a law is only constitutionally invalid when declared to be so by the courts.

Purported laws that are in breach of the laws of the land, or are constitutionally invalid, have no legal validity—they are not laws. I also suggest that laws which are in breach of a government's public commitments ought to be considered invalid or unjust. Where a government commits to a course of action, or acts in such a way as to generate an expectation that the government will act in a particular way, then it is unjust for it to renege on that commitment. Many jurisdictions recognize a doctrine of "legitimate expectations," which has been explained as follows: "If a public body engages in a practice of acting in some way sufficient to generate a social rule, then the court will provide a remedy if that body breaches that rule, unless there is good reason to the contrary."[19]

To take an example, in Victoria, section 10 of the Charter of Human Rights and Responsibilities Act 2006 states that a person must not be subjected to medical experimentation or treatment without his or her full, free, and informed consent. Despite this, during the coronavirus pandemic, the Victorian government imposed mandates which required large sections of the population to receive a Covid-19 vaccine. Those who failed to comply lost their jobs and were unable to do basic things such as enter shops and cafés. Many people were effectively coerced into receiving a vaccine in order to keep their jobs. Being coerced into receiving a medical procedure from fear of losing one's livelihood is not "free and informed consent." This is a clear breach of a right which is supposedly guaranteed by Victorian legislation, and so, even though the government's mandate was not unlawful under Australian law, it was unjust and wrong.[20]

Laws That Exceed the Authority of Government

The fifth category of exemption are laws that unjustly interfere in areas where it is not the business of governments to interfere. Such laws may not require a person to sin or disobey a direct biblical

19. Farrah Ahmed, Richard Albert, and Adam Perry, "Enforcing Constitutional Conventions," *International Journal of Constitutional Law* 17, no. 4 (2019): 1146, 1159.

20. This paragraph simplifies the legal position somewhat: under section 7 of the *Charter Act*, rights may be limited in a proportionate manner to achieve legitimate policy goals. I have discussed this issue in a bit more detail in Benjamin Saunders, "Human rights implications of mandatory Covid-19 vaccinations in Victoria," ABC, October 8, 2021, https://www.abc.net.au/religion/human-rights-and-mandatory-covid-19-vaccinations/13577278.

mandate, and so would not fall within the categories already mentioned. These laws would nevertheless be unjust, an intrusion of the civil law into realms where it has no business intruding. Although there is no direct biblical mandate to disobey, it is reasonable to suggest that such laws are beyond the scope of the legitimate authority of the civil government. Jesus said that we should "Render to Caesar the things that are Caesar's, and to God the things that are God's" (Mark 12:17), which implies that there is a distinction between what is Caesar's and what is God's—in other words, that there are things that belong to one and not the other—and thus that there are limits to the scope of the civil ruler's authority.

The Christian tradition has attempted to characterize these limits in a variety of ways. The Lutheran tradition emphasizes the inviolability of conscience, which the civil ruler must not attempt to interfere with.[21] The neo-Calvinist tradition emphasizes the principle of sphere sovereignty, which argues that there are different domains of life such as church, state, family, education, and so on. Each domain has its own "law" and purpose and ought not to intrude into the other domains.[22]

The Roman Catholic tradition has emphasized the distinct jurisdictions of church and state.[23] The Presbyterian tradition has emphasized that there is a spiritual government in the church which is distinct from that of the civil ruler, thereby establishing limitations on the power of civil government.[24] It is for the church to determine such things as its doctrine, worship, discipline, and government, and the civil ruler has no business attempting to regulate such matters.

---

21. Luther, "Temporal Authority," 295.

22. Abraham Kuyper, "Sphere Sovereignty," in *Abraham Kuyper: A Centennial Reader*, ed. James D. Bratt (Grand Rapids: Eerdmans, 1998).

23. *Catechism of the Catholic Church* (Staten Island: St Pauls Publishing, 1994), 542 [2245].

24. *Westminster Confession of Faith*, XXIII.3; XXX.1.

Thus, the Christian tradition has overwhelmingly affirmed, as a necessary deduction from scriptural principles and the various domains of life that God has established through the created order, that there are limitations to the legitimate scope of the civil ruler's authority. Laws that exceed this authority are unjust.

In this regard, there is a distinction between laws which expressly single out churches for discriminatory treatment, and laws of general application which happen to impact churches. Some laws are expressly targeted at Christians or churches, seeking to regulate or discriminate against them. Such laws may be unreasonable or unjust on the basis that they overstep the civil ruler's authority. Laws of general application which have an impact on churches are, in my view, different. To take an example, in many places permission is required from a council to undertake building work on a property. This would require churches to get permission before renovating or extending their buildings. Although this impacts churches, these laws do not expressly single out Christians or churches, and so I suggest that there is no improper intrusion into the church's domain.

Examples of laws that go beyond the civil ruler's proper role include laws that have prevented parents from raising or educating their children in a manner consistent with their fundamental beliefs and principles, or laws that have allowed for the removal of children from their families in unjust situations.[25] Other examples include a law that requires a religious school to employ people who do not share the school's values, a law that requires an accommodation provider to allow its facilities to be used to promote something that is diametrically opposed to its beliefs, or a law that deems a parent's calling his child by pronouns that are not preferred by the child to be family violence.

---

25. There are situations in which it would be right to remove a child from his or her parents—namely, where that is necessary to protect the child from physical or sexual abuse.

Laws That Infringe Rights

The final category is laws that infringe rights or liberty. The Christian tradition has affirmed that people possess rights that exist by virtue of the creation of humans in the image of God, the natural law, and the obligations in the Decalogue relating to worship, life, marriage, and property.[26] Because the first commandment mandates that all people worship the one true God, this means that people must have a right to do so, and civil rulers may not attempt to prevent people from worshiping. The obligation to work to provide for one's family (1 Tim 5:8) implies the rights to work and to move freely to obtain the work needed to earn a living. It is widely accepted today that people possess rights by virtue of their dignity as human beings and that governments should protect and respect their rights. These rights are pre-political rights which cannot be infringed or taken away by the civil ruler. Civil laws which infringe rights are invalid and unjust.

However, there are several difficulties with asserting that laws which infringe rights are unjust. Scripture does not provide an authoritative list of civil rights which should be protected by civil law, and there is difficulty in defining the scope of the rights which may not be infringed. People disagree about which rights ought to be protected, about the relative importance of rights, and about which rights should prevail when there is a conflict. Most rights are not absolute but can be limited to pursue other legitimate ends. Even important rights such as free speech and property rights may be limited to accommodate the rights or interests of others.

We all agree that free speech is a good thing. We all agree that free speech is not absolute. But we do not agree on where the line should be drawn. Should my right to free speech entitle me to say offensive and insulting things about other people? What if the things I say are based on my sincerely held religious beliefs? Should my right to free speech entitle me to say things that are offensive on racial grounds?

---

26. John Witte, *God's Joust, God's Justice: Law and Religion in the Western Tradition* (Grand Rapids: Eerdmans 2006), 31–49.

Can I slander someone under the guise of free speech if that might damage their reputation? Is it different if the person is a politician or running for public office? Where is the line between insulting someone and slandering them? Am I allowed to post inflammatory material on the internet which stirs up hate or violence? What if I did not intend for my post to stir up hate or violence, but it happened to have that effect?

Determining that a law is unjust because it infringes rights or liberty is not always an easy matter. A law might infringe someone's right to do something, but that law might be justified because it protects the rights of others. A law may infringe someone's liberty in order to achieve a necessary and legitimate purpose. Human rights law typically recognizes that many rights may be limited, provided that the limitation is justified and proportionate.

However, some rights *are* absolute. The International Covenant on Civil and Political Rights (hereafter ICCPR) states that some of the rights in the covenant, such as the right to life and the right to freedom of religion, are "non-derogable"—that is, they cannot be limited or infringed in any way.[27] A law which infringes a non-derogable right is unjust and wrong. For example, the ICCPR states that "no one shall be subjected without his free consent to medical or scientific experimentation." A law which coerces a person into taking an experimental medical treatment is contrary to the person's human rights and is unjust.

Rights which are not absolute may be limited in a proportionate manner in order to achieve a legitimate purpose. It is typically considered legitimate to imprison someone who has committed a criminal offence, even though this limits the person's freedom. In

---

27. ICCPR article 6 (right to life), 7 ("No one shall be subjected to torture or to cruel, inhuman or degrading treatment or punishment. In particular, no one shall be subjected without his free consent to medical or scientific experimentation"), paragraphs 1 and 2 of article 8 (prohibition on slavery), 11 (no imprisonment for inability to fulfil a contractual obligation), 15 (no retrospective criminal punishment), 16 (right to recognition as a person before the law) and 18 (right to freedom of thought, conscience and religion).

principle, it is legitimate for civil law to limit people's rights in order to prevent the spread of a highly contagious and deadly disease.

"Proportionate" means essentially that the limitation on rights should not be more restrictive than is necessary to achieve that legitimate purpose. Different people will have different views on what is reasonable and proportionate, and therefore whether an infringement of a right is unjust. This suggests that caution is often warranted when deciding that laws are unjust on the basis that they infringe rights.

INTERPRETING LAWS

It is worth making a few brief remarks about how legislation is interpreted, because this is relevant to the question of obedience. Before deciding whether a law is unjust, and whether to obey or disobey the law, it is first necessary to determine what the law means. Interpreting legislation is complex—it is not as simple as "the law means what it says."

This is for two reasons. First, some level of uncertainty is inevitable in most legal documents. Despite the best efforts of legal drafters, it is not possible to remove all uncertainty from a law. There can be debate about what a particular word means or whether it applies to a particular class of conduct. Laws are often applied in circumstances that were not foreseen by their drafters. Laws may conflict with each other or appear to mean something other than what was intended.

Second, under the Anglo-American system of government, it is the courts that have the role of authoritatively determining the meaning of legislation. The meaning of a law is the meaning that the courts give to it—not the meaning intended by the legislature or the executive. Courts interpret legislation so as to give effect to the intention of the legislation as expressed objectively in the words used—that is, the subjective intention of the lawmaker is irrelevant. Laws may be "read down" to ensure that they are constitutionally valid.

When interpreting legislation, courts apply recognized principles of interpretation. Courts interpret legislation in light of the "mischief" that the legislation is intended to address—that is, the problem or defect with the existing law that the legislation aims to correct. Another important canon of interpretation is the principle of legality, which means that the courts interpret legislation in a rights-compatible way; unless the legislation clearly and unambiguously interferes with fundamental rights, the courts will interpret the law in such a way that it does not interfere with rights.[28]

Much more could be said, but that would be beyond the scope of this book. The point, when considering the question of whether Christians may disobey an unjust law, is that the meaning of a law is not always self-evident. It is not unusual for the courts to interpret a law contrary to the intentions of its drafters. Sometimes, obnoxious laws can be construed in a more benign manner. A law which appears to interfere with rights may be interpreted such that it does not in fact have that effect. Where there is uncertainty about the interpretation of a law, and there often is, that uncertainty can be resolved in a rights-friendly way.

This is not a blank check to reinterpret laws to suit our personal wishes. Laws are sometimes passed that *are* obnoxious, and it is not possible to give them a less obnoxious reading. Sometimes laws infringe rights, and they clearly express an intention to do so. Nevertheless, sometimes it is possible to interpret laws in such a way that disobedience is unnecessary.

SHOULD CHRISTIANS DISOBEY UNJUST LAWS?

In this chapter, we have considered what makes a law just and what makes a law unjust. However, this does not answer the question of whether Christians are entitled to disobey unjust laws. I noted earlier that there is a distinction between the question of whether a law is unjust and the question of whether a person should submit to it. In some circumstances, Christians ought to submit to laws that are

---

28. Coco v. The Queen, 179 CLR 427, 437 (1994).

unjust. That is, a law being unjust is a necessary, but not sufficient, condition for disobedience.

To be clear, I am not suggesting that there is any validity or legitimacy whatsoever in an unjust law: an unjust law is a contradiction in terms. Justice is of the essence of law, and so an unjust law is not a true law. A civil government which enacts unjust or invalid laws exceeds its authority. Nevertheless, Christians have a mandate to obey that goes beyond just laws.[29] How then do we determine whether to obey or disobey an unjust law?

As noted above in the section "What Is an Unjust Law?," Scripture teaches that there are situations in which Christians ought to disobey unjust laws.[30] From such passages, we can see two clear situations in which Christians are expected to disobey civil laws. Christians ought not to obey laws which would require them personally to sin or do evil, and they ought not to obey laws which would prevent them from obeying a biblical mandate such as praying or speaking the gospel. The basic principle of obedience to civil law is that, where it is not possible to obey God and the civil ruler at the same time, Christians should obey God rather than man.

Are there any additional circumstances in which Christians may disobey the civil law? I suggest that there are, and I offer the following principles in thinking through this question.

First, Christians ought to lean toward obedience rather than disobedience. Given the clear command to obey our rulers (Rom 13:1–7) and the imperative of following the example of Christ, who willingly suffered injustice (1 Pet 2:21–25), there ought to be a presumption of obedience. The starting principle for Christians ought to be to obey civil laws, even unjust laws, and to be prayerful and cautious before disobeying.

Second, Christians have a clear duty to disobey laws which require them to do evil. In this regard, it is important to bear in

---

29. 1 Pet 2:13–25; 3:8–17; 4:12–19.
30. E.g., Exod 1:15–21; Dan 3, 6; Acts 4:19–20.

mind that laws come in different shapes and sizes. Some laws are commands, requiring a person to do or not do something. Some laws provide remedies or a right to take legal action where certain conduct occurs, for example where a person causes harm to another. Many laws are facultative, empowering people to do certain things, sometimes imposing conditions upon doing certain things: "If you want to do X, you must do it in this way." Sometimes the things permitted under such laws are unjust or wrong, such as laws which permit brothels to operate. Other laws specify the legal consequences for doing certain things such as writing a will.

The point of this discussion is that only certain types of laws will raise questions of obedience for Christians. Laws which allow or permit immoral things but do not require Christians to be involved with these activities should not raise questions of conscience; Christians ought simply to have nothing to do with them. Christians need not visit a brothel or have an abortion. In these situations, we can obey God and the civil ruler.

The main types of laws which will raise questions of obedience are laws which require Christians to do something immoral or laws which attempt to prevent Christians from carrying out a biblical duty. In these cases, the mandate of disobedience is clear: Christians ought to disobey laws which require them to participate in evil or prevent them from doing something they ought to do. The law which requires medical practitioners to refer a person seeking an abortion to another medical practitioner effectively forces them to participate in something that is evil, and so the law should be disobeyed.

Thus, conscience is an extremely important factor in considering civil disobedience. Governments have no moral right to require a person to do something against his or her conscience. However, this does not give us permission to disobey every law we happen not to like. Conscience relates to a person's fundamental beliefs and her views about right and wrong, as defined by the moral law. Simply disagreeing with a law, or believing that a particular law is beyond the proper role of civil government, is not a warrant for disobedience.

A law that requires churches to obtain council approval to renovate their buildings is inconvenient, but it does not require churches to do anything immoral or improper and so does not raise questions of conscience. We may think that it is beyond the proper role of civil government to establish a taxpayer-funded healthcare system by law, but (depending on the detail) this may not raise questions of conscience.

Should Christians disobey laws that infringe their rights and liberties? Laws that infringe rights and liberties may be unjust and wrong. But this does not mean it is always a good idea to disobey such laws. Christians should be motivated primarily by the gospel and love for others rather than their own self-interest, and insisting on one's rights does not sit easily with the biblical attitude of willingness to suffer wrong. In Matthew 5:39, Jesus instructed his disciples not to resist evil; from this verse, Martin Luther argued:

> A Christian should be so disposed that he will suffer every evil and injustice without avenging himself; neither will he seek legal redress in the courts but have utterly no need of temporal authority and law for his own sake. On behalf of others, however, he may and should seek vengeance, justice, protection, and help, and do as much as he can to achieve it.[31]

Luther considered that Christians should not be motivated by self-interest but rather by the interests of others, and they should be willing to suffer wrong where only their interests are concerned, consistent with Jesus's words in Matthew 5:39. But in the service of others, Christians may disobey unjust laws. (Rosa Parks is a good example of how disobeying unjust laws may serve the interests of others.)

Can Christians disobey laws where only their rights are at stake? The book of Acts records Paul's response to various injustices that were committed or permitted by the ruling civil authorities in breach

---

31. Luther, "Temporal Authority," 291.

of his rights. At times Paul submitted to such injustices (e.g., Acts 14:19). On other occasions, Paul asserted his rights; for instance, he insisted on being escorted from the city of Philippi by the magistrates (Acts 16:37) and narrowly avoided being flogged in Jerusalem by reminding the centurion of his Roman citizenship (Acts 22:25–29). He also exercised his right to appeal to Caesar (Acts 25:11–12). While the purpose of the appeal to Caesar appears to have been so that he could carry out ministry in Rome, this does not appear to have been the motivation in the earlier passages, but rather to insist on his rights as a citizen.[32]

There is some biblical precedent, therefore, for asserting one's legal rights and insisting that civil rulers and governments comply with applicable legal obligations. In some situations, it is legitimate to assert one's legal rights in the face of laws or executive orders that infringe those rights. It may be legitimate to disobey laws that infringe rights.

The fourth consideration is witness to the gospel. It will often be wise to obey laws, even unjust ones, for the sake of witness. Aquinas said that unjust laws "do not bind in conscience, except perhaps in order to avoid scandal or disturbance, for which cause a man should even yield his right," quoting Matthew 5:40–41.[33] If we are to follow the example of Christ, who suffered unjustly (1 Pet 2:21–25), then obeying unjust rulers and their laws can be an important gospel imperative and a way in which Christians demonstrate that they belong to Christ. Turning the other cheek and not insisting on our rights shows that our treasure is in a kingdom that is not of this world. Insisting on our rights may show that our treasure is in this world. A person who insists on his right to bear arms and brings a weapon to a church service may send the message that he has more concern for the things of this life than the life to come.

---

32. Boyd Reese, "The Apostle Paul's Exercise of His Rights as a Roman Citizen as Recorded in the Book of Acts," *Evangelical Quarterly* 47 (1975): 138, 142.

33. Aquinas, *Summa Theologica* IaIIae 96:4, in Dyson, *Aquinas: Political Writings*, 144. See also IaIIae 104:6.

On the other hand, this imperative cuts both ways. Complying with or not speaking out against evil laws for fear of punishment would be cowardice and could seriously damage the church's witness. There are numerous instances in the history of the church where Christians have failed to oppose evil laws.

In some church denominations, a spirit of legalism has come to dominate, such that compliance with civil law is a paramount consideration, even where such compliance causes harm to the church and damages gospel unity. Such a risk-averse mindset may send a message that the church is no different from other worldly bureaucracies, concerned with liability and compliance more than the gospel. This has the potential to damage the witness of the church.

The fifth principle is to consider the likely consequences of one's actions, which is a key part of wisdom. Civil rulers, and the laws they enact, are blessings given to us by God for our good. They restrain anarchy and promote order and peace. Widespread disobedience to civil law may plunge a legal system into chaos. Christians are told to pray for those in authority, "that we may lead a peaceful and quiet life, godly and dignified in every way" (1 Tim 2:1–2). Promoting peace is an important function provided by rulers and an important goal for Christians. If a likely consequence of disobedience is the promotion of or contribution to a breakdown of respect for civil law, then this should be an important consideration in any decision whether to disobey. An imperfect legal system is better than none.

On the other hand, disobedience could have beneficial consequences in some circumstances. Lawmakers today acknowledge few constraints on their powers beyond that of public opinion. And yet they are subject to God's authority and will be held to account for their rule (2 Cor 5:10). Disobedience to civil law is one way in which lawmakers can be confronted with the limits of their power. In the right circumstances, therefore, and done in the right way, disobeying an unjust civil law could be a powerful witness to lawmakers, showing that they are not omnipotent. Summarizing Martin Luther King Jr.'s argument in his 1963 "Letter from Birmingham

Jail," J. Budziszewski writes that when considering civil disobedience, protesters must first

> disobey the unjust law only after attempts to change it through
> discussion with the authorities have been exhausted. Second,
> when protestors disobey, they must do so for the sake of jus-
> tice rather than revenge, they must do so publicly rather than
> in secret, they must give a public explanation of their rea-
> sons for disobedience, and they must publicly accept the legal
> penalties for disobedience. Protestors should offer no resis-
> tance whatsoever, even if spat upon, beaten with nightsticks,
> sprayed with high-pressure fire hoses, bitten by police dogs,
> and carried off to prison.[34]

Sixth, I noted above that unconstitutional laws have no legal
validity—they are simply not laws. There is no obligation to obey
laws that are constitutionally invalid or contrary to the law of a particular jurisdiction. However, I suggest that Christians should be
cautious before disobeying laws on the grounds of constitutional
invalidity. It will usually be wise to obey laws that are thought to be
unconstitutional unless and until they are struck down by the courts.
Another prudent course is to rely on legal advice from a competent
lawyer before taking the step of disobeying laws on constitutional
grounds. Christians may also challenge the constitutional validity of
laws in the courts, provided they have the means to do so.

Finally, Christians ought to approach the question of civil disobedience with a robust doctrine of Christian liberty, and with scant
concern for the things of this passing age. Christians have been
redeemed from the guilt of sin, the wrath of God, and the curse of
the law, and they have direct access to and union with Christ, free

---

34. J. Budziszewski, *Companion to the Commentary* (Cambridge: Cambridge
University Press, 2014), 192–93. See also H. D. Thoreau, "Resistance to Civil
Government," in *Æsthetic Papers*, ed. Elizabeth P. Peabody (Boston: The Editor, 1849),
189–211; M. K. Gandhi, "For Passive Resisters," *Indian Opinion*, October 26, 1907.

from any earthly intermediary.[35] Martin Luther wrote that "every Christian is by faith so exalted above all things that, by virtue of a spiritual power, he is lord of all things without exception, so that nothing can do him any harm."[36] These are powerful and challenging words: nothing done by an earthly ruler can do any harm to the Christian.

Civil laws can only ever be outward, affecting the body or possessions. The Christian is united to Christ, and nothing in this world can touch or interfere with that union. Christians can submit to earthly laws which are merely outward without compromising their fundamental freedom, which is in Christ.[37] Luther railed against those who "want to show that they are free men and Christians only by despising and finding fault with ceremonies, traditions, and human laws."[38] We are bought with a price (1 Cor 6:20) and can submit to those things we disagree with. Obeying even unjust laws does not touch the Christian's fundamental status.

The New Testament treatment of slavery is a good example of this. Slavery, and laws permitting slavery, would today be seen as obviously and uncontroversially contrary to the moral law. And yet in the New Testament, slaves who became Christians are told to remain in their position as slaves, recognizing their freedom in Christ, and are told to obey their earthly masters.[39] That is, slaves were commanded to obey laws permitting slavery, notwithstanding that those laws were unjust. The Christian's freedom in Christ enables her to submit to earthly authority, even unjust earthly authority.

The basic principle of civil disobedience is that where it is possible to obey God and civil law at the same time, Christians should do so. Where it is not possible to obey God and the law, Christians should

---

35. *Westminster Confession of Faith*, XX.1.

36. Martin Luther, "The Freedom of a Christian," trans W. A. Lambert, in *elected Writings of Martin Luther: 1520–1523*, ed. Theodore G. Tappert (Minneapolis: Fortress, 2007), 30.

37. See also Calvin, *Institutes*, 4.20.1.

38. Luther, "Freedom of a Christian," 48.

39. 1 Cor 7:17–24; Eph 6:5–8; Col 3:22–24; 1 Pet 2:18.

obey God rather than man. Where civil laws force Christians to participate in something that is contrary to the moral law, Christians ought to resist those laws.

Beyond these black and white categories, there is some scope for Christians to disobey unjust laws. Sometimes it is legitimate to assert one's legal rights, sometimes it is not. Sometimes obedience to unjust laws will present a powerful gospel witness, at other times it will not. Sometimes obedience to unjust laws will have beneficial consequences, other times not.

It should be apparent from this chapter that there is not a one-size-fits-all answer to the question of when to disobey an unjust law, and that acting rightly demands considerable wisdom. In considering the right course of action, Christians should approach disobedience cautiously and should have regard to the principles of gospel witness and the service of others, holding lightly to the things of this age.

VI

ERRORS *to* BE AVOIDED

The purpose of this book is not to engage in a polemical exercise, but to present a positive account of how Christians should think about law. I have thus not engaged in detailed refutations of other views. Nevertheless, there is value in briefly examining some other views about Christianity and law, both to guard against error and also so that the true position may emerge with greater clarity. This chapter does not engage in a detailed refutation of such views, but simply aims to point out the main issues.

THEONOMY

One error to be avoided is theonomy, which has been a minority view (albeit a vocal one) in the Christian tradition. The basic principle of theonomy is that God's law contains an authoritative standard for civil laws throughout all ages. Theonomy is committed to the continuing bindingness of the Old Testament civil laws and the desire to bring all of life, including civil government, under the lordship of Christ.

Theonomists argue that all laws enacted by civil governments must be expressly authorized or warranted in Scripture. Any law which is not positively authorized in Scripture, whether by express command, logical deduction, or necessary consequence, is unlawful or wrong. That is, it is not enough for a civil law not to be forbidden by Scripture; for a civil law to be legitimate, there must be something in the Bible expressly authorizing that law.

So, to take an example, is a law that redistributes wealth from the rich to the poor a legitimate law? Obviously giving money to the poor is not wrong; it is not against God's law. Taxation is also not wrong (Rom 13:7). But this is not enough. Theonomists argue that something more is necessary: there needs to be something in Scripture that expressly provides that it is part of the role of civil government to redistribute wealth in this way.

Theonomy draws a binary contrast between theonomy and autonomy: civil laws are either based on God's law or (sinful) human reason. There is no middle ground. For every question of civil law, there is a correct answer which is consistent with Scripture. Theonomists place little emphasis on wisdom or prudence in enacting civil laws. The question of the legitimacy of civil law is a binary question of faithfulness to God's law or not.

Theonomists affirm the perpetual bindingness of the Mosaic civil laws, including the applicable sanctions and punishments, and argue for the abiding validity of the Mosaic law in exhaustive detail.[1] They typically reject the moral-civil-ceremonial distinction (see chapter 2), arguing that the civil laws are as binding today as the moral law. More nuanced theonomists recognize that the Mosaic civil laws do not apply today in precisely the same way as they did under the old covenant but need to be translated to the New Testament context. This

---

1. Greg L. Bahnsen, *Theonomy in Christian Ethics*, 3rd ed. (n.p.: Covenant Media Press, 2002), 41–90.

can have the effect of transforming them into something that looks like a very different set of obligations than their original context.[2]

Theonomists are also committed to the view that Scripture is an exhaustive code regulating civil law—that is, the Old Testament laws are a blueprint for modern civil law. If every civil law must be authorized by Scripture, then Scripture must provide a comprehensive standard against which to measure civil law.

Theonomy is not the mainstream teaching of the Christian tradition, and, in my view, it is incorrect for three main reasons. First, the mainstream Christian view is that the Old Testament laws were an application of the eternal moral law (or natural law) to a particular context and therefore were perfectly adapted for Israel. They were not addressed to any other nation and are not intended to be a blueprint for all societies at all times.

The Old Testament laws were given within a particular context, especially the redemptive-historical context of Israel as a covenant nation, and that context does not continue to exist under the New Testament. The people of God are now the church. As such, the Old Testament civil laws cannot be considered binding in their original form, and those things that pertained specifically to Israel—such as the particular punishments and sanctions imposed by the law—are not binding on modern nation states.

Nevertheless, the Old Testament laws are not irrelevant; they have much to teach us about justice and the principles of the moral law. While they are not binding in precisely their original form, the underlying moral principles reflected in the Mosaic laws remain applicable today, including to modern civil government, provided the law is carefully translated to the New Testament context.

Second, Scripture is not, and is not intended to be, an exhaustive blueprint for civil law. The Bible tells us everything we need to know to be thoroughly equipped for the Christian life (2 Tim 3:16–17). That

---

2. For an example, see Joel McDurmon, *The Bounds of Love: An Introduction to God's Law of Liberty* (Publisher: Independently Published, 2019), 50–61.

is, according to Scripture's own testimony about itself, it is sufficient to equip the Christian to live a life pleasing to God; it does not claim to be a comprehensive treatment of civil law and government. There are many things for which law is necessary that are not addressed in Scripture. Even where the Mosaic laws do stipulate laws about something, the laws are typically selective rather than comprehensive, assuming the existence of social norms and intervening in limited ways (e.g., Exod 21:7–11).

Another way of illustrating this point is that, under the New Testament, the people of God is the church, not Israel or any nation-state. It is widely recognized that the New Testament "by design, does not give us an exhaustive manual of church polity. It does not prescribe every conceivable detail relating to the government of the church."[3] And if Scripture does not exhaustively regulate every aspect of church government, then it would seem decidedly strange for it to exhaustively regulate every aspect of civil law. Notwithstanding its desire to be faithful to Scripture, the theonomist approach is unbiblical in that it seeks to press Scripture into answering questions it was not intended to answer.

Finally, theonomy is incapable of delivering the certainty its proponents desire. Theonomy contemplates a binary choice between God's law and human law and promises a clear, biblical, and certain answer to every question of law. But it cannot deliver on that promise.

The Bible comprehensively tells us the content of the moral law. But having a clear *moral* principle does not translate to a clear *legal* principle. According to Scripture itself, civil law needs to permit some sins to account for the hardness of the people's hearts (Matt 19:8; Mark 10:5). And even where we can deduce a clear legal principle from Scripture, there are multiple possible ways of implementing this into civil law. Questions of wisdom and judgment are inescapable. There is a need for wisdom and prudence in applying

---

3. Guy Prentiss Waters, *How Jesus Runs the Church* (Phillipsburg, NJ: P&R Publishing, 2011), 49; Bannerman, *The Church of Christ*, 2:204–5, 209–11.

the principles of the moral law to the changing circumstances of a nation-state, and civil lawmakers have freedom in determining which laws are necessary and the detail of those laws.

This means that there is not a binary choice between God's law or human wisdom—both are necessary. The dichotomy between God's law and human law is a false one (except, of course, where human wisdom is in opposition to God). And this means that there is rarely complete certainty, or one single correct answer, when enacting civil law. Theonomy cannot deliver the certainty promised by its proponents.

CIVIL LAW AND GOVERNMENT AS INHERENTLY EVIL

Some argue that the institutions of law and government are inherently evil and call for Christians to have nothing to do with them. Writers in this vein emphasize strongly both the radical demands placed by Christ on his followers, especially in the Sermon on the Mount, and the example set by Christ himself. Christians are called to love, suffer, serve, submit, forgive, and not insist on their legal rights,[4] which is a very different pattern from the coercion and compulsion typical of earthly law and government. John Howard Yoder argued that secular government is "the province of the sovereignty of Satan."[5] The Christian's calling is to submit to unrighteous secular authority, and the very existence of the church proclaims Christ's victory over the earthly powers.

The church has traditionally reconciled the Sermon on the Mount with other passages of Scripture such as Romans 13 by drawing a distinction between Christians acting in their personal capacity and acting while holding office. Dietrich Bonhoeffer rejected such a distinction, arguing that Jesus "is the Lord of all life, and demands

---

4. Matt 5:38–42; Rom 12:20; 1 Pet 2:21–23.
5. John Howard Yoder, *The Politics of Jesus: Vicit Agnus Noster* (Grand Rapids: Eerdmans, 1972), 195, 203.

undivided allegiance," and that the distinction is an unworkable one.[6] Therefore, when Jesus called his disciples to patiently endure evil, this applies to Christians in whatever capacity or office they hold, and there is no "exception." Christians ought not to countenance any form of violence or war, even if they hold office. Given the inherently coercive nature of civil government, this obviously makes it difficult for Christians to hold any kind of civil office.

These views have radical implications. For instance, a system of property rights depends for its existence on the recognition and enforcement of those rights in civil law. Those mechanisms depend for their efficacy on being backed up by the coercive sanctions of the state. The only reason property rights work is because the government will enforce those rights if they are infringed. By holding property, Christians are depending on the coercive mechanisms of the state and thereby legitimating them. The implication of the views of Yoder and Bonhoeffer is that it is morally impermissible for Christians or the church to hold property. According to this logic, it would also be impermissible for a church to lease or own property to hold services of worship, and it would be impermissible for Christians to enter into any legally binding contract whatsoever (because they depend ultimately on enforcement by the government). If pressed to their conclusion, these views logically demand the total withdrawal of Christians from many aspects of society.

In evaluating these views, it is helpful to read passages such as the Sermon on the Mount in light of the totality of the revelation in Scripture. Although there are important points of discontinuity, there is also substantial continuity between the Old and New Testaments. As has already been noted (see chapter 2), many of the radical demands in the Sermon on the Mount are consistent with the teachings of the Mosaic law. Underlying that law and giving content to its specific commands was the imperative to love God and neighbor,

---

6. Dietrich Bonhoeffer, *The Cost of Discipleship*, trans. R. H. Fuller (London: SCM Press, 1948), 123–24.

which included loving one's enemy. In addition, the law also contained coercive and punitive elements. These things were not considered to be inconsistent with the "loving" or "gracious" elements, but also as giving effect to the same underlying imperative. Therefore, there is no sharp distinction between law and love.

Indeed, the law was given by God, and therefore it must be consistent with God's character. God's character maintains consistency with all of his attributes at all times. In God, there is no contradiction between law and love. This also means that love underlies all the institutions of law and government. Romans 13 teaches that God has "instituted" and "appointed" the institutions of civil government, including the ruler who wields the coercive power of the sword. And if God is love as well as just, then God has appointed civil authorities and lawmakers lovingly in order to restrain evil and promote the good (Rom 13:4).[7]

Thus, notwithstanding that they frequently fail to be perfect, law and civil government are a blessing, a good thing, and necessary in a fallen world. To do justice to the teaching of Scripture, it is therefore necessary to recognize both the legitimacy of the coercive institutions of civil law given by God, as well as the need for Christians to be radically "other worldly" by forgiving, being willing to suffer, and shunning violence and revenge. The eschatological, institutional, and theological distinctions noted earlier are necessary to account for scriptural teaching as a whole: although they are temporal, external, and provisional, civil authorities are necessary and good. This undercuts the basis of the views of writers such as Yoder and Bonhoeffer.

---

7. See Benjamin B. Saunders, "The Loving Sword: The Implications of Divine Simplicity for Law and Love," in *Christianity, Ethics and the Law: The Concept of Love in Christian Legal Thought*, ed. Zachary R. Calo, Joshua Neoh, and A. Keith Thompson (Abingdon: Routledge, 2023), 112–29.

TWO KINGDOMS, OR WHOLLY SEPARATE
REALMS, SEPARATELY GOVERNED

Some approaches to political theology today conceive the world to
be divided into two distinct realms: there is a civil sphere, governed
by natural law, and there is the sphere of the kingdom, which is
governed by Scripture. In its extreme forms it can lead to a view
that there is one law for the church and a different law for the world,
such that Scripture has little or no applicability outside the church.
Darryl Hart has argued that the view of the *Westminster Confession* is
that "faith and public policy have little to do with each other."[8] David
VanDrunen has argued that political institutions and the church are
separate realms and that "Christians are not to seek the transformation of political institutions according to the moral pattern of
Christ's kingdom."[9]

It is certainly a standard part of Protestant teaching that there
is a unique government in the church,[10] and so there is a sense in
which Christ rules the church in a distinct spiritual manner. There
is something unique about the church, considered from a corporate and institutional point of view: the church is more than just an
aggregation of Christians, and the church's nature and role are not
the same as the calling of individual Christians.[11] It is also true that
the kingdom of God is not to be equated with social and political
transformation. Some form of the two-kingdoms idea is consistent
with these aspects of scriptural teaching.

However, to the extent that the two-kingdoms approach con-
fines the kingdom within the church, or denies the applicability of
Scripture outside the church, or denies that Christianity has any

8. Darryl Hart, *A Secular Faith: Why Christianity Favors the Separation of Church and State* (Chicago: Ivan R. Dee, 2006), 70.

9. David VanDrunen, *Politics after Christendom: Political Theology in a Fractured World* (Grand Rapids: Zondervan, 2020), 119.

10. *Westminster Confession of Faith*, XXX.1; *Belgic Confession*, article 30.

11. Kevin DeYoung and Greg Gilbert, *What Is the Mission of the Church? Making Sense of Social Justice, Shalom, and the Great Commission* (Wheaton, IL: Crossway, 2011), 232–33.

political ramifications, or argues that things that are wrong in the redemptive sphere are permissible in the civil sphere, in my view it is incorrect.

Scripture has important social and political implications and contains the clearest and most authoritative statement of the moral law (which is universally applicable). There is a very important need for the application of natural law principles within the sphere of the church, although it is beyond the scope of this book to argue this in any detail.[12] That is, natural law applies within the church as well as the civil kingdom, and Scripture applies within the world as well as the church. Therefore, it is not the case that there are two wholly distinct realms which are separately governed, but there are important areas of overlap between them. Further, the kingdom can be (and historically has been) a model for the civil realm, as illustrated by scriptural passages such as Matthew 20:25–28 and Luke 22:24–30.

It should be noted that there are different ways of defining the two kingdoms. Some advocate for the two kingdoms to be understood as internal and external (that is, the realm of conscience over against everything else);[13] some conceive the two kingdoms in eschatological terms, representing the future kingdom of Christ and the present secular age;[14] others give greater emphasis to the institutional manifestations of the different kingdoms.[15] In my view, all of these variants capture something of the truth, but none are complete in and of themselves.[16]

---

12. This is recognized in the *Westminster Confession of Faith*, I.6.

13. On this approach, see W. J. Torrance Kirby, *Richard Hooker's Doctrine of the Royal Supremacy* (Leiden: Brill, 1990), 41–51.

14. On this approach, see Matthew J. Tuininga, *Calvin's Political Theology and the Public Engagement of the Church: Christ's Two Kingdoms* (Cambridge: Cambridge University Press, 2017).

15. See, e.g., David VanDrunen, *Natural Law and the Two Kingdoms: A Study in the Development of Reformed Social Thought* (Grand Rapids: Eerdmans, 2010), 176–89.

16. See further Benjamin B. Saunders and Simon P. Kennedy, "Characterizing the Two Kingdoms and Assessing Their Relevance Today," *Calvin Theological Journal* 53, no. 1 (2018): 161.

REJECTION OF NATURAL LAW

Many Protestants are suspicious of the idea of natural law. R. J.
Rushdoony thought that the doctrine of natural law was "heretical
nonsense."[17] The reasons for this suspicion include the following. First, natural law seems to be inconsistent with the Protestant
emphasis on the primacy of Scripture. As the *Westminster Confession*
put it: "The whole counsel of God concerning all things necessary
for His own glory, man's salvation, faith and life, is either expressly
set down in Scripture, or by good and necessary consequence may
be deduced from Scripture: unto which nothing at any time is to
be added, whether by new revelations of the Spirit, or traditions
of men."[18] Scripture is sufficient to teach us everything necessary
to live a life pleasing to God, so why do we need another source of
moral teaching additional to what is contained in the Bible? Human
reason often goes astray, even to the extent of calling "evil good and
good evil" (Isa 5:20), and so we should be wary of human speculation
which is not founded on scriptural principles.

A second and related reason is that God alone has the right to
authoritatively bind our consciences. As put by Charles Hodge, "The
people of God are bound by nothing but the Word of God."[19] To quote
the *Westminster Confession* again: "God alone is Lord of the conscience,
and has left it free from the doctrines and commandments of men,
which are, in any thing, contrary to His Word; or beside it, in matters of faith, or worship. So that, to believe such doctrines, or to
obey such commands, out of conscience, is to betray true liberty of
conscience." A doctrine of natural law has the potential to impose
extrabiblical moral demands on the consciences of God's people,
which is beyond the authority of any person, pope, or council. Take
contraception as an example. The Roman Catholic Church teaches

---

17. Rousas John Rushdoony, *The Institutes of Biblical Law* (Phillipsburg, NJ:
Presbyterian and Reformed Publishing, 1973), 9.

18. *Westminster Confession of Faith*, I.6.

19. Charles Hodge, *Systematic Theology* (New York: Charles Scribner & Co., 1872),
1:183.

that "every action which, whether in anticipation of the conjugal act, or in its accomplishment, or in the development of its natural consequences, proposes, whether as an end or as a means, to render procreation impossible" is intrinsically evil.[20] Protestants are likely to ask: What authority does the Roman Catholic Church have to impose such a prohibition?

A third reason is that natural law seems to downplay the distinctive, supernatural, Christocentric revelation of Christianity. For some theologians in the Reformed tradition, a general revelation, knowable through universally accessible reason, "creates an autonomous locus of theological and moral reflection that is severed from grace and God's revelation in Jesus Christ." Karl Barth considered that natural law reflects a more "natural" and "reasonable" religion which empties Christianity of its miraculous and Christological core.[21] Stanley Hauerwas argued that natural law was culturally assimilationist, such that the content of Christian ethics was "little different from the consensus of whatever culture [Protestants] found themselves a part."[22]

It is beyond the purpose of this book to consider this issue in detail.[23] I argue that it is necessary to accept some form of natural law in order to be consistent with Scripture. At the very least, it is necessary to affirm that there exists a moral law which is applicable to all people at all times, the same in substance as the Ten Commandments. This law is knowable through reason and conscience, although that knowledge is corrupted by sin and is not sufficient to provide a saving knowledge of God. Perhaps the most valuable contribution a doctrine

---

20. *Catechism of the Catholic Church* (Staten Island: St Pauls Publishing, 1994), 570 [2370].

21. J. Daryl Charles, "Protestant Bias against the Natural Law: A Critique," *Journal of Lutheran Ethics* 10, no. 3 (2010).

22. Stanley Hauerwas, *The Peaceable Kingdom: A Primer in Christian Ethics* (London: SCM Press, 1984), 52.

23. Interested readers are encouraged to consult works such as Stephen J. Grabill, *Rediscovering the Natural Law in Reformed Theological Ethics* (Grand Rapids: Eerdmans, 2006).

of natural law has to make is the idea of created order, helping to clarify that the moral law is not an arbitrary set of requirements given at God's whim on Mount Sinai, but reflects his character and the nature of the world he has made. Importantly, the idea of natural law is not an attempt to construct an autonomous system of morality and does not deny the need for Scripture, which contains a clear statement of the moral law. Natural law has long been an important part of Protestant thinking about law and morality.[24]

---

24. The *Westminster Confession of Faith*, the classic confessional statement of Reformed theology, teaches or assumes a doctrine of natural law; see Benjamin B. Saunders, "Hidden in Plain Sight: Natural Law and the Westminster Confession of Faith," *Westminster Theological Journal* 84 (2022): 177.

CONCLUSION

I n this book I have sought to lay out key principles to guide Christians as to how to think biblically about law. I have sought to re-articulate the historic Christian tradition of jurisprudence for today's context, emphasizing both the radically distinct nature of Christianity and its impact on law, and also the freedom available to lawmakers in enacting laws. I have examined the different types or categories of laws contained in the Bible, their contemporary applicability, and the different purposes the law serves. I have sought to explain how civil laws are made and how Christians should respond to the civil laws that have been enacted in particular contexts.

I have emphasized the significant areas of continuity between the Old and New Testaments, especially with regard to the substance of the obligations comprehended in the law. This suggests the continuing animating power and relevance of the Old Testament law. However, there are also significant areas of discontinuity, and the Mosaic law cannot be simply applied today without careful translation to the New Testament context. The traditional distinction between moral, ceremonial, and civil law is a helpful way of navigating both the continuity and discontinuity of biblical law.

Throughout this book I have sought to re-orient our views both of civil law and biblical law. It is, perhaps, common to have too high a view of civil law and too low a view of biblical law. That is, there is typically a high level of confidence in the power of civil law to change human behavior: if we get the right laws, we will get the right outcomes. While law can change human behavior to some extent, it can only operate on the external person, and civil laws can never change the heart. We therefore need modest expectations for what civil law has the capacity to achieve.

By contrast, there is often a negative attitude toward biblical law, with many seeing such law as a set of arbitrary and even absurd restrictions. Against this, I have emphasized that biblical law, although typically framed in negative terms as a series of prohibitions, has positive as well as negative dimensions, reflects God's character, and is consistent with the order of creation. The church has arguably not done well at emphasizing the positive aspects of the law.

One theme of this book is the principle of natural law: the universally applicable standard of morality that is given and knowable outside special revelation. Natural law is often viewed with suspicion in Protestant circles: We have the authoritative and clear teaching of Scripture, so why do we need to appeal to notions of natural law?

I have argued that natural law is an integral element of biblical teaching, necessary to account for the express teaching of Scripture and also to account for key biblical concepts, such as the accountability of all people to the moral law. Another important implication of natural law is that it emphasizes that the moral law is not simply an arbitrary set of commands given at Mount Sinai to a particular people but something which is embedded in creation and knowable by all. In this book I have adopted the standard Christian view that the content of natural law is broadly equivalent to the Ten Commandments.

The Reformed tradition has usually held that the Mosaic law is an application of the principles of the natural law to a particular context. This helps explain the applicability of the moral law today and also explains the relevance of the Israel-specific judicial laws: the laws in their original form are no longer binding, but the underlying moral principles embodied in those laws help elucidate the logic of the moral law and have continuing applicability.

The Mosaic law gave allowances for human sinfulness, permitting things such as divorce and slavery that were clearly wrong. If this was permissible in Israel—among God's chosen, holy people—how much more is it applicable in modern secular nation-states? Therefore, even where there is an applicable moral principle, this does not always neatly translate into a legal principle. Not all sins ought to be crimes, and human sinfulness may need to be accommodated in civil laws.

Even where an applicable legal principle can be discerned, this does not neatly translate into a precise form of law: enacting laws to achieve a certain goal involves many policy and design choices. One reason for this is that the moral law speaks at a high level of generality and does not prescribe in detail what laws are necessary. Both of these steps—translating a moral principle into a legal principle, and translating a legal principle into law—require a considerable degree of wisdom and prudence.

Another key theme of this book has been that Christians ought not to view law as a binary choice between faithfulness and unfaithfulness, as if there is one scripturally correct answer to every question of law. Binary choices such as these do exist, but often lawmaking is not a simplistic choice between God's law and autonomy. For many questions of law there will be a range of legitimate choices, and it is necessary to employ both God's law and human reason.

The Scriptures are detailed and contain much about law. But they do not answer every conceivable question about law. What this means is that while attempting to obtain a direct scriptural answer for every issue of law is a worthy goal, in practice it means clothing merely human opinions with divine authority.

LAW AND LEGAL TRADITIONS

The discussion in this book has been deliberately abstracted from a discussion of any particular legal systems, seeking instead to lay out fundamental principles. In practice, of course, laws are not made in a void, divorced from real circumstances and context. That context significantly constrains the process of lawmaking.

There are two main ways of making law. One is by the courts, through the common law and decided cases. The law is often developed through changes to the common law; such changes are incremental, modifying or extending the application of existing doctrines in the light of new fact situations. Under the common law model, the law is a stable but non-static system of doctrines and remedies. The common law is constantly changing in an incremental way as the boundaries of the law are tested. When deciding cases, judges are constrained by legislation and prior case law.

The other main way of making law is through legislation. Legislatures typically have more freedom when enacting laws, having greater ability to repeal or modify existing laws, and are not constrained by the discipline of needing to decide particular cases. Yet that freedom is not absolute. Legislation must be consistent with the governing constitutional framework and generally consistent with other laws. That is, there needs to be an internal coherence to the legal system as a whole, and attempts to radically change legal doctrines are often not successful. Courts have developed interpretive principles that govern the interpretation of legislation and can defeat the intention of the legislature when statutes go too far.

Both courts and legislatures are therefore significantly constrained by the existing legal system and prior cases. There is no totally blank slate when it comes to enacting laws. More than this, the existing structures and doctrines of the legal system are thought to embody the wisdom of centuries to the problems of law. Some earlier thinkers thought that common law embodies the natural law, and that common law is an important means of discovering the natural law.

Thinking well about law therefore requires not simply an abstracted understanding of the Ten Commandments divorced from any particular historical and legal context. Those enacting laws in any context must ensure they do so in a way that is consistent with the established traditions of a particular legal system. This is consistent with the theme of contextualization I have emphasized throughout this book.

THINKING ABOUT LAW CONFESSIONALLY

As I have noted throughout this book, the Christian tradition (includ-ing the Lutheran, Reformed, and Roman Catholic churches) had a largely shared catholic understanding of law prior to the seventeenth century, and perhaps even well into the twentieth century. Thinkers such as Thomas Aquinas have had a profound impact on both the Roman Catholic and Protestant views of law. That is no longer the case. The Roman Catholic and Protestant churches have gone their separate ways, and within the Reformed tradition, law is a casualty of the increasingly polarized divisions relating to political theology.

Given this, it is worth emphasizing that the Christian tradi-tion contains an immense wealth of literature regarding law which can guide our thinking today. Of course, the creeds of the church and other non-canonical writers are not infallible and may from time to time need correcting. For instance, it was a widely held view in the sixteenth and seventeenth centuries that the civil ruler ought to enforce the first four commandments of the Decalogue. Notwithstanding that this remains the official confessional position of many Presbyterian churches,[1] most Christians today (in my view rightly) would not accord such a role to the civil ruler. The truths of the Scriptures need careful rearticulation in every age.

Nevertheless, we ought to be careful before departing from the historic teaching of the church on any topic, including law. Elevating individual private judgment above that of the church in

---

1. *Westminster Confession of Faith*, XXIII.3.

the interpretation of Scripture is "a recipe for theological chaos," as
church history attests.[2] Many of the errors and problems with contemporary thinking about law could have been corrected by reference
to the historic catholic teaching of the Christian tradition about law.

COMBINING TRANSFORMATION
AND COMMON GROUND

Often the debate over Christ and culture is a debate about whether
we should be transformational or whether we should emphasize
common ground. Two-kingdoms advocates typically emphasize
common ground and natural law (especially in the civil sphere),
and they are reluctant to use the terminology of transformation.
Kuyperians or neo-Calvinists consider that we ought to adopt a
transformational approach to law—that is, we ought to have a distinctly Christian approach to law which is radically different from
the views of law held in the non-Christian world. Proponents of this
approach consider that natural law, with its emphasis on common
ground and universally knowable principles, is an enemy of transformational thinking.

This book has argued that Christians must be radically distinct,
but also that there are limitations to transformational thinking. It
is difficult to maintain consistently a transformational approach in
relation to every legal question, from the minutiae of road rules to
whether parliamentary or presidential systems of government are
preferable. As a result, transformational approaches all too often
shrink-wrap around a core range of pet topics, usually abortion
and marriage on the Christian right, race relations and refugees
on the Christian left. While of course these issues are important,
this shrink-wrapping means that in practice the church has little to
say on many significant issues that we face in the twenty-first century. Addressing these issues may require not a special Christian

---

2. Alister E. McGrath, *Reformation Thought: An Introduction*, 4th ed. (Malden, MA:
Wiley-Blackwell, 2012), 102.

insight, but the application of wisdom and principles we hold in common with non-Christians. The irony is that, while transformational approaches are loath to recognize areas of freedom or common ground, the failure to do so results in an inability to be truly, consistently transformational.

This should not be taken as a rejection of transformationalism. Christians are specifically commanded not to be conformed to this world, but to be transformed by the renewal of our minds (Rom 12:2). What is needed is a more realistic, and biblical, understanding of those things that truly are transformational rather than exaggerated claims about a radically distinct set of beliefs about every single thing. While it is certainly true that, as Kuyper famously said, "there is not a square inch in the whole domain of our human existence over which Christ, who is Sovereign over *all*, does not cry: 'Mine,' " Kuyper himself recognized that Christ does not rule over every square inch of human existence in precisely the same way.[3] Recognizing legitimate areas of common ground removes the burden of always being transformational, a burden which is ultimately unsustainable. By freeing us up from the need to discover a distinctly Christian way of boiling an egg and driving a car, we can boil eggs and drive cars in the ordinary manner and focus our attention on the things that really are distinct from the non-Christian culture.

In this book, I have argued that we need to both be transformational and recognize common ground. Indeed, we can only be truly transformational insofar as we recognize significant space for common ground. I argue, therefore, not that we need to abandon our transformational commitments, but that we need to recognize their proper scope. On the one hand, then, the problem with transformationalism is that it is too transformational: it attempts to make

---

3. Abraham Kuyper, "Sphere Sovereignty," in *Abraham Kuyper: A Centennial Reader*, ed. James D. Bratt (Grand Rapids: Eerdmans, 1998), 488. Kuyper wrote: "This perfect Sovereignty of the *sinless* Messiah at the same time directly denies and challenges all absolute Sovereignty among *sinful* men on earth, and does so by dividing life into *separate spheres*, each with its own sovereignty" (467–68).

absolutely everything into a radically different Christian doctrine, which is a project that is doomed to failure.

However, we also have the opposite problem: our transformationalism is not radical enough. We live in an age which faces huge challenges, where technology has redefined even human nature itself. By and large, however, the church contents itself with simplistic pronouncements on a core range of pet topics (such as abortion, marriage, and refugees), with a few Bible verses thrown in for good measure. We fight the symptoms but ignore—or worse, are complicit in—the root causes. We are unwilling to undertake deep analysis of our modern condition, whether due to the Protestant concern with conscience or because we are unwilling to place ourselves in the crosshairs of controversy.

The problem with our transformationalism, then, is that we are not nearly transformational enough. Perhaps the deepest irony of all is that we cannot be truly transformational because we fail to truly grasp the implications of the creational order. In short, we fail to appreciate the natural law tradition. The most profound critics of modern thought have been those who truly understand human nature and the way that it has been undermined by the logic of technological development. It is not that natural law would allow us to claim divine sanction for merely human opinions, but that a profound grasp of natural law allows us to fully appreciate the stark difference between Christianity and modern ways of thinking.

ACKNOWLEDGMENTS

I am grateful to Simon Kennedy, Matthew Deroon, Phillip Young, and Elliot Ritzema for providing valuable comments on earlier versions of this book, and for those who have challenged and helped refine my thinking over the years, especially Darren Middleton, Benjamin Nelson, and James Playfoot. I would like to thank my daughter, Theodora Saunders, for preparing the indexes so competently.

Any views expressed in this book are solely those of the author. *S. D. G.*

FURTHER STUDY

For study of specific passages of Scripture which relate to law, Alastair Roberts's chapter-by-chapter commentary on the Bible is an immensely valuable resource: https://audio.alastairadversaria.com.

The Westminster Larger Catechism contains a valuable exposition of the moral law and the Decalogue in questions 91–148.

A helpful distillation of key principles relating to law is found in "Evangelicals and Catholics Together on Law: The Lord of Heaven and Earth. A Joint Statement by Evangelical and Catholic Legal Scholars," printed in *Journal of Christian Legal Thought* 3, no. 1 (2013): 2–10.

Also recommended is Robert F. Cochran Jr. and David VanDrunen, eds., *Law and the Bible: Justice, Mercy and Legal Institutions* (Downers Grove, IL: IVP Academic, 2013).

Thomas Aquinas's "Treatise on Law" (questions 90–108 of the *Summa Theologica* IaIIae) has had an immense impact on the Protestant and Roman Catholic traditions. Most of his "Treatise on Law" can be found in R. W. Dyson, ed., *Aquinas: Political Writings* (Cambridge: Cambridge University Press, 2020).

Cambridge University Press has published a valuable series of books on Christianity and law, including several books on great Christian jurists throughout history: https://www.cambridge.org/core/series/law-and-christianity/6D77992447E6BD14E748AE05E137D92B.

VALUABLE PRIMARY SOURCES FROM A REFORMED AND LUTHERAN PERSPECTIVE

Calvin, John. *Institutes of the Christian Religion*. Edited by John
    T. McNeill. Translated by Ford Lewis Battles. Louisville:
    Westminster John Knox, 1960. See especially chapter 8 of
    book 2, and chapter 20 of book 4.

Chemnitz, Martin. *Loci Theologici*. Translated by J. A. O. Preus. St.
    Louis: Concordia Publishing House, 1989 [1594].

Gerhard, Johann. *On the Law*. Edited by Benjamin T. G. Mayes and
    Joshua J. Hayes. Translated by Richard J. Dinda. St. Louis:
    Concordia Publishing House, 2015 [1613].

Junius, Franciscus. *The Mosaic Polity*. Edited by Andrew M. McGinnis.
    Translated by Todd M. Rester. Grand Rapids: CLP Academic,
    2015.

Turretin, Francis. *Institutes of Elenctic Theology*. Edited by James T.
    Dennison Jr. Translated by George Musgrave Giger. 3 vols.
    Phillipsburg, NJ: P&R Publishing, 1992. See especially 2:1–167.

Zanchi, Girolamo. *On the Law in General*. Translated by Jeffrey J.
    Veenstra. Grand Rapids: Christian's Library Press, 2013.

VALUABLE SOURCES ON NATURAL LAW

Budziszewski, J. *What We Can't Not Know: A Guide*. San Francisco:
    Ignatius Press, 2010.

Grabill, Stephen J. *Rediscovering the Natural Law in Reformed
    Theological Ethics*. Grand Rapids: Eerdmans, 2006.

McCall, Brian M. *The Architecture of Law: Rebuilding Law in the
    Classical Tradition*. Notre Dame, IN: University of Notre Dame
    Press, 2018.

Porter, Jean. *Natural and Divine Law: Reclaiming the Tradition for
    Christian Ethics*. Grand Rapids: Eerdmans, 1999.

VanDrunen, David. *Politics after Christendom: Political Theology in a
    Fractured World*. Grand Rapids: Zondervan, 2020. Chapter 5 of
    this volume contains a very helpful discussion of natural law.

OTHER VALUABLE SOURCES

Aroney, Nicholas, and Ian Leigh, eds. Christianity and
 Constitutionalism. Oxford: Oxford University Press, 2022.

Berman, Harold J. *Law and Revolution: The Formation of the Western Legal
 Tradition*. Cambridge, MA: Harvard University Press, 1983.

_____. *Law and Revolution II: The Impact of the Protestant Reformations
 on the Western Legal Tradition*. Cambridge, MA: Belknap Press,
 2003.

McIlroy, David. *A Biblical View of Law and Justice*. Milton Keynes:
 Paternoster, 2004.

Schutt, Michael P. *Redeeming Law: Christian Calling and the Legal
 Profession*. Downers Grove, IL: InterVarsity Press, 2009. This
 is a helpful resource aimed specifically at lawyers.

Witte, John. *Law and Protestantism: The Legal Teachings of the Lutheran
 Reformation*. Cambridge: Cambridge University Press, 2002.

_____. *The Reformation of Rights: Law, Religion, and Human Rights in
 Early Modern Calvinism*. Cambridge: Cambridge University
 Press, 2007.

SUBJECT and AUTHOR INDEX

abortion, 8, 22, 78, 117, 125, 134, 140, 141, 142, 143, 143n55, 155–56, 168, 192, 194

accountability, 9, 18, 32, 115, 119, 134, 137, 188

adultery, 42, 50, 69, 76, 82, 84, 94, 106, 125, 151

Alexander, Frank S., 30n28, 136n46

Armacost, Barbara E., 32n31

Althusius, Johannes, 126, 15n8, 110n4

Ames, William, 50n19

Andrewes, Lancelot, 50n19

Aquinas, Thomas, 91, 93, 101, 103, 110, 138, 148, 156, 170, 191, 45n9, 95n48, 104n68

Augustine of Hippo, 27, 74, 110, 156n13

Australian Constitution, 128

Bahnsen, Greg L., 58n32, 65n37, 92n42, 176n1

Banner, Stuart, 129n34

Bannerman, James, 45, 178n3

Bavinck, Herman, 110n5

Beck, Randy, 25n17

Belgic Confession of Faith, 182n10

Benson, Iain, 116n13

Berman, Harold J., 30n28, 135n41

Bible and law, as a foundation for human law, 13, 27, 110, 130–31

as non-exhaustive legal code, 4, 12, 58, 112–13, 151, 154, 177–78

concern for vulnerable, 28, 76, 98–99, 124, 133

threefold division of law, 45–48

Blackstone, Sir William, 143

blasphemy, 85, 127, 129

Bolton, Samuel, 142n54

Bonhoeffer, Dietrich, 179, 180, 181

Book of Concord, 6

Brown, Christopher Boyd, 66n46

Brunner, Emil, 19, 21, 20n14

Bucer, Martin, 148, 66n45, 99n56, 100n60

Budziszewski, J., 172, 135n42,

Bullinger, Heinrich, 91, 51n21, 71n61, 91n40, 98n53, 99n56

Burgess, Anthony, 24n15

Burnside, Jonathan, 12n1, 100n58

Calo, Zachary R., 35n40, 181n7

Carson, D. A., 115n12

Catechism of the Catholic Church, 32n32, 49n18, 52n23, 87n25, 90n35, 100n61, 161n23, 185n20

ceremonial law, 45, 46, 47, 48, 55, 56, 57, 86

Charles, J. Daryl, 3n5, 185n21,

Charter of Human Rights and Responsibilities Act 2006 (Vic), 160

Chavura, Stephen A., 129n33

Chemnitz, Martin, 51n22, 71n61, 142n54

Christendom, 114, 115, 128

Christian liberty, 29–30, 172, 173, 184
Christian view of law, 3, 4, 9, 11, 14, 19, 23, 94, 109, 126, 136, 141, 177, 188
church,
  and risk-aversion, 171
  as institution, 28–29, 31, 130, 182
  nature of, 54, 59, 60, 177–78
  role of, 114–15, 182
civil government,
  and church, 28–29, 31, 161
  and religion, 130
  and restraint of evil, 25–26, 29, 35, 171, 181
  as God's servant, 25, 35, 94, 112–13, 121, 141,
  external and coercive nature of, 28, 30, 33, 122, 128, 158, 173, 181, 188
  legitimacy of, 29, 113, 181
  outward nature of, 127–28
  provisional nature of, 29, 127, 181
  public health and, 153
  public order and safety, 138–39
  religion and, 130
  role of, 83, 94, 110–13, 117, 127–28, 141, 162, 169, 191
  scriptural ambivalence towards, 26, 113–14
  tension with kingdom of God, 28, 113–14
civil law,
  allowance for human sinfulness, 124–25, 178, 189
  and first table of the Decalogue, 126–30
  and second table of the Decalogue, 126–30
  and moral law, 13, 27, 110, 130–31
  and restraint of evil, 25, 35, 71, 171, 181

  and the church, 130, 162
  and the people, 18–19, 122–23, 171
  coercive nature of, 28, 127, 181
  continually changing, 15, 120
  criteria for validity of, 150, 156–57
  directive power for the good, 121–22, 125, 131
  inability to change the heart, 19, 25, 30, 122, 128, 130, 188
  interpretation of, 165–66, 190
  making of, 116–21
  priorities for today, 130–37
  role of, 25–26, 94, 122
civil obedience, 26, 92, 123, 134, 145, 146, 148, 149, 150, 155, 165, 167, 168, 174, 91n38
civil disobedience, 146, 149, 166, 167, 168, 171, 172, 173, 174
Clark, R. Scott, 132n38
Cochran Jr., Robert F., 25n17, 32n31, 35n40
Cole, R. Alan, 77
common good, 32, 122, 131, 156, 157
common grace, 151
common ground, 11, 21, 22, 192, 193
common law, 129, 190
conscience, 10, 23, 29, 33, 34, 38, 42, 44, 49, 81, 127, 134, 146, 156, 157, 158, 161, 168, 169, 170, 183, 184, 185, 194, 50n19, 102n66, 158n18, 164n27
constitutional law and constitutionalism, 31, 159
constitutional validity of laws, 150, 159, 165, 172
context, 5, 6, 7, 15, 16, 27, 28, 44, 45, 46, 47, 48, 54, 55, 59, 60, 61, 64, 80, 99, 111, 112, 123, 124, 125, 126, 137, 140, 151, 176, 177, 187, 188, 190, 191
contextualization, 14, 15, 150, 191

courts, 34, 55, 58, 63, 91, 100, 159, 165, 166, 169, 172, 190
covenant of works, 24
Covid-19,
  church's response to, 2, 7
  law and regulations relating to, 2, 133–34, 157, 160
  mandatory vaccination, 160
created order, 2, 17, 18, 21, 24, 25, 27, 42–44, 49, 52, 69–70, 79, 86, 90, 132, 156, 162, 186, 188, 194
creation mandate, 24, 25
creeds and confessions, 191
Crowley, J. D., 102

Dabney, Robert L., 130
Dawkins, Richard, 33n34
decalogue,
  as summarized in the two great commandments, 53, 74
  as summary of the moral law, 10, 27–28, 38, 49–51, 73, 81, 107
  division into two tables, 74, 126
  principle for interpreting, 73–79
  Ten Commandments as synecdoches, 50
DeYoung, Kevin, 182n11
Dicey, A. V., 109n1
disobedience. *See* civil disobedience
divorce, 94, 96, 97, 117, 123, 124, 125, 189
Dobbs v. Jackson Women's Health Organization, 142n53
Dumbrell, William J., 56n27

Enns, Peter, 32n31
environment, 116, 117, 135
equity, 34, 60, 153
euthanasia, 22, 125, 146
executive, 5, 34, 134, 159, 165, 170

family, 18, 22, 29, 30, 31, 40, 89, 97, 131, 132, 161, 163
family violence, 1, 162
federalism, 32, 128
First Amendment, 150
Forde, Gerhard O, 64, 65n39
Forsythe, Clarke, 142
free speech, 163, 164
freedom of lawmakers in enacting law, 11, 13, 18, 22, 107, 110, 134, 141, 151, 152, 154, 171, 179, 187

Gandhi, Mohandas K., 172n34
Gascoigne, John, 129n33
George, Robert P., 122n20
Gerhard, Johann, 51, 64, 83, 71n61, 76n10, 84n18
Gilbert, Greg, 182n11
Gillespie, George, 138n49
gospel,
  social and political implications of, 152, 182
  witness to, 170–71, 174
Grabill, Stephen J., 3n5, 185n23
Grantham, Ross, 6n6, 122n21, 135n41
Gray, Kevin, 99n57
Gray, Susan F., 99n57
Grudem, Wayne, 45n10, 48n16, 58n33
gun regulation, 4, 6, 8, 61, 137, 139, 140, 153, 154

Hains, Todd R., 66n46
"hardness of heart" principle, 123, 125, 178
Hart, H. L. A., 136n44
Hart, Darryl, 182
Hauerwas, Stanley, 185
Helmholz, R. H., 35n38
Hemmingsen, Niels, 77n12

Hodge, Charles, 127, 184, 148n3, 154n11
Holy Spirit, 57, 66, 67, 68, 70, 122, 151, 184
human rights, 1, 3, 20, 31, 32, 33, 34, 136–37, 158, 160, 164
Hunter, James Davison, 121

image of God, 10, 20, 23, 24, 25, 33, 43, 74, 77, 92, 141, 163
Innes, David C., 110n4
injustice, 18, 28, 34, 47, 104, 112, 167, 169, 170
International Covenant on Civil and Political Rights, 158, 164, 34n36
interpretation of laws, 165–66, 190
Ishay, Micheline, 136n45
Israel, 10, 12, 16, 28, 38, 40, 41, 44, 46, 53, 55, 59, 60, 64, 80, 81, 85, 86, 88, 91, 93, 99, 100, 112, 123, 124, 129, 177, 178, 189

Johnson, Gary L. W., 65n42
Jordan, James B., 130, 12n1
judicial laws, 45, 46, 48, 51, 58–64, 189
Junius, Franciscus, 95n48, 112n7
just laws, 131, 145, 150, 155, 167
justice, 18, 24, 25, 26, 27, 28, 31, 34, 55, 93, 100, 104, 105, 126, 130, 131, 132, 138, 151, 167, 169, 172, 177, 181
justification, 64–65

Keller, Timothy, 15, 65, 82n16
Kennedy, Simon P., 17n10, 91n38, 183n16
King, Martin Luther, 171
kingdom of Christ, 26–28, 29–30, 66, 115, 182–83

Kirby, W. J. Torrance, 183n13
Koyzis, David T., 115n12
Kuyper, Abraham, 193, 29n24, 121n35, 161n22

law,
    and conflict with Christian values, 3, 27, 113–16
    and love, 74, 180–81
    and the Christian, 64–71
    and vulnerable, 18, 125, 133, 141
    as a guide to Christian living, 64–71
    as a means of salvation, 64–71
    different meanings of in Scripture, 44–45
    non-Christian approaches to, 109, 136–37
    sanctification, 64–71
    written on the heart, 10, 21, 24, 27, 42, 44, 49, 54
lawmakers,
    as accountable to God, 9, 18, 27, 28, 171
    cultural change and, 121–22
    directive power for the good, 121–22, 125, 131
legal positivism, 109, 136
legislature, 31, 58, 116, 149, 150, 190
legitimate expectations, 160
Locke, John, 101
lordship of Christ, 9, 23, 28,
Luther, Martin, 33, 66, 67, 74, 82, 85, 157, 169, 173, 12n1, 30n27, 33n35, 34n37, 71n60, 94n45, 114n11, 128n29, 158n15, 161n21
Lutheran approaches to law, 2, 51, 66, 74, 161

marriage, 12, 18, 22, 24, 31, 33, 43,
    94, 95, 97, 117, 123, 126, 131,
    132, 163, 192, 194
McCall, Brian M., 13n4
McDurmon, Joel, 46n11, 177n2
McGarvey, J. W., 88
McGrath, Alister E., 192n2
McNeill, John T., 3n5, 12n1, 45n9,
    110n4, 148n5
medical practitioners,156, 168,
Meilaender, Gilbert, 103n67
Melanchthon, Philip, 66, 67, 12n1,
    99n56, 101n65, 148n4
Mill, John Stuart, 122, 123n22
Moo, Douglas J., 44n6
moral law,
    and created order, 2, 17, 18, 21, 24,
        25, 27, 42–44, 49, 52, 69–70,
        79, 86, 90, 132, 156, 162, 186,
        188, 194
    and human nature, 76
    and God's character, 76–77, 181,
        186, 188
    and love, 74, 180–81
    and the Decalogue, 10, 27–28, 38,
        49–51, 73, 81, 107
    as a foundation for human law, 13,
        27, 110, 130–31
    as a means of salvation, 70–71
    as a rule of conduct, 10, 55, 70–71
    as internal and external, 75, 79, 93
    as predating Decalogue, 38–41
    as relatively indeterminate, 12, 137,
        140–41, 150–51
    as summarised in the two great
        commandments, 53, 74
    as universally applicable, 9–10, 14,
        15, 23, 27, 31, 38–39, 44, 59,
        60, 81, 131, 183, 188
    continuing applicability of, 45–47,
        55, 64–71
    knowability of, 10, 38–39, 49

    loss of belief in, 6, 135
    New Testament and, 46–47, 68–69
    place of in sanctification, 64–71
    role in justification, 70–71
    three uses of, 71
Mosaic law,
    and concern for vulnerable, 28, 76,
        98–99, 124, 133
    as application of the moral law, 28
    as particularization of the
        Decalogue, 51, 75
    contemporary applicability, 45–48
    offices of prophet, priest, and
        king, 32
    parapet law, 16, 48, 61–64
    selective and illustrative nature of,
        12, 124, 178
    threefold division of law, 45–48
Muller, Richard A., 3n5
Müller, Wolfgang P., 143n55
murder, 10, 12, 13, 47, 39, 69, 77, 78,
    92, 93, 106, 141, 142, 143, 151
Murray, John, 113n8

Naselli, Andrew David, 102
natural law, 10, 13, 15, 19, 27, 31, 33,
    35, 38, 42, 44, 49, 52, 59, 60,
    69, 81, 83, 84, 87, 91, 92, 93,
    95, 101, 103, 109, 110, 112,
    131, 132, 138, 140, 151, 163,
    177, 182, 183, 184, 185, 186,
    188, 190, 192, 194
neo-Calvinism, 161
new covenant, 54, 68, 86
New Perspective on Paul, 65n42
Noahic covenant, 25, 46
Noble, Alan, 90n35
non-Christians, 9, 11, 19, 23, 41, 55,
    114, 136, 144, 150, 151, 192,
    193
Noonan, John T., 143n55

O'Donovan, Oliver, 113, 128
over-regulation, 6

pandemic, 1, 2, 4, 7, 117, 133, 134,
      154 157, 160. *See also* Covid-19
parents, 45, 90, 91, 92, 97, 105, 142,
      162
Parks, Rosa, 169
Paul, Darel E., 121n19
Pendleton, Philip Y., 88
Perkins, William, 50n19
politics, 6, 20, 22, 136, 151, 152
Pope Leo XIII, 129,
Pope Paul VI, 158n16
principle of negative liberty, 159
principles for thinking about law,
      9–19
privacy, 119, 120, 133
procedural fairness (due process),
      18, 34–35, 105, 138
property, 22, 31, 33, 97–103, 131, 158,
      163, 180
proportionate justice, 25, 104,
      135–36
public opinion and law, 18–19,
      122–23, 171
punishment for crime, 135–36

reason, 10, 18, 34, 42, 44, 70, 77, 83,
      140, 151, 156, 157, 176, 184,
      185, 189
Reno, R. R., 96, 97n51
religious freedom, 33, 34, 133, 158,
      164
restitution, 135
retributive justice, 25
road safety laws, 5, 14, 16, 62, 117,
      152, 154, 192
Roberts, Alastair, 75n5, 106n74
Roe v. Wade, 142
Roman Catholic approaches to law
      (including the Magisterium)

2, 32, 49, 52, 74, 100, 161,
      184–85,191, 52n23
rule of law, 32
Rushdoony, Rousas John, 184,
      58n32, 64n37

Sabbath. *See* Ten Commandments:
      Fourth Commandment
Sacks, Jonathan, 100n58, 101n62
sanctification, 64, 65, 69, 70, 71
Schaeffer, Francis, 149, 154
Schleitheim Articles, 52n24
schools, 2, 162,
Second Helvetic Confession, 49n17
self-defense, 93, 137, 138, 139, 140
separation of powers, 32, 149
sexuality, 3, 5, 20, 22, 94, 96, 114,
      117, 118, 132, 134
Silcock, Jeffrey G., 66n46
sin and human law, 83, 97, 126, 127,
      189
slavery, 27, 54, 59, 80, 86, 87, 88, 99,
      124, 125, 129, 130, 173, 189,
      164n27
Smith, James K. A., 77
sovereignty, 31, 193, 179, 193n3
spectrum of transformation, 11, 19,
      22, 140, 141, 152
sphere sovereignty, 161, 183, 192
St. Germain, Christopher, 34n37
Stephen, Leslie, 109n1
subsidiarity, 32
surveillance capitalism, 133

Taylor, Charles, 118n14, 119n16
technocracy, 133, 134
technology and human nature,
      89–90, 132, 134, 194
Ten Commandments,
   First Commandment, 33, 39, 40,
      46n14, 69n57, 81–83, 128,
      163

Second Commandment, 39, 40, 46n14, 69n57, 83–84

Third Commandment, 46n14, 69n57, 85, 129

Fourth Commandment, 43–44, 46, 54, 69, 74, 85–90, 99, 128, 129–30

Fifth Commandment, 40, 46n14, 54, 69n57, 73, 90–92, 105, 126

Sixth Commandment, 16, 39, 40, 43–44, 46n14, 61, 69n57, 77, 78, 92–94, 102, 141

Seventh Commandment, 40, 43–44, 46–7n14, 50, 51, 69n57, 76, 94–97

Eighth Commandment, 33, 47n14, 69n57, 97–103

Ninth Commandment, 40, 47n14, 51, 69n57, 77, 103–5, 126

Tenth Commandment, 47n14, 69n57, 73, 74, 106–107

theonomy, 175, 176, 177, 178, 179,

Thoreau, H. D., 172n34

Tierney, Brian, 100n59

Towerson, Gabriel, 143n55

transformation, 11, 14, 19, 182, 192,

transformationalism, 5, 192, 193, 194

Tregenza, Ian, 129n33

Trueman, Carl R., 33n34, 94n46

Tuininga, Matthew J., 29n25, 183n14

Turretin, Francis, 50, 90, 45n7, 53n25, 70n59, 84n20, 93n43

two great commandments, 53, 69, 74

two kingdoms, 182, 183, 192

unbelievers, 11, 20, 54, 151

United States Constitution, 150

Universal Declaration on Human Rights, 136

universal healthcare, 153, 154, 169

unjust laws, 8, 30, 145, 148, 149, 151, 155, 156, 157, 159, 166, 167, 169, 170, 172, 173, 174,

Ursinus, Zacharias, 12n1

vaccines, 2, 160

values, 3, 4, 5, 6, 22, 34, 78, 97, 101, 116, 117, 118, 119, 120, 121, 131, 132, 135, 138, 141, 162, 175

VanDrunen, David, 42, 182, 12n2, 17n11, 25nn17–19, 29n26, 32n31, 43n5, 151n8, 183n15

Viret, Pierre, 76n9

virtue, 10, 17, 33, 60, 81, 106, 121, 123, 135, 163, 173

Vitoria, Francisco de, 128n30

Vos, Geerhardus, 56n26, 76n6

Walton, John H., 75nn4–5, 104n69

Warfield, Benjamin B., 86, 87n23

Waters, Guy P., 65n42, 178n3

Watson, Thomas, 142n54

Wenham, Gordon J., 56, 45n10, 51n22, 57n29, 88n30, 136n43

Weemes, John R., 143n55

western legal tradition, 7, 30, 33, 34

Westminster Confession of Faith, 60, 87, 127, 182, 184, 23n15, 45n9, 49n17, 59n34, 70n59, 161n24, 173n35, 183n12, 186n24, 191n1

Westminster Larger Catechism, 79, 50n19, 80n14, 84n19

Wilder, Laura Ingalls, 88, 89n33

will of God, 11, 67, 110, 111, 123, 146

Willson, James M., 147

Winslow, Octavius, 68

wisdom, 11, 14, 16, 17, 18, 19, 41, 62, 63, 76, 77, 102, 103, 112, 126,

132, 140, 141, 143, 150, 151,
152, 154, 171, 174, 176, 178,
179, 189, 190, 193, 58n33,
105n72
Witsius, Herman, 45n9
Witte, John, 30n28, 33n33, 136n46,
163n26
Worth, Jennifer, 143n57

Yoder, John Howard, 179, 180, 181
Yogyakarta Principles, 137n4

Zanchi, Girolamo, 15, 124, 12n2
Zuboff, Shoshana, 133n40
Zwingli, Ulrich, 123n23

SCRIPTURE INDEX

OLD TESTAMENT

Genesis

1:26–28 ....23, 42, 43
1:27–28 24
1:28 24,
2:1–3 ....24, 43
2:2–3 86
2:15 ....24, 43
2:16–17 24
2:18–25 ....24, 43
2:19–20 43
2:24 43
2:24–25 .... 95n47
3 .... 24 n16
3:9 34
3:15 26
4:11 39
4:26 39
6:5–8 .... 40n2
8:20–9:17 25
9:4 46
9:5–6 141
9:6 .... 43, 92, 141n51
9:20–27 40
11:1–9 .... 40n2
12:1–3 26
12:10–20 .... 40n2
18:21 .... 35n38
19 .... 96, 41n4
19:5–6 44
19:12 40
19:13 40

Exodus

1:15–21 ..... 155, 167n30
19:5–6 .... 59, 125
20:1–17 27
20 ....23, 73, 76, 86
20:2 .... 64, 80
20:3 81
20:4–6 83
20:7 85
20:8–10 85
20:11 86
20:12 .... 54, 90
20:13 ....10, 92
20:14 94
20:15 97
20:16 103
20:17 106
21:2 ....87, 99
21:2–6 .... 88n32
21:2–11 .... 28n22, 76n8
21:7 5
21:7–11 ....124, 178,
                12n3
21:12–14 92
21:29 93
22:2–3 138

20:1–2 44
20:9 40
34 .... 40n2
38:6–10 .... 40n2

22:3 139
22:21–27 .... 133n39
21:22–25 ....141n51
22:22–27 .... 28n22,
              76n8, 99n55
22:28 85
23:1–3, 6–8.......... 104
23:4–5 53
23:9 .... 28n22, 76n8,
                  99n55
23:10–19 .... 87n26
31:12–18 .... 87n26
34:28 73
35:1–3 .... 87, 87n26
35:10, 26, 35 17

Leviticus

4:1–5:13 57
5:1 104
11:10–12, 20, 42 46
18:1–30 .... 76, 94
19 50
19:3–8, 17–26 ....46n12
19:8 46
19:9–10 .... 98n54
19:12 85
19:13 .... 48, 98, 99n55
19:14, 33–34 ..... 28n22,
                  76n8
19:15 104
19:16 .... 93, 103

19:17–18 93
19:18 .....52, 53, 69n56, 74n2
19:26 46
19:29 91
19:32 91
19:35–36 98
20:9 58
23 .... 87n26
23:1–3 ...87n27, 88n30
23:22 ...... 28n22, 76n8, 98n54, 99n55
23:40 .... 88n28
24:10–16 85
24:22 104
25 .... 87n26
25:1–8 ....87n27
25:13 ....87, 99
25:13, 23, 28, 42 88n32
25:14–17 98
25:15–16 99
25:23 100
25:23–55 . 28n22, 76n8
25:35–38 99
25:42–43 88

Numbers

15:32–36 87
32 .... 88n32
35:30 ....105n71

Deuteronomy

4:6 41
4:6–8 77
4:12–18 ....83n17
4:13 73
5:1–33 ....73, 76, 86
5:6 80
5:6–21 27
5:7 81
5:8–10 83
5:11 85

5:12–14 85
5:12–15 ....43, 54
5:15 86
5:16 90
5:17 ....10, 92
5:18 94
5:19 97
5:20 103
5:21 106
6:1–11:32 75
6:4–5 .... 81, 82
6:4–9 .... 79, 74n2
6:5 .... 53, 69n56
10:4 73
10:12–13 82
10:17–19 . 28n22, 76n8
12 75
12:4–14, 31 83
13 129
13:1–14:21 75
13:12–14 ....105n71
14:1 10
14:22–16:17 ..75, 87n26
14:24–26 .... 88n29
14:24–29 .... 88n28
14:28–29 28n22, 76n8
15:1 ....87, 99
15:7–11 ....75n3
15:7–15 ... 28n22, 76n8
15:12–15 99
15:26–29 .... 88n28
16:11, 14–15 ...... 88n29
16:9–12, 13–15 .. 88n28
16:18–20 105
16:18–18:22 .... 75, 91
16:19–20 104
17:4–7 ....105n71
17:5 104
17:6 .... 35n39
17:7, 12 .... 60n36
17:8–20 . 32n30, 91n37
17:11–12 91

17:16–17 .... 32n29
17:18–20 .... 32n31
18:1–8, 14–22 ....91n37
18:15–22 .... 32n29
19 93
19:1–22:8 ....75, 93
19:4–7, 11–13 92
19:14 93
19:15 ....13, 35n39
19:15–21 ....93, 104, 105n71
19:19 .... 60n36
21:10–14 ......124, 12n3, 28n22
21:18–21 93
21:21 .... 60n36
22:1–7 93
22:8 .... 16, 48, 61, 93
22:9–23:14 75
22:10–11 37
22:13–30 94
22:21, 22, 24 .....60n36
22:25 51
23:1 37
23:15–24:7 75
23:19–20 99
23:24–25 .... 98n54
24:1–4 ....97, 123
24:6 98
24:7 .... 60n36
24:8–16 75
24:14–15 98
24:14–18 ....105n70
24:16 104
24:17 .... 133n39
24:17–22 . 28n22, 76n8, 99n55
24:17–26:19 75
24:19–22 .... 98n54
25:11–12 5
25:13–16 98
26:1–15 106

26:12–13 . 28n22, 76n8
27:19 ...... 28n22, 76n8
28:1–68 54
29:29 110

Joshua

6 .... 41n4
8 .... 41n4
10 .... 41n4
11 .... 41n4
13 .... 88n32

Judges

21:25 .... 35n40

1 Samuel

13:14 80
15:22 47
17 140

2 Samuel

11 .... 96, 106,
                     106n73
12 .... 32n30
13 96

1 Kings

3:28 17
12:6–19 17
21:1–29 ....104, 106n73

Job

12:12 17

Psalms

1:1–2 79
2:1–12 ....27n20
2:12 28
19:7 17
19:7–11 79
40:6 47
51:6 47

82:3 .... 28n22, 133n39
82:3–4 141
118:9 26
139:13–16 ....141n51
146:3 26
146:9 ....28n22

Proverbs

1:7 17
3:7 17
4:23 122
5:15–19 .... 95, 95n47
6:6–8 17
8:15–16 17
9:10 17
11:2 17
11:14 17
13:1 .... 7, 17
13:20 17
14:31 39
14:34 131
15:1 17
15:22 17
15:31 17
16:12 131
18:17 ..... 17, 105, 35n39
19:20 17
25:21–22 140

Ecclesiastes

12:14 27

Song of Solomon

1:1–4 .... 95n47
2:3 .... 95n47
4:11–16 .... 95n47
5:1, 4–5 .... 95n47
7:6–13 .... 95n47

Isaiah

1:12–14 47
1:17 ....28n22

5:20 ....44, 184
10:1–2 ....28n23, 150
13:1–23:18 .... 41n4
40:18 ....83n17
42:1 27
42:4 27
58:3–4 47
58:13 88
66:3–4 47

Jeramiah

1:5 ....141n51
5:28 ....28n22
22:16 82
31:33–34 68
46:1–51:64 .... 41n4

Ezekiel

23 84
25:1–32:32 .... 41n4
35 .... 41n4
38:1–39:29 .... 41n4

Daniel

3 .... 155, 167n30
4:1–37 .... 41n4
5:1–31 .... 41n4
6 .... 155, 167n30

Hosea

4:12–14 84
6:6 47

Amos

1 41
1:13 ....28n23
2 41
2:4 .... 41, 81
3:2 81
4:1 ....28n23
8:4–6 ....28n23

Zephaniah

2 .... 41n4

Micah

6:6–8 47

Zechariah

7:10 ....28n22, 75n3,
                    133n39

Malachi

3:5 ....28n22

NEW TESTAMENT

Matthew

1:21 26
3:17 81
4:10 ...... 46n14, 69n57
5:9 140
5:17 26
5:17–20 68
5:21–22 . 46n14, 69n57
5:21–26 93
5:21–37 .... 76n7
5:21–32 .... 111n6
5:21–48 .... 51, 53, 68
5:27–28 46n14, 69n57
5:27–30 94
5:33–37 46n14, 69n57
5:38–40 .... 52, 53
5:38–42 ..... 147, 179n4
5:39 .... 140, 169
5:40–41 170
5:43–48 53
7:12 74
12:36 27
15:4 ...... 46n14, 69n57
15:9 51
15:10–20 122
17:5 81
18:16 ... 46n13, 105n72
19:3–9 97
19:8 ....123, 141, 178
19:18 .... 46–7n14,
                    69n57
19:19 ....46n14,
                    69nn56–57
19:22–24 115

20:25–28 183
22:15–22 112
22:36–40 69n56, 74n2,
                    76n7
22:37–40 .... 53, 81
23:25–26 48
25:40 .... 133n39
26:26–29 57
27:51 56
28:18 23
28:18–20 26

Mark

7:7 51
10:4 178
10:4–9 97
10:5 .... 123, 141
10:5–12, 19 ....46n14,
                    69n57
10:6–9 .... 95n47
10:19 .... 46–7n14,
                    69n57
10:23–25 115
12:13–17 112
12:17 161
12:28–31 .... 69n56
12:29–31 81

Luke

1:41–44 ....141n51
4:8 .... 46n14, 69n57
4:18–19 88
6:31 74
10:7 ....57n31

11:39–41 48
12:11 .... 114, 27n20
12:15 .... 97, 47n14,
                    69n57
13:1–3 112
14:26 92
16:18 .....47n14, 69n57
18:20 .... 46–7n14,
                    69n57
20:20–26 112
21:12 ....27n20
22:24–30 183
22:36 138
24:25–27 56

John

2:19–21 57
3:16 82
4:24 ....83n17
5:17 43
5:26–29 27
6:39 26
8:44 103
14:6 103
14:15 69
14:26 70
15:20 113
17:17 70
19:11 28

Acts

2:31–36 23
3:22 56
4:19–20 ... 155, 167n30

4:23–28 114
5:3–4 .....47n14, 69n57
5:17–42 .... 114n10
6:8–8:3 .... 114n10
10:15 55
10:9–15 ....47n15
11:1–18 ....47n15
12:1–19 .... 114n10
14:19 170
15 ....47n15
15:20 .... 46n14, 69n57
16:6–40 .... 114n10
16:37 170
17:1–9 .... 114n10
17:29 ....83n17
17:30 123
21:27–26:32 .... 114n10
22:25–29 170
25:11–12 170

Romans

1:18....................44, 55
1:18–20 42
1:18–23 24
1:20 ....54, 82
1:21–23 106
1:23 ....83n17
2:14–15 .... 10, 24, 42, 44, 54
2:24 85
3:4 103
3:9–20, 23 70
3:19 44
3:20 71
3:21......................26
3:21–22, 28 70
3:26 26
3:31...................68, 71
4:5 ....65n41
4:15.....................69
5:12–18 ....24n16
5:18–19 26

5:19...................... 81
6:14–15 .... 64, 71
6:15 69
7:12......................77
7 70
7:7–12 71
7:23 44
8:1 ....65n41
8:7........................24
8:7–8 70
8:18–23..................26
8:19–23 ....24n16
8:32......................82
11:36 23
12:2......................11
12:17–19 140
12:20 ....179n4
13 .... 147, 179
13:1 ....7, 23
13:1–4 141
13:1–5 71
13:1–7 ..35, 91, 112, 145, 146, 150, 167
13:4 .....25, 94, 112, 113, 181
13:7 176
13:8 71
13:8–10 69
13:9 .... 46–47n14, 69n57
13:9–10 .69n56, 111n6
13:10 74

1 Corinthians

2:6–8 ....27n20
5:1 ....55, 151
5:7–8 57
5:12–13.................. 61
5:13 48
6:9–10 ....69n58
6:16–18..................43
6:19–20 57

6:20 173
7:2–5 .... 95n47
7:17–24 .... 173n39
7:19 69
9:3–14 .... 57n31
9:20......................71
9:21......................71
9:24–27................65
11:1 .... 68n54
11:23–26............... 57
12:3 122
15:20....................57
15:25 26

2 Corinthians

3:6........................64
5:10 .... 27, 171
5:21......................26
9:6–11 .... 57n31
10:5 11
13:1 ..... 46n13, 105n72

Galatians

2:16 ....65n41
3:13.....................26
3:23 64
3:28 55
5:3 44
5:17.....................70
6:2........................69
6:10 98
6:19–21 ....69n58

Ephesians

2:8 ....65n41
4:15 103
4:25 ....103, 47n14, 69nn57–58
4:28 ....47n14, 69n57
5:3–5 .... 69n58
5:25–33 .... 95n47

6:1–3 ....54, 46n14, 69n57
6:4 ....91n39
6:5–8 .... 173n39

Philippians

2:1–11 .... 68n54
2:12 65
3:9 ....65n41
3:13–14 65

Colossians

1:15–20 23
1:20 26
2:3 17
2:13–15 70
2:16 ....87n27
2:17 56
3:5 106
3:5–9 ....69n58
3:21 ....91n39
3:22–24 ....173n39
4:5 .... 41n3

1 Thessalonians

4:12 .... 41n3

1 Timothy

2:1–2 ...35, 112, 113, 171
2:2 133
3:7 ....41n3
5:8 ....163, 91n39
5:17 91
5:17–18 .... 57n31

5:19 ..... 46n13, 105n72
6:10 ....106n73

2 Timothy

3:16 56
3:16–17 ...... 37, 60, 177
3:17 ....17, 37

Titus

1:2 103
2:14 57
3:1 ....146, 150
3:7 ....65n41

Hebrews

4:8–11 88
5:5–6 56
7:18 64
8–10 ....47n15
8:5 56
8:13 ....55, 64
9:12 57
9:22 57
10:1 64
10:4 56
10:5–6................47
10:12 57
11:16 26
13:4 .... 95n47
13:7 91

James

1:5 17
1:25 77

3:17 ....105n72
4:1–2 ....106n73

1 Peter

2 147
2:5 57
2:9 59
2:12 .... 41n3
2:13–14 141
2:13–17 ....147, 148
2:13–25 ....167n29
2:18 ....173n39
2:18–20 147
2:18–25 ....147n2
2:21–23 ......148, 179n4
2:21, 24 .... 68n54
2:21–25 ....167, 170
2:24 70
3:8–17 ..147n2, 167n29
4:3 ....69n58
4:12–19 ....147n2, 167n29

1 John

1:9 57
2:1 69
3:4 69
5:3 71

Revelation

1:10 54
17:12–14 ....27n20
21:1–4 26